CONTEMPORARY CHALLENGES FOR VOCATIONAL EDUCATION

Edited by
Katy B. Greenwood

American Vocational Association

Staff Editor: Ruth A. Sievers

ISBN: 0-89514-037-3

Published 1981 by
The American Vocational Association, Inc.
2020 North Fourteenth Street
Arlington, Virginia 22201

CONTENTS

Introduction 1

I. A New Era for Job Training 3

Options for the 1980s: Changing Lifestyles, Economy
and Information, *Egils Milbergs* 5

Finding Work: Some Trends, Predictions and
Laments for the 1980s, *Edward D. Berkowitz* 15

Vocational Education in an Era of Supply-Side
Economic Policy, *Marvin Feldman* 23

II. Re-Examining Value Bases 35

Historic and Continuing Debates Over
Terminology, *Kenneth C. Gray* 37

Redefining the Work Ethic for the 1980s,
Paul Sultan 49

Early Values Underlying Vocational
Education, *Melvin D. Miller* 63

Cultural Foundations of Black Leadership,
Sonja H. Stone 71

**III. A Growing Network of Vocational
Educators** 83

The Changing Fortunes of CETA,
William Mirengoff 85

Apprenticeship Training and Vocational Education
as Partners, *Robert W. Glover* 97

The Growing Trend of Business and Industry
Training, *Richard A. Swanson and
Brian P. Murphy* 105

IV. Reflecting on Past Effectiveness 113

The Persistent Frustrations of Vocational Solutions
to Youth Problems, *W. Norton Grubb and
Marvin Lazerson* 115

A Response to the Criticisms of Job Training by
Revisionist Historians, *Paul Joseph Ringel* 129

A Perspective on Vocational Education's
Contribution, *Eli Ginzberg* 143

The Effects of Job Training, *Morgan V. Lewis and
Donna M. Mertens* 149

V. The Continuing Challenge to Meet Individual and Special Needs 167

Does Job Training Serve the Needs of People?
Edwin L. Herr 169

Increasing Opportunities for Entrepreneurs, *Robert
E. Nelson and James A. Leach* 179

Women in Vocational Administration: Why So Few?
Kermeta "Kay" Clayton 189

VI. Strengthening Curriculum and Instruction . .195

The Promise and Limitations of Competency-Based
Instruction, *John D. Skinkle* .197

Employability Skills Training: A Weapon Against
Youth Unemployment, *Dolores M. Robinson* 207

An International Perspective on Secondary School
Vocational Education, *Beatrice Reubens* 217

VII. New Issues and New Directions for the 1980s 225

The Role of Vocational Education in Economic
Development, *Krishan K. Paul and Ellen A. Carlos* .227

Vocational Education and Reindustrialization,
Rupert N. Evans 237

Vocational Education in the Economic Development
Enterprise: Policy Options, *Leonard A. Lecht* 253

Multi-Agency System Linkages and Coordination,
Clyde Maurice 275

Yearbook Authors 291

Index 297

INTRODUCTION

The field of vocational education will face challenges during the 1980s that are unparalled in its history. Recognizing those challenges is the first step toward addressing them. Examining alternative ideas that respond to the current scenario will assist the field to move forward in the 1980s in a realistic and positive direction. Ultimately, the wisdom behind policy decisions will be furthered by the extent that the field can collectively focus, in a deliberate and careful manner, on the necessity of meeting challenge and change.

Thus, whether the choices taken by vocational educators in the future will reflect traditional practices and values or will chart new patterns of education-for-work configurations will be influenced by how the field begins to respond to the changing environment during the early 1980s. This yearbook is intended to initiate those deliberations toward collective awareness and response. It will perhaps suggest more questions than answers and provide more alternatives than clear direction. The aim is to stimulate the cadre of vocational educators to focus on the uniqueness of the 1980s and the contemporary challenges that must be addressed by a field that has, over a period of more than 60 years, been able to adjust, change and respond to the influences of the times.

Contemporary Challenges for Vocational Education is divided into seven sections. Authors were sought who could provide innovative ideas in examining various approaches to education for work. Certain questions guided the organization of this yearbook, of which at least seven became dominant as the yearbook took form:

1. It appears that the 1980s are going to be considerably different from the 1960s and 1970s. *What changes have occurred that are central to planning and delivering education for work in the 1980s?* Authors were sought who would provide a frame of reference for viewing the 1980s as a unique and changing time. Their views are included in Section I, "A New Era for Job Training."
2. A basis for judging the need for continuity became the underlying quest for Section II, "Re-Examining Value Bases." *Given the changing environment of the 1980s, what value premises and practical applications can be relied on to guide the future of education for work?* Four authors in this section provide a basis for debating values useful for contemporary times.
3. A realization that networks, rather than single delivery systems, began to be the dominant characteristic of education for work in the 1970s

guided the inclusion of the next section. One of the most significant shifts in employment policy during the 1960s and 1970s has been the deliberate creation by federal policy of alternative job training opportunities. Section III, "A Growing Network of Vocational Educators," asks *what are the potential partnerships for delivering quality but flexible approaches to job training in the 1980s?*

4. Sections IV, V and VI *all* reflect the need to rethink challenges from the near past that continue to trouble the field of vocational education. Section IV, "Reflections on Past Effectiveness," reflects the varying viewpoints of its four authors. Even though these questions will continue into the 1980s, this section gives an overview and status summary of *how effective has the field of vocational education been?*

5. Throughout the 1960s and 1970s, meeting the needs of special populations became a dominant challenge for vocational education. Targeted set-asides for handicapped individuals, for disadvantaged persons, for minorities, for women, for limited English-speaking persons and for the displaced homemaker were infused into employment policy without exception. For the 1980s, two questions pose new challenges for the field. *How can vocational education facilitate women to provide quality leadership in policy development, in program management and in conceptual administration of education-for-work programs? And, how can the preparation of entrepreneurs be strengthened?* Section V, "The Continuing Challenge to Meet Individual and Special Needs," addresses these questions.

6. Continuing debates during the 1980s will focus on *how do we teach, what do we teach and where do we teach vocational skills?* Section VI, "Strengthening Curriculum and Instruction," provides a sampling of views on these questions.

7. Section VII, "New Issues and New Directions for the 1980s" responds to the query of *how can vocational education meet the emergencies identified by current economic and social indicators?*

This yearbook recognizes that for the field of vocational education, the ultimate force for meeting challenges and for being effective lies with the vocational teacher, who, on a day-to-day basis, is attentive to preparing his or her clients for a dynamic labor market. *Contemporary Challenges for Vocational Education* offers some cavaets for providing a policy structure that will best accommodate the educational practices in whatever setting the future will bring.

K.B.G.
College Station, Texas
August 1981

SECTION I

A NEW ERA FOR JOB TRAINING

In this section, Egils Milbergs sets the stage for examining the 1980s by pin-pointing significant changes that will affect planning for quality job preparation: lifestyles, economy and information.

Edward Berkowitz outlines trends, predictions and laments for finding work in the 1980s, and Marvin Feldman explains the implications for vocational education that must be understood within a "supply-side" economy.

These three authors together provide a scenario for contemporary times from which vocational educators can envision the need for new strategies, as well as improvement of old strategies, in the exercise of preparing people for the world of work.

OPTIONS FOR THE 1980s: CHANGING LIFESTYLES, ECONOMY AND INFORMATION

Egils Milbergs

The United States and advanced industrial nations are in a period of fundamental transition from a resource intensive materialistic-based society to a conserving and information-based society. And as is typical of past periods of socioeconomic transition, the 1980s will be characterized by ambiguity—subject to multiple interpretations—complexity, conflict and turbulence.

THE GOLDEN ECONOMIC ERA

Between 1948 and the late 1960s, this nation experienced a fantastic period of economic growth. The U.S. economy grew at 4 to 5 percent annual rates in real terms. The Japanese and German economies had growth rates twice as impressive. Resources were very cheap, accessible and easily exploited.

Technology was the productivity-driving engine of our economy. It replaced labor, solved problems and vastly improved our material well-being. Government attitudes tended to be laissez-faire. Private enterprise concentrated on its economic mission of growth, profits and meeting the market needs of millions of Americans, not on social objectives.

Organizations became more centralized and grew larger as we applied new managerial concepts. Our economic and political system was internationalized through the rapid development of the multinational corporation, and through military and foreign aid. It was a fantastic two decades of expanding growth, profits and steady rises in the standard of living for Americans.

Discontinuities in the 1960s and 1970s

As we moved into the 1960s, clouds began to gather on the sociopolitical horizon. We moved into an era of accelerated change and intensifying conflicts; compelling changes in social attitudes and assumptions emerged.

Americans no longer maintained unquestioning beliefs in economic growth, technology, foreign policy, government and U.S. superiority in the world.

The postwar golden economic era came to a watershed as basic industries matured, foreign competition intensified and resource costs and risks rose. Inflation grew from 1 to 1.5 percent in the early 1960s to about 13 percent in the last two years. Not since World War II had there been two years of back-to-back double-digit inflation. Happiness and security were no longer being provided by exploitation of scarce resources. Our massive consumption of energy and materials contributed to global competition, conflicts and vulnerability. Technology lost its automatic constituency. Nuclear power, once viewed as a logical extension of mankind's innovation, created a fear that we may not have the knowledge, skills and capabilities to control the secondary costs of certain kinds of technology. Institutions like government and corporations grew enormous in size and complexity, leading to complications in managing these enterprises.

Social movements—of consumerism, environmental concerns, minority and feminist awareness, holistic health, voluntary simplicity—challenged traditional value patterns and authority systems. These movements gave rise to radically new perceptions of where America's future should be focused.

International events, such as those in Iran and Afghanistan and growing worldwide terrorism, gave rise to the belief that the United States was rapidly losing control of its political, moral and military leadership role in the world.

Today, we seem to be entering an age of pessimism. People expect higher prices, more resource shortages and no increase in their standards of living. Books about the coming financial collapse and the new dark age are popular. H.L. Mencken's acrid observation of an earlier time—that people are so cynical and pessimistic nowadays that when they smell flowers, they look for a funeral—could just as well apply to the present. To many Americans, the past looks better than the present and the present looks better than the future, an historical reversal from the attitudes of the golden economic era.

THREE ALTERNATIVE FUTURES

What are the alternative scenarios of the 1980s? The first scenario is *economic optimism*. Some experts suggest that we are living in a temporary period of adjustment. With sufficient motivation and political will, we will have the knowledge, management expertise and resources to return to a sustained period of economic expansion. This scenario assumes the United States establishes more disciplined fiscal and monetary policies and restores economic incentives through reduction of marginal tax rates and regulatory burdens. It assumes no fundamental shortage of resources. Technology is the stimulus, particularly in the area of energy, as we successfully advance nuclear and coal programs. A more conservative value system emerges in the country. We rely more on marketplace solutions, not government solutions. Free trade policies are promoted to expand world markets.

The second scenario is *economic drift*. Many academicians perceive the business civilization in decline—a fundamental end to the capitalistic era, for it no longer provides a solution to society's expectations. There is a collapse of national cohesion and faith in the American dream. This scenario assumes we lose control over key issues such as energy, inflation and productivity growth rates. Americans, confronted with adjusting their lifestyles to lower real income growth and diminished expectations, support

6

the emergence of new socialistic and national planning movements. Business is squeezed by higher costs, government regulations and a soft economic outlook. Trade protectionism is on the rise in this scenario to protect jobs, and confidence in the international economic system ebbs. The conflict between Third World nations and advanced economies intensifies.

The third scenario is *changing values*. The distinguishing characteristic of this scenario is change in the basic value premises governing Americans. In this scenario, the driving forces of the golden economic era—industrialization, technological rationality, specialization, centralization, materialism—appear less valid in a world of increased interdependence, complexity and limited resources. We make a transition from something Kenneth Boulding called the "cowboy economy," driven by economic growth, to a "spaceship-earth economy," in which humanity's lifestyles and resources reflect the way resources are used in nature. There exists a key concern with person-centered ecological values as opposed to economic values, an emphasis on conservation and self-sufficiency and a reduction to the lowest feasible level of the throughput of matter and energy, particularly nonreplenishable matter and energy.

This future depends more on a "soft" energy path of renewable energy resources—solar, wind, biomass—as opposed to hard technology such as nuclear, oil shale and coal liquefaction. Decentralization, neighborhood power, community-based economic systems and local self-reliance become important phrases heard throughout the United States. Some social analysts see the country developing a culture of liberation away from larger, more complex systems toward more personal control and self-sufficiency.

TRENDS TO WATCH

We have three important trends to watch for in the 1980s: a shift in social values, economic restructuring and the emergence of the information society.

Changing Lifestyles

In the 1980s population growth as a whole will slow, more Americans will be living in the Sunbelt and the persons who made up the tidal wave of the baby boom will be entering their most productive years. Although traditional values of outer-directedness, materialism, success and conformity will still be embraced by the majority in the coming decade, there will be rapid growth in the emerging values of:

- Quality over quantity
- Persons over institutions
- Individualism over conformity
- Sufficiency over abundance
- Experience over materialism
- Meaningful over the impressive
- Knowledge over power

7

• Concern for responding personally to society and global issues. Society will be more decentralized, diverse and grow more elaborate.

A key issue for the 1980s is how society deals with the conflict between persons advocating traditional values and those supporting new values. In the 1980s the nation will in effect have two elites holding very different values, each with considerable influence. Historically America has been dominated by the *achiever* way of life—growth, profit, specialization, materialism and competition. The emergence of new values and the reality of resource and social constraints contrary to the achiever viewpoint may well lead to a period of social turbulence. New-values people will emphasize ecology, cooperation, conservation and self-management.

Increasing pressure on government and corporations to decentralize will develop. Workers and voters will not want to be bossed around. They will want to be more involved and to share in decision-making. For this reason and others, the large corporation is likely to become a looser confederation or network of smaller working units than the hierarchical command/control structure that exists today. It is not that people will lose the work ethic. Rather, they will be less driven by income alone and organizational loyalty and more motivated by specific tasks, the people they work with, how the job relates to life goals and the desire for more autonomy.

A major redesign of the working environment can be expected. Persons who are aware of and subscribe to the new values will want to exchange linear lifestyles—the education box to the work box to the retirement box—to a more diversified pattern of two or three career changes, lifelong education and leisure sabbaticals.

More personal institutions such as families and familial relationships, small businesses, religious activities and local community institutions will be strengthened with the shift toward new values. The negative pressures will be on remote institutions, big corporations and big government. As a consequence people will be regaining more control of work, entertainment and education. The trend of government growth in the economy may be flattened as more people take personal responsibility for services traditionally provided by government.

Economic Restructuring

Reversing the degeneration of the U.S. economy and its underlying productive capacity will constitute one of the greatest challenges of the 1980s. Today our economy is much less dynamic. Our competitive position is considerably diminished from that of 20 years ago. Between 1960 and 1980 our world market share of manufactured goods fell from 25 to 18 percent. The underlying rate of inflation has dramatically accelerated. Business is hedging, taking the short-term defensive view because risks are up and rewards are down.

Consider that our rate of productivity growth—the key to increasing our standard of living—is one of the lowest of the advanced industrial nations. In the past three years our productivity growth rate actually fell, although it should be pointed out that productivity growth rates are declining for many nations. A whole host of factors have contributed to this poor performance in productivity, but one key factor is that the U.S. economy has emphasized consumption at the expense of savings and investment. The United States is experiencing a severe case of stagflation, because our savings rate has been declining and now stands at half that of West Germany and France and less than one-fourth the rate of Japan. Couple these data with our low capital investment rates and it is no surprise that foreign competitors are giving us an economic beating—but remember we are getting beat with products we all love.

Another disturbing and similar trend is the technological recession experienced since the mid-1960s. Historically, our investment in research and development has been the principal factor contributing to improving productivity, real growth, employment and balance of payments. However, the percentage of gross national product the United States has invested in research and development (R&D) has been declining since the mid-1960s, while our competitors have increased their R&D considerably.

As a consequence, prevailing economic conditions forecast slower economic growth, a continuation of inflationary pressures and a restructuring of basic industries. In each instance, we can expect specific conditions to prevail.

Slow economic growth. Without a major change in economic policies, the United States will not return to the high-growth rates of the golden economic era. The main constraints in achieving higher rates of growth will be energy uncertainties, continued low-productivity rates, slower growth of the labor force and regulatory complexity. A slower growing economy combined with high inflation rates would inevitably lead to a new wave of social and political stresses among labor, management, consumers and government.

Inflation pressures will continue. Since it is difficult to restrain wage increases by tying them to productivity improvements, inflation will be the principal method of adjusting standards of living to lower, real levels of income. We would rather accept rising prices than falling incomes. Inflation is being institutionalized through price indexing of wages, pensions, transfer payments and debt instruments.

Restructuring of basic industries. With slower growing markets, increasing resource costs, a difficult regulatory environment and more foreign competition, we can expect profitability to remain low in basic industries —primary metals, textiles, autos, paper and packaged goods. This will be particularly true for energy-intensive processing industries and those that make energy-intensive products. A major restructuring will occur as we scrap our excess/obsolete capacity (e.g., to produce autos and steel), reorganize by merger or acquisition (foreign capital playing an important role), attempt to introduce new automated processing technology and transfer capital and labor to new growth sectors. In the coming decade we

9

can expect competitive pressures from the newly industrializing countries such as South Korea, Taiwan, Mexico, Brazil and Saudi Arabia.

The failure of Keynesian demand economics to deal with the problems of inflation, low productivity and employment leads me to believe that public economic policy will focus increasingly on the problems of supply: capital formation, technology innovation, education and resources. We need to channel more incentives toward savings and investment. Today's tax system is designed on the concept of distributing wealth and income more equitably than on generating productive investment. However, we cannot distribute income and wealth before it is created.

The Information Society

While our society is struggling with energy/resource problems and restructuring our basic industries, we need to recognize that we have a future. Our material-based economy is shifting towards a communication, information and knowledge-based society. The materials of our society are becoming more expensive, but the bits, the information bits, are becoming cheaper. Prior to 1900, most of us were farmers in the agricultural economy. Between 1900 and 1955, most of us were factory workers in the industrial economy. But now, the majority of us are information workers—managers, professionals, clerks, office workers—pushing around words, symbols and paper. The strategic resources of the industrial era were physical resources —in the 1980s it is going to be knowledge, data, information and communications. Knowledge is renewable and cannot be depleted. In relative terms, we will be trading fewer resources and goods and we will be trading more and more information, knowledge and culture in the 1980s.

What will make this information society possible on a scale never before imagined is the microprocessor (the silicon chip), the new wealth-generating device of the future. It is an elegant piece of sand, but it is a development as significant as the automobile. Whereas previous technological advances such as the automobile extended our physical mobility, the chip will extend our intellectual and mental capacities. This chip is now being used by computer companies and telecommunication industries, but soon it will be replacing on a broad scale electromechanical parts in devices such as watches, calculators, controls on automobiles, washers and television sets. We will be installing this "intelligence" in thousands of products.

Instead of taking problems to a large mainframe computer, we will take the computer to the problem via that small chip. Some examples of microelectronic applications presently being developed are: pocket entertainment, the office of the future, automated factories, industrial robots, new communicating devices for the deaf, home entertainment systems, personal computers for educational activities and new uses for the television set, to name just a few.

Computers in the 1980s will perceive the world around them using mini-cameras, microphones and other sensors. They will reason, using common sense, through something we call artificial intelligence. Computers will act

10

as expert consultants and people will converse with them in ordinary English.

The merger of the computer and communications field is coming. Computers will become linked together into a worldwide communications system. We can expect an explosion of new entertainment, publishing and information services. The smart terminals of the 1980s will give world-wide access to people, entertainment and information on a two-way basis.

What are the social implications of this exciting new technology? This is much more difficult to assess. Microelectronics will be the critical technology for all advanced nations in improving industrial products, office automation and consumer products. A lot of value can be added to products and services with little additional cost. According to some estimates, the world electronic market will approach $400 billion a year by 1990. Attesting to this, governments in Japan, France and West Germany are making significant funding commitments to software systems and product applications.

The training and retraining of human resources—designers, engineers, software specialists, managers and workers—will be much more important than capital. Silicon valley faces continuing shortages of highly skilled technical personnel. This shortage continues to provide us with a major educational challenge.

Impact on Productivity

Microelectronics will also have an important impact on productivity. By the year 2000, 25 percent of manufacturing assembly jobs, many of which are dangerous and monotonous, could be replaced by programmable robots. As a result, there will be startling increases in productivity— doubling or tripling in some cases. The ultimate in automation is coming when robots assemble robots. The office environment will begin to replace paper with electronic mail, data storage, electronic transmission and computer-aided design applications. We may be able to dramatically increase the productivity of professionals such as lawyers, doctors, architects, engineers, managers and financial analysts. So far office automation has focused on the activities performed by secretaries and typists, but in the 1980s we will see more emphasis on the work of managers, professionals and technicians.

Another impact of microelectronics will be employment shifts. Clearly, certain jobs will be eliminated, some will be restructured and new jobs will be created. This employment shift will create a problem of transition that will need to be effectively managed and, in some cases, may require close cooperation among the private sector, government and educational institutions.

The revolutionary aspects of the microelectronics movement are the possibilities with respect to education, leisure and work. When the home computer is coupled with other advances in satellite relays, telecommunications and fiber optics, two important factors emerge. First, this tech-

11

nology will revolutionize locational decisions. Information-intensive activities may be conducted in any part of the country or the world as long as access exists to a telephone line, cable or a satellite system. The cost of using this technology will essentially become independent of distance. Second, there will be a decentralizing impact. Since all members of the system who have a terminal can share the same information base, this will tend to break up concentrations of power and hierarchies.

Impact on Home Life

We will be able to work, play, learn and stay at home with integrated home information appliances. Consider, instead of getting a three-pound *New York Times,* the news will be available automatically personalized to individual need. Travel scheduling will allow the would-be excursionist to automatically find the cheapest fares and to make reservations from the comfort of the home. Department store catalogs will become available over cable TV systems. With 30,000 books published every year, electronic computer libraries, through search algorithms, will help readers find something useful. Electronic mail will even enable the sending of love letters instantly—people will have their own cryptographies.

It will not be unusual to find people doing 30 percent of their work in their homes—by telecommuting. Savings will be accrued in commuting time, fuel costs and will result in a more intimate family life. Business will be conducted with associates overseas by using teleconferencing at a fraction of the cost in time and expense associated with today's business travel. Education will be brought back into the home. Schools will manage, rather than teach. They will provide materials, develop computer-based curricula and testing and provide certification.

Television will change from the "plug-in-drug" it is today. While millions of people are linked together today by tuning into the same visual image, these people are nevertheless isolated. The coming video computer and communications revolution will change all that and make television an extension of the *individual's* life, not the major television networks'.

Privacy will certainly be a key issue to be carefully examined. Because the new technology will be so cheap, it will be easy to maintain extensive records on people: individual tax records, credit ratings, medical and educational records and a myriad of others. Serious questions will be raised as to access and use of this information. We will probably have to contend with increased computer crime as the number of sophisticated users increases.

The final point to consider concerns the "knows" and "know nots." During the 1980s we are going to have a new information elite. We used to talk about the "haves" and "have nots," those who had control of land and resources and those who did not. Now we will talk about the "knows" and the "know nots." The "knows" are the people who are comfortable with and can take advantage of this new technology. The "know nots" will be the people who do not understand, are frustrated with or are threatened by this new technology.

Opportunities for Response

Events have brought us to an evolutionary crossroad and we are now on a new learning curve for the 1980s. The successful organization of the 1980s must be prepared to deal not only with the expected, but also with ambiguity and surprise. In this regard, planning will be conceived more as a learning process that embraces alternative interpretations of the future.

We will need managers who have finely-tuned external perceptions, entrepreneurial skills, less emotional attachments to tradition and more orientation toward longer term economic and social payoffs. New tools will need to be developed: early warning and scanning systems, monitoring networks, contingency planning and issue management systems. We will also need new mechanisms for conceiving and implementing joint ventures between the public and private sectors, domestically and internationally.

In seeking answers to the issues of the 1980s, we are recognizing that the United States is in a profound revolution of lifestyles—a restructuring of the global economic order and technology. Accepting the ambiguity of the 1980s may well turn out to be the easiest task. Much harder tasks of interpretation, judgment and action lie ahead.

FINDING WORK: SOME TRENDS, PREDICTIONS AND LAMENTS FOR THE 1980s

Edward D. Berkowitz

Those interested in preparations for the world of work can breathe a little more easily these days; they no longer have to devise ways for a sluggish economy to absorb vast numbers of potential workers. The labor force has swallowed the baby boom and the women's movement generations, and employment statistics now look more favorable. The number of people aged 16 to 24 will drop over 16 percent during the 1980s, and fewer inexperienced women will seek entry into the labor force.

These simple demographic facts have benevolent consequences. During this decade, members of the labor force will have greater experience than has been the case for some time. Output per worker and income per worker should increase. Inexperienced workers should become more scarce, making it easier for young, old and female workers to find jobs (President's Commission, pp. 17-31).

OLD PROBLEMS PERSIST

Despite this stroke of statistical luck, old problems will persist in the decade ahead and will frame the decade's major policy dilemmas. The fundamental problem stems from the labor market's dual nature. At the risk of oversimplifying, one might say that the American economy now proceeds along two tracks—the fast and the slow. People with high technology or "super" service skills work in the fast track, and for these trained and motivated people, jobs are available. Even a casual glance through the want ads in a regional newspaper such as the *Boston Globe* reveals a plethora of opportunity at "high tech" establishments for those who know the secrets of software or who can solve other technological mysteries.

Life along the fast track poses few problems for government or industry. When the returns on an investment in training are high, people seek that training and companies devise the means of providing it.

Boom times do create tensions. New England engineers complain, for example, that local universities do not respond to their needs as effectively as California universities accommodate the needs of "silicon valley." The town of Lowell, Massachusetts, worries that the surge in employment stimulated by the Wang Corporation may end with the abruptness that characterized the demise of that town's textile trade, while Houston residents fear that a change in government priorities may suddenly stop the growth of defense-related industries. Dealing with the problems of an expanding economy, however, is a skill at which Americans have a great deal of practice and at which they excel. Life along the fast track, then, proceeds at its own quick pace and requires little government response.

Concern for Those on the Slow Track

The slow track, by way of stark contrast, is the site of many public policy problems. For those Americans who have made the "wrong" educational choice—they opted for a PhD in history or English instead of a degree in electrical engineering—or for those who lack even the basic skills, life in the next decade will continue to be difficult. The over-educated or "mis-educated" group contains relatively few members and even fewer who are poor; this group will continue the process of skill adjustment in the decade ahead. Problems for the unskilled are much more complex and so interrelated that it becomes difficult to untangle all the factors involved. Public policy must concentrate during the next decade on those individuals whose life patterns consign them to this slower track and which offer them little means of switching from one track to the other.

A MACROECONOMIC APPROACH

What are the available options to improve the chances of this group obtaining employment? One is to adopt a macroeconomic strategy by trying to improve the performance of the nation's economy. The hope is that such improvement will offer help to the unskilled by creating jobs that require little previous experience. To use a favorite Washington idiom, the benefits of economic growth will trickle down to those at the lower end of the income scale. The idea is that instead of trying to match a large pool of applicants with a small number of jobs, government should work on increasing the total number of jobs. In such a view, job training programs have a lower priority than do macroeconomic adjustments, such as decreasing personal and corporate income taxes or lowering government spending.

This option contains much that is valuable. Money does trickle down, and economic growth—not job training programs—is the surest means for ending poverty. To return to the example of Lowell, one can see how a successful regional economy stimulates the development of service industries, often located in urban centers. The growth of the Wang Corporation in Lowell fuels the renaissance of downtown Lowell and to the extent that restaurants, boutiques and dry cleaners lead to the employment of youth, minorities and other unskilled workers, then economic growth does indeed filter down. In addition to the growth of service industries, these same high-tech operations also create a demand for a certain amount of low-tech work—the mail must still be delivered, typing (even on a slick word processor) needs to be done.

Reducing Poverty

Viewed from a national level, the relationship between economic growth and economic well-being appears to be well established. Lower income workers know intuitively that growth acts as a magnet, highly imperfect to be sure, that pulls people out of poverty. The official poverty figures tend to bear out this intuition. During the 1960s the nation managed to reduce the poverty rate substantially; during the 1970s, when the rate of economic growth and of output per man hour slowed considerably, progress in eradicating poverty took place at a much slower rate. The official poverty figures, flawed by their omission of in-kind transfers but still valuable indicators of trends in earned income, showed no improvement from 1970 to 1977.

So creating economic growth is an important strategy for helping people to find work. By this time enthusiasts of the slower growth society—those who spoke of the emptiness of American life in decades past—now must yield to a prior concern for the emptiness of American bellies. Not surprisingly, the attainment of economic growth has rejoined the list of unambiguous political goods favored by all politicians and opposed by none.

The macroeconomic option holds out the dangerously false promise of solving the entire problem. It is necessary to remember that those people remain who are immune to economic growth. The unemployment rate can fall to zero and those people will still fail to join the labor force. The hardcore unemployed, marooned on the slow track, tend to be inner-city residents; a disproportionate number of them belong to a racial minority and live in a family headed by a woman. Clearly, further options are required for these people, so that they can be more than invisible residents of another America—or a social dynamite with a long fuse.

LABOR MARKET DEREGULATION

Among the options trotted out for the "disadvantaged" are a set of proposals that amounts to the deregulation of the labor market. Such issues may form the cutting edge of political debate for the next decade. In the past, the trend toward deregulation has affected markets for goods and services and in the public's mind, the term is associated with such popular causes as reducing air fares. But the concept applies to other markets as well, including the market from which businesses choose employees.

At present many regulations affect this labor market. Employers need to pay minimum wages set by government statute and to compensate workers for disabilities incurred in the course of employment. As some economists have long argued, such regulations may create problems. Often an inexperienced worker cannot produce as much as the minimum costs of paying for that worker. Even if a suitable entry-level position can be found, a firm may have no incentive to spend additional money on training the worker.

Offering Incentives to Industry

Some believe that the solution to this problem lies in a strategic lowering of the minimum wage and other employment regulations, so that the costs of hiring members of a particular group are lowered, giving industry the incentive to hire from that group. The proposal of this type that has shown the most political durability calls for a youth differential in the minimum wage. There are, however, obvious limitations. The proposal targets youth and ignores other disadvantaged workers, and it fails to provide incentives for employers to train the young workers whom the law causes to be hired. One way around this problem is to create a program that pays industry a bounty for every member of a target group it hires and trains. This stipend could equal the difference between a socially acceptable wage and the value of the worker's productivity. Proponents of this approach say it represents a realistic way of providing the disadvantaged with training. Opponents note that it rewards industry far more than it benefits members of the disadvantaged class. The members of this class might be better off with a cash stipend that allows them to purchase their own training.

Giving unencumbered cash grants to the poor, including vouchers that can be used only for training, is an idea that is not yet ripe. Nor is that time likely to arrive in the next decade. Not to put too fine a point on it, the United States does not engage in blatant redistribution of income. Members of Congress are much more comfortable providing the poor with opportunity, as opposed to cash. The imperatives of the political process, then, have produced a host of manpower and training programs, and this is a third option to provide the disadvantaged with jobs.

WORK TRAINING PROGRAMS

This idea of government-financed training programs was most recently implemented through the Comprehensive Employment and Training Act of 1973 (CETA). A creative consolidation of the federal government's manpower training programs, CETA accelerated a trend toward actual work experience in place of intensive training. Despite this conceptual breakthrough, CETA floundered on the shore of the economy's poor performance during the 1970s. Over the course of the decade, the emphasis shifted from the disadvantaged or structually unemployed to another group—those more skilled workers who had lost jobs because of the recession. Instead of sticking to the slow track, CETA served as a respite for the miseducated or for the temporarily unemployed members of the baby boom generation.

Furthermore, the contents of the program varied from prime sponsor to prime sponsor; many were local governments that used CETA slots to fund municipal jobs. By the time a new administration arrived in Washington in 1981, CETA had acquired the same mistrust that Republicans had once reserved for Franklin D. Roosevelt's Works Progress Administration (WPA): it was a boondoggle and a means by which Democrats funded their big city machines.

Finding Work: Some Trends

Irresistible Political Appeal

CETA was only the latest misadventure in a long history of government manpower and training programs. The sequence of failures owed its continuity to the political appeal that lies behind the very concept of such programs. In the most fundamental sense, government efforts to give people opportunity play well in Peoria and elsewhere. To use what may be the nation's oldest political cliche, such programs help people to help themselves and, one might add, without giving the poor an undue advantage over the established. Even better for political decision-makers, proponents of training programs often claim that such programs cost very little, or better yet, make money for the government. The rhetoric of investment quickly attaches itself to such programs; who can resist a socially beneficial venture that pays society dividends? In the case of manpower training programs, then, rhetoric and slick intellectual packaging have consistently overpowered the historical record. The fact that such programs seldom deliver on their promises is less important than the programs' irresistible political appeal.

Both Republicans and Democrats have a piece of the manpower and training promise. Which aspects a politician endorses depends upon whether he or she desires to do something about the disadvantaged *per se* or about the many programs intended to help the disadvantaged. Manpower and training can serve the primary purpose of mainstreaming the disadvantaged into the economy's fast track or the secondary purpose of separating the disadvantaged from the dole. Whatever the motive, the programs often come out the same.

CETA, for example, descends directly from the Manpower Development and Training Act of 1962 and the Economic Opportunity Act of 1964—products of the Kennedy and Johnson administrations. The opportunities inherent in manpower and training programs played a major factor in the passage of these acts.

Hubert Humphrey once explained that Walter Heller, the chairman of Kennedy's Council of Economic Advisors who helped to draft the initial war on poverty proposals, thought that "poverty was not only wrong; it was something we could not afford . . . Johnson agreed with that. Investing in the poor to lift them up, to make them independent, was economically feasible" (Miller, 1980). The war on poverty was politically feasible in part because it was economically feasible.

The Promise and Problems of Workfare

This sort of rhetoric works as well for conservatives as for liberals. The current U.S. President has an interest in a set of work training programs known as "workfare." When he governed California, President Reagan helped to create the Community Work Experience Program and he hopes to make this program a model for fundamental reform of the welfare system. The idea is to get some productivity for the state's welfare dollar

19

and it is a good idea. Welfare recipients learn about the nature of work and they also perform socially useful projects in their communities.

Beyond the promise of both CETA and workfare, however, one discovers a dismaying reality—the programs do not function all that well.

CETA and the current federal workfare program for welfare mothers, called the Work Incentive Program, and given the wonderfully euphuistic acronym of WIN, operate in conflict with one another. CETA, for instance, provides its participants with better wages than does WIN. Separate bureaucracies produce separate programs and fragment the manpower and training efforts of the various states.

Reagan's California experience illustrates other, more general difficulties with workfare and, by extension, with other manpower and training programs. The programs often do not meet their numerical goals and they cost a great deal. Their quality varies from place to place. Stressing numerical goals can cause program administrators to engage in the practice of creaming, accepting the easy cases and rejecting those who need help the most. These practices are as old as the manpower and training programs themselves; one need only read the historical records of such respected programs as the vocational rehabilitation program, which counsels the handicapped and attempts to get them jobs. This record holds the comments of one influential rehabilitation supervisor who told his fellow workers not to spend money on "shut in cases" and to concentrate on "better material" (Berkowitz & McQuaid, 1980). The spirit of his instructions have been followed in many other manpower programs in many other years.

As for Reagan's California program, the Governor announced that he wanted 800,000 welfare recipients to be placed in community jobs. In the years that the program operated, it made 9,627 job assignments; the most optimistic accounts ascribe a 25 percent success rate to the program. The job assignments that were made failed to stem the rise in welfare rates and the greatest increase in the rate came in the locations with workfare programs. The program itself cost $570,000. Commenting on the spotty nature of the program, a California legislator told the *New York Times* that the success of workfare varied from county to county depending on "how hyped up the county welfare director was" (Turner, 1981).

The problems with workfare in California have failed to deter the President. Forgetting that the WIN program is already in place and ignoring the weight of the historical record, he now wants to extend the concept to the entire nation. Workfare remains a good idea which in practice often fails to deliver on its promise. It is such a good idea that it is immune to criticism in spite of the evidence of its past problems.

CONCLUSION

So the 1980s bring with them three options for the unskilled who travel the slow track of the labor force. The options are not mutually exclusive, and some combination of them will doubtlessly be followed. There will be a major effort to stimulate the nation's economy and to lower the unemployment rate. There will be some attempt to relieve employers of burdensome regulations and perhaps there will be an accompanying effort to induce those employers to hire from the pool of disadvantaged workers. Finally, there will be some variant of workfare, an effort to substitute work for cash assistance in an attempt to lower welfare costs and increase production.

As these various programs and actions unfold, it is important to remember that no one of these options will give those on the economy's slower track the skills they need to move from one track to the other. The available technology to effect this move is poor, despite all the advances in program evaluation that have been made since the mid-1960s. One is left with the uneasy feeling that what the disadvantaged really need is money so they can purchase the means necessary to participate in the economy's fast track. That, however, is not likely to happen in the decade ahead. In the meantime, we might content ourselves with our demographic good luck; many members of the baby boom and many women have been absorbed into the labor force. Those problems, if not many others, with be less pressing in the 1980s.

REFERENCES

Berkowitz, E., & McQuaid, K. Bureaucrats as social engineers: Federal welfare programs in Herbert Hoover's America. *The American Journal of Economics and Sociology,* 1980, *39*(4), 321-336.

Miller, M. *Lyndon: An oral biography.* New York: Putnam 1980.

President's Commission for a National Agenda for the Eighties. *The American economy—employment, productivity, and inflation in the eighties, Report of the panel on the American economy.* Washington, D.C.: Government Printing Office, 1980.

Turner, W. Workfare program in California got mixed reviews. *New York Times,* March 18, 1981.

VOCATIONAL EDUCATION IN AN ERA OF SUPPLY-SIDE ECONOMIC POLICY

Marvin Feldman

The nation is witnessing an historic shift in official approach to employment policy and this shift should have profound implications for vocational educators. It-is most recognizable as a waning of influence of "demand-side" economics and the ascendance of an alternative called "supply-side" economics. Since the Great Depression, a commitment to maintain something called full employment has been the centerpiece of public policy. That, I think, will not change. The method for meeting this commitment—the management of overall economic demand according to the teachings of an infant science called macroeconomics—will change, and I think, change radically.

THE END OF AN ERA

In late summer of 1980, the Joint Economic Committee of Congress issued a statement that marked the end of an era in public policy. The report said bluntly that the American economy cannot be "fine tuned" anymore. It reviewed the six recessions since World War II and concluded that "government attempts to shorten the duration or reduce the intensity of recessions through countercycle programs . . . have been ineffective." The report was all but unanimous. The committee's eight Republican members approved it and eleven of twelve Democrats.

This was an immense and sudden change. Just four years before, the committee report reflected the economic orthodoxy that had set the direction of public policy since 1946. It expressed full confidence that the economy could be managed, and reproached the Ford Administration for doubting it. "Administration officials," it said, "speak as though they had heard nothing of the progress (of the highly developed discipline of economics) in the past 40 years," in an evident reference to the publication of John Maynard Keynes' *General Theory* in 1936. It sternly admonished the administration to stop purveying ignorance.

Now the committee had almost unanimously repudiated these 40 years of "progress." What was reprehensible ignorance four years ago had become the new economic wisdom.

But the renunciation of the Keynesian gospel has become commonplace for a fairly simple reason. A central proposition of the Keynesian model was that unemployment and inflation had a neat, inverse relation to each other, like the two ends of a seesaw. If unemployment went up, inflation would go down and vice versa. This relation was so fixed and predictable (if charted it produced a clean line called the Phillips curve) as to provide a marvelous policy instrument. This soothing assumption was integral to public policy.

But then in the 1970s, things began to go haywire. We began to have stagnation and inflation at the same time—"stagflation" it was called, and the Keynesian edifice began to crumble. Paul Samuelson, who beyond any doubt had been most responsible for the almost instant apotheosis of Keynes in the 1940s, confessed sheepishly that "experts feel less sure of their expertise."

James Callaghan, as British Labor Party's Prime Minister, said with a clarity rare in politics:

> We used to think that you could just spend your way out of a recession and reduce employment by cutting taxes and boosting government spending . . . that option no longer exists . . . it only worked by injecting bigger doses of inflation into the economy followed by higher levels of unemployment as the next step.

That is the history of the last twenty years.

The American voter expressed himself emphatically, electing a president who promised supply-side economic policies, purging a whole class of liberal demand-side senators and electing a Republican majority to the Senate for the first time in a quarter of a century.

We have clearly come to the end of an era. Events had already dictated the change. The election was merely the punctuation.

Effects of the Great Depression

It had all begun, about 50 years ago, when, on what we still call Black Thursday, the bottom fell out of the American economy. The crash was not a single shock but a crushing series of shocks. Black Thursday was October 24, 1929; then came Black Tuesday. Then for a while every day was Black. Some investors cried uncontrollably. Others kicked the tickers. A few—although not nearly so many as legend suggests—went to the roof and jumped. But the collapse of the stockmarket was just the beginning.

Looking back, the bottom line of the depression, when we finally reached it, was literally terrifying:

- GNP had fallen by half;
- nearly half the nation's factories had shut down;
- big board stocks had lost four-fifths of their value;
- 5,000 banks had closed their doors;
- 15 million people had lost their jobs and a million families had lost their homes;
- 18 million Americans were on relief.

The Great Depression was a national mortification. Men rode the subways all night to keep warm. People put I.O.U.'s in church collection plates. Illinois Wesleyan accepted vegetables for tuition. For the first time in our history, more people left the United States than came. The Russians advertised for 6,000 skilled workers and 100,000 Americans applied.

More and more Americans began to believe that the moment working people had dreaded since the beginning of industrialization had come at last. It seemed that the world's work was done. This recession wasn't like the others from which, sooner or later, we had moved on to even higher levels of productivity. This was the end of the line, the awful fulfillment of a collective premonition that the machine was the enemy of the working man. It had lured him off the land, then, when the work was finished—when the last car anyone wanted was assembled, when the last house had been built, when the last washboard had come off the assembly line—left him to starve. The work was done—or seemed to be—and the people who had burned their bridges were terrified.

It is part of the abundant mythology that America—if not the whole industrial world—was close to revolution in those dark times. But scholars who have studied unemployed people carefully find that unemployment, far from galvanizing working people, reduces them to a frightened impotence. John Garraty writes that jobless protests were "sporadic, unfocused and merely rhetorical." A reporter described the 1932 bonus marchers as "the army of bewilderment" who behaved with a "curious melancholy." Another reporter, who after seven months of driving across the country, was most of all outraged by the unemployed workers' "passive acceptance of their condition."

The Beginnings of Demand-Side Economics

Franklin Roosevelt was merely expressing my father's barber shop wisdom when he told an audience of businessmen in 1932 that America's great era of growth (which had exploded after the Civil War) was over. "Our task now, he said, "is *not* discovery or exploration of natural resources or . . . producing more goods. It is the soberer, less dramatic business of administering resources and plants already at hand." More growth could be dangerous. The American economy, which in 50 years had lifted a whole nation of refugees from poverty, had finally reached the unforgiving winter of its maturity.

We had, Roosevelt said, "produced too much too fast." Now the problem was a strange, new economic phenomenon called "under-consumption." A few weeks later Roosevelt was elected to the presidency. And what he had told that business audience became the basis for nearly half a century of public policy. It marked the beginning of the era of demand-side economics and became the declaration of a war on production that would last for 50 years.

The problem was, or seemed to be, that the economy was producing more than the people could afford to buy. So the first homespun stage of the struggle against production began, bizarre only because it was so innocently direct and literal. When the price of crude oil fell to 10 cents a barrel, Oklahoma's Governor "Alfalfa Bill" Murray sent troops to stop oil

25

production. The federal government paid farmers to plow crops under and kill little pigs.

Almost from the beginning, there was tremendous pressure for government spending to get the economy moving. "We saved our way into the depression," wrote one business economist with impeccable conservative credentials, "we must squander our way out of it." A group of "scientific economists," assembled by William Randolph Hearst to support a proposed $5 billion program of public works, said that most economists had been pushing the idea of public spending in depressions to restore purchasing power for 10 years.

But Roosevelt resisted deficit spending. He thought the economy was suffering from an elusive "structural defect" and that pump-priming could at best be a stop gap until that defect was found and corrected.

He was, at the beginning at least, much more interested in programs like The National Recovery Act, which sought to adjust production more accurately to demand. Government spending was for relief.

Keynes and His General Theory

Keynes and Roosevelt met early in his administration but neither was much impressed. Roosevelt said he couldn't make heads or tails of what Keynes said to him and Keynes, with polite restraint, expressed surprise at Roosevelt's limited economic knowledge.

But it was Keynes in the end who probably had the largest influence. He published his *General Theory of Employment, Interest and Money* in 1936 to a waiting world. The book, surely the most controversial and influential of our time, caused a revolution in economic theory and, shortly, in public policy.

Keynes' severest critics called the book a masterpiece. It was, like most great works, the elaboration of a vision and the Keynesian vision, as Joseph Schumpeter has pointed out, was the vision of a world run down, in which the spirit of enterprise was flagging, investment opportunities drying up, in which saving has thus lost its usefulness and become a problem—a society, in short, that found itself "baking cakes in order not to eat them."

The reader will be relieved to know that I do not intend to recapitulate the complex propositions of Keynes' *General Theory*—merely to summarize them crudely in a sentence or two. The Keynesian diagnosis was that an industrial economy could come to rest with less than all of its resources employed because there was a tendency for saving to exceed investment opportunities. A free economy did not, as classical economists contended, tend to provide full employment. It tended, instead, not to. This stagnation and the mass unemployment that was its cruel, intolerable consequence could be remedied by appropriate—if necessary, massive—doses of public spending.

The validity of Keynesian doctrine seemed to be massively confirmed, not by the New Deal—that experience was equivocal—but by mobilization for war. Unemployment stood at 16.7 percent when the Hitler-Stalin Pact was signed in August, 1939. In a few months unemployment had disappeared like magic. Federal spending jumped from $9 billion in 1939 to more than $100 billion in 1945. In 1941, the federal deficit was $5 billion; two years later it was $55 billion. The economy so recently pronounced senile was booming.

The Keynesian therapy was promptly built into the Full Employment Act of 1946. The government committed itself to maintain full employment, confident that the means were now at hand.

The Expense and Experience of "Full Employment"

It became the most costly government undertaking in the history of the world, including the Pyramids and China's Great Wall. Unemployment was the central problem in an industrial society. It was the government's task to fix it. The best approach was a "macro" approach, to create employment on a grand scale by stirring up the whole economy by stimulating consumption.

Production would take care of itself. It would tend to follow automatically if demand were kept strong. We no longer killed little pigs or set cornfields on fire or sent troops to stop oil production. Our active antagonism to production had cooled. But an official indifference to the need to maintain and expend productive capacity was built into public policy.

By 1960, the acceptance of Keynes was nearly universal. If the economic waters receded and left some stranded on high ground, macroeconomics meant flooding the whole landscape, raising the whole level and setting them afloat again. There was a powerful tendency to let the microeconomic details take care of themselves. It was an era of an overpowering emphasis on the demand-side of the economic equation—the stimulation of consumption. Policy approaches that emphasized the supply-side—those concerned directly with production (capital formation, enterprises and vocational education)—were consigned to the shadows.

What gave extra appeal to Keynesian analysis was its repudiation of the role of saving. The resentment of capitalism's inequalities suddenly had a powerful rationalization. Classical economists had taught that economic progress depended on saving and that the rich, who saved most, were most necessary to progress. Keynes stood this proposition on its head. Saving was not only not necessary, it was the principal *cause* of mass unemployment.

An Indifference to Capital Formation

Prosperity, he wrote, far from being dependent on the abstinance of the rich, is more likely to be impeded by it. Elsewhere he put it more bluntly: "The unequal distribution of income is the ultimate cause of unemployment." So rather suddenly, public policies of what had become the cradle of capitalism became indifferent to the need for capital formation, if not hostile to it.

But a few years later, just about three decades after the full employment act was passed, the Keynesian honeymoon was over. The Joint Economic

Committee had made it official with only one dissenting vote. The voters seemed to agree, electing the first supply-side majority in the Senate in post-war history.

What now? It seems that if the details are obscure, the general outlines of the next era of economic policy are already clear. It will be an era of emphasis on the supply side. It will be an era guided by the kind of economics which reacknowledges that what's good for General Motors, and all the other individual enterprises born and unborn, is good for the country. It will be an era which reemphasizes capital formation. It will be an era that reemphasizes productivity. It will be an era in which the new buzz words will be revitalization, reindustrialization, recapitalization. And more important, for vocational educators, it will be an era of reaffirmation of the centrality of effective vocational education as a *primary* answer to the employment problem. Vocational education is the educational component of a supply-side approach to full employment.

A NEW EMPHASIS FOR VOCATIONAL EDUCATION

The Joint Economic Committee recommended a new emphasis on vocational education. Alfred Malabre, the widely-read *Wall Street Journal* columnist, in his most recent book calls for vocational education as the way "to bring down joblessness with a minimum of inflationary pressure."

For half a century, public policy-makers wanted to know what to do about unemployment. They called on Harvard's macroeconomists. They were interested in broad, overall, systematic, macro approaches. They were interested in monetary and fiscal policy. Unemployment was the central problem, but no one sought the counsel of vocational educators.

Policy-makers were not much interested in capital formation. They were comparatively indifferent to enterprise. It was a period of capital punishment, benign indifference to productivity and a kind of bored tolerance of vocational education.

Now all that is changing. Unemployment is still the central problem; it will always be in a specialized economy. But demand-side medicine has been found to have dangerous side effects. It has been pronounced hazardous to our economic health.

The Postindustrial Society

Now policy-makers will be looking in new directions for *supply-side* policy initiatives. They will be looking to vocational educators. I hope we will be ready.

I think the beginning of readiness must be fuller recognition that we are moving into a postindustrial society—and that our mission as vocational educators is thus being elementally altered. We must still teach skills, but we must teach skills of a different and somewhat unfamiliar order.

We can find the character of these new demands in the full recognition that it was not just Keynesian policy that was wrong—the whole Keynesian premise was wrong. The Keynesian vision was wrong. We have been so

28

preoccupied with the application of demand-side policies, that we have forgotten to reexamine the social diagnosis on which they were based.

Demand-side policy was built on the idea that the American economy was mature, that it had used up its frontiers, that its capacity for growth, as Roosevelt put it, was nearly over. That mournful assessment, painfully plausible in the 1930s, was clearly mistaken. Since then we moved to a whole new generation of technology—and then another and then another. Now we are on the edge of a technological revolution so vast in its possibilities that futurist Alvin Toffler calls it "The Third Wave."

Nevertheless, the idea that job opportunities are dwindling—that people wanting work are a problem, rather than an opportunity for progress, has worked its way deep into the collective subconscious. We have tended to see the employment question as one of rationing a limited resource rather than releasing a boundless one.

That is the central anomaly of industrial America: there is plenty of work but not enough jobs.

Certainly there is plenty of work to do. There are plenty of people who want better houses, better clothes. There are plenty of people who want to get on with the rebuilding of our decaying urban centers. Plenty of more mature and discriminating consumers want better products of better quality.

Boundless Opportunities for Work

There's plenty of work to do in putting society on a recycling basis. This, alone, is an exciting possibility. By converting industrial processes to reuse waste materials, we will realize half a dozen important ambitions all at once. We can protect the environment, produce better products of better quality that take less energy to make and run on less energy, and as a bonus, improve the balance of payments by reducing imports of raw materials.

There is a staggering agenda of work that needs doing, but a nagging shortage of jobs. This, I think, is the overlooked result of the macroeconomic view of society, which along with other misconceptions, saw the work force as a great, inert shapeless mass—an industrial proletariat—which somehow had to be fully employed.

But the supply-side policy revolution suggests an altogether different view. It suggests that we must begin to prepare young people for work that will always be abundant—and not for jobs that will always be scarce.

John Dewey, that unread and misunderstood genius of education theory, wrote that a proper conception of industrial education would "prize freedom more than docility, initiative more than automatic skill, insight and understanding more than capacity to recite lessons or executive tasks under the direction of others." Dewey was suggesting that we prepare young people to be self employable either on their own or inside organizations—that we prepare them for work rather than for jobs.

Almost accidentally, my institution has found that it is preparing people to create their own work. An increasing number of the graduates at the

29

Fashion Institute of Technology, where I am president, start their own businesses when they leave. We find that we have not equipped them to fill jobs, but to find work. It may be one of those small distinctions with immense consequences.

These graduates may, in turn, be providing work—or jobs—for others. This is precisely the metabolism of economic growth. The economy grows as new businesses are formed. Big businesses are less a cause of economic growth than one of growth's results. Small businesses are the principal support of new ideas, new economic growth and of new work opportunities.

A Return to Entrepreneurship

A few more years ago, in a simple study that became a landmark, the M.I.T. Development Foundation compared job formation in 16 companies over a five-year period. Six of these companies were seasoned giants with sales in the billions. Five were fairly large companies with reputations for innovation. Five were smaller, new companies built on new technologies.

The sales of the six largest companies, such as Bethlehem Steel and General Electric, grew 11.4 percent a year. But their employment rolls increased at the rate of only three-fifths of 1 percent a year. Altogether, they created only 25,000 new jobs.

The sales of the five large innovative companies, such as IBM and Xerox, increased at 13.2 percent a year and their employment rolls increased at the rate of 4.3 percent a year. These five companies created 106,000 new jobs.

The sales of the five small high technology companies such as Data General and Computer Graphics increased 4.2 percent a year. Their employment rolls increased at the rate of 4.1 percent a year. Their sales totaled less than a thirtieth of the sales of the six giants, but they created 10,000 more jobs—35,000 altogether.

Something like a national rediscovery of the indispensable role of the entrepreneur—for a while an endangered species—is loose in the land. Vocational educators need to get out in front of it.

Studies suggest that entrepreneurs tend to be poor performers in school. "For the first time in my life," one remembered, "I realized I wasn't wierd or a misfit; I was an entrepreneur." But often, entrepreneurs are dropouts. This could mean clearly that conventional educational programs are neglecting the nurture of the imagination. The Marxists have accused us, to quote one of them, of "creating the personality and cognitive traits that enable individuals to function effectively in bureaucratic work organizations." Maybe they're right. Maybe we've been taming people instead of inspiring them.

That suggests another frontier—the larger task of making work within organizations more entrepreneurial. Large corporations may some day operate as "confederations of entrepreneurs." What is most promising about this emerging mode is its flexibility, its expandability. It is a much more hopeful, forward looking, dynamic vision than the melancholic static vision that underlay the Keynesian era.

And, above all, it permits a larger, more optimistic vision of the future of industrial man. It can mean the end of the industrial proletariat. It can mean the perception of working people not as interchangeable digits in a gray mass called the work force, but as increasingly autonomous self-supervising individuals who look forward to a rich and intense life after work.

Liberal Education and Vocational Relevance

Higher education was, originally, frankly elitest. Right up until the American Revolution, Harvard students, for example, were listed by social rank.

In those days, common people were flatly forbidden to "walk in great boots" or otherwise imitate the behavior of their betters. It was a rigidly hierarchical society. Colleges educated the tiny elite destined for the ministry or for the professions or for the easy responsibilities of class and privilege. The education provided was in its essentials, a liberal education—one learned skills in other ways.

But as the great democratic tradition blossomed in the United States as it blossomed nowhere else in the world before, more and more people aspired to more and more education. And the model was the kind of liberal arts education intended for an aristocratic minority—many of whom had no need to earn a living. "Do you smoke?" the great lady asks her daughter's suitor in an Oscar Wilde play. "Good," she replies when he admits hesitantly that he does, "I think every young man should have an occupation of some kind."

But as America democratized, the mark of the new mass mobility became a college education originally intended for the indolent or for the professional scholar. In 1900, 200,000 students went to college. Last year, the figure was 11 million. But the vocationally impractical curriculum simply did not suit the real world imperatives of the new masses. And so somewhere along the line—liberal educators began to make an uneasy, tormented case for the relevance of irrelevant education. The consequences have been disastrous—for the great liberal tradition of education and for millions of students who have been seduced into believing that liberal education has a vocational relevance that it simply does not, cannot, and should not have.

Now, as a secondary consequence, the culturally indispensable liberal tradition is being discredited because in practice it fails to do what it never should have been represented as doing. And we vocational educators are witnessing an unwelcome reaction against liberal education.

What Does "Over-Educated" Mean?

This situation has grotesque consequences. We read in the papers that thousands of young people are "over-educated." How can a civilized person know too much? How can a common man who struggled for centuries for the leisure that would free him from his exhausting struggle

31

for survival, for some contemplation and personal civilization, be "over-civilized?" It is absurd. A student can know more than he or she needs to know to program a computer or sell an insurance policy or manage a supermarket, but to be "over-educated?"—the word is to me, as an educator, an obscenity.

Clearly the rehabilitation of vocational education to include the liberal arts adapted to the needs of a mass aristocracy has become an urgent necessity. And the anomaly is that vocational educators are best able to make the case for the liberal arts. We do not have to pretend that they're vocationally relevant. We can say, more forcibly than the liberal educators, that liberal arts are vocationally irrelevant, but that they have a desperate importance of their own.

I've lately been haunted by a puzzling, perplexing, heart-rending book entitled, *What Went Wrong,* by an English craftsman. He's writing about British working people who have largely achieved the material goals they sought half a century ago—and who now have no sure sense of purpose. They are asking, with a terrible urgency, whether there can be life after work or only an emptiness to be filled by passive entertainers, recreational chemicals and a bored and heavy indolence.

The Jeffersonian Ideal and Its Application to Today

In other words, we may be finding that the unemployment problem has two related dimensions: *not only have we left some people wholly unemployed, but we have left unemployed the most human qualities of practically all working people.* And as we solve the second, less visible problem, the first may simply disappear. The crisis in macroeconomics may mean that the Jefferson ideal, which for two centuries stopped at the factory gate, may at last be finding its way indoors.

Jefferson's hope that America would remain a nation of independent farmers was much more than sentimental pastoralism. He saw it as necessary to the maintenance of a durable democracy in which the participants were financially and physically independent, not conditioned in their employment to some habit of subordination.

Jefferson believed that widespread economic independence through self-employment on the land was the best defense against a familiar tendency for democracies to degenerate into some form of tyranny.

In spite of his passion for gadgets, Jefferson was uneasy about the prospect of industrialization. He shared one historian's concern that it might "blunt people's imaginations and ethical sensibilities, alienate them from their environment and perhaps even serve as a new instrument of tyranny."

And the organizational patterns early generations of technology seemed to dictate justified this concern. But now it appears that emerging generations of technology may enable decentralization and the transformation of customary mechanical, authoritarian and bureaucratic relationships into more entrepreneurial ones.

We have simply taken a long detour to the Jeffersonian ideal—not as a nation of farmers, but as a nation of essentially autonomous, self-supervising, equal entrepreneurs, working within nonauthoritarian conclaves.

New Questions for Research

What does all this mean for research? I believe it suggests a new research dimension. I think we need studies in education for entrepreneurship—not just the indispensable descriptive studies of who is doing what, where, how and with what apparent result. Education for entrepreneurship is evidently a rapidly growing field. The statistics of nonfarm self-employment began to rise in the 1970s after a full century of decline. And we need to look more closely at qualities like initiative and imagination and learn how our approaches must be altered to nurture them best.

But even more important is the reduction of the emerging vision of a demassified work force to a specific and actionable one. The first step, I believe, is a sustained, systematic effort to redefine the terms of employment.

We need answers to a whole family of new questions. It is said that someday soon we will pay people for modules of work done. To what extent is employment now defined this way? In what fields? To what effect? Can reasonable comparisons be made? Is the work module method more productive, more cost effective, more satisfying? How can existing conventional job descriptions be reshaped into work definitions? Should we not begin a continuing conversation with managers, production engineers, accountants and academicians about the opportunities and problems involved? What is the state of the art? Is so-called "responsibility accounting" a base on which we can build? Can the idea of "management by objectives," already familiar in the executive suite, be extended to all employees? How might educational programs be modified to prepare people for entrepreneurially defined work? What retraining might be necessary if work is redefined? Or can a word like "training" be properly applied to preparation for self-supervised work?

There are some larger questions. How do we redirect the insane accumulation of short-term remedial job training programs toward long-term preventive programs in our public schools and colleges? How can we redirect federal spending on education to serve the part-time working student? How can we redirect manpower training dollars to extend the school day and year to give students time to make choices, work together and share common experiences?

Full employment will always be the central domestic concern in a specialized society. But our approach to achieving it is fundamentally changing. The premises of a half century are being put aside and the search for new ones has begun. It is a time of extraordinary opportunity for all of us.

This piece was originally prepared for the National Center for Research in Vocational Education. A reprint may be obtained by ordering OC 70 for $2.20 from the Publications Office, The National Center for Research in Vocational Education, 1960 Kenny Road, Columbus, Ohio 43210.

SECTION II

RE-EXAMINING VALUE BASES

Four authors examine, in this section, historical themes that will require further definition in the 1980s. Kenneth C. Gray points to the continuous debates over education-for-work terminology and emphasizes the need for acceptable and relevant terminology for contemporary times.

Paul Sultan establishes the need for a contemporary work ethic for the 1980s and forecasts the significant role that vocational education can play in establishing such an ethic. Melvin D. Miller identifies from history those values that have served the field well and distinguishes these from past practices that have also served the field.

Sonja Stone looks at the attributes that have guided black leadership in vocational education over past decades and identifies the impetus for including new ethnic-cultural bases from past black leadership into new programs of leadership for tomorrow.

HISTORIC AND CONTINUING DEBATES OVER TERMINOLOGY

Kenneth C. Gray

It was an impressive group that gathered in Chicago in 1908 for the first annual meeting of the National Society for the Promotion of Industrial Education (NSPIE). While efforts to attract Samuel Gompers, the labor leader, had failed, many prominent personages were present. Jane Addams, the progressive reformer, was to address the group as was James Van Cleave, president of the National Association of Manufacturers (NAM). First to speak was Charles Eliot, president of Harvard. His opening remarks were predictive of coming terminology debates.

"There is a great deal of confusion about the meaning of the term industrial education," stated Eliot. "Industrial education ought to mean trade schools, and nothing but trade schools" (NSPIE), *Bulletin No. 6*, p. 9). Yet despite the crisp definition by the Harvard professor, less than a year later the NSPIE Board of Managers took the position that high school industrial education programs were not trade schools (NSPIE, *Min.*, Dec. 1909). After 1909 the NSPIE avoided the term "trade school" because of the emotional response it brought from labor and industrialists. The NSPIE had learned quickly that terminology is not something to be taken lightly. The lesson still holds today.

The labels given to training efforts would appear to be a simple question of description or semantics. But as suggested by Kotler and Levy (1969, pp. 10-15), public agencies will find it increasingly necessary to conduct classic marketing functions to insure a continuing flow of both clients and funds. Vocational education is no exception. The names of services will be as important in the future as the names of consumer goods have been in the past. These labels bring forth images to potential consumers and supporters that can be counterproductive. This is one message of history that this chapter will convey.

What follows is not an exhaustive chronology of the origin of present vocational education terminology; such an account would easily take a volume. Instead the objective is to provide what Henry David (1977) has termed "feed forward" signals from our history to those who would consider terminology changes. First to be examined will be the historical explanations of why vocational education terminology seems to have both class specific and social efficiency connotations. Second, this chapter will document the terminology debates that accompanied the legislative drive for the Smith-Hughes Act, the original 1917 federal vocational education funding law.

One intent will be to illustrate that it was politics, not pedagogy, that led to the adoption and defining of the term "vocational education."

NEGATIVISM TOWARD TRAINING TERMINOLOGY

Not everyone responds positively to training terms. Commenting on industrial education in 1913, John Dewey (pp. 374-377) worried that programs were being promoted by manufacturers in order to provide "a better grade of worker to exploit." Labor leader John Golden's reaction to the term "trade schools" was a bit more curt—he dismissed them as "scab hatcheries" (NAM, 1908, p. 5). There are historical reasons why many still adhere to the old saw that vocational education is great, but for someone else's kid. Those who would consider new terms to market vocational education might begin considering the roots of this conventional thought.

The term "industrial education" is the forerunner of the more general term "vocational education." The origin of "industrial education" was most likely the industrial schools that developed in the 1800s in England and then in America. Since the seventeenth century, job training had been the common solution to indigent youth. The original social institution for this purpose was the colonial type apprenticeship. Both the 1601 English Poor Law and the 1647 Massachusetts Bay Colony's Old Deluder Satan Act authorized involuntary indenturing of poor children. When industrialization made the traditional apprenticeship obsolete, the industrial school developed to take its place as the provider of training for young wards of the state.

Early Industrial Schools: Class Specific

As mass production and urban cities spread during the mid to late 1800s, so, too, did the industrial school. The 1883 report of the U.S. Commissioner of Education (p. cxii) listed 79 such institutions. Only two of this group were receiving any public support and more than half were run by religious organizations. For our consideration, what is most revealing about the 1883 listing is that it was part of a larger composite of all schools for orphans, dependent children and delinquents.

Seemingly without exception, nineteenth-century industrial schools were for youth on the fringes of society. This can be contrasted with another vocational movement of the times: manual training. Those who attended manual training programs were frequently sons of prominent manufacturers including James Van Cleave (NSPIE, *Bulletin No. 6,* 1908, p. 65). The clientele of industrial schools had no such connections. As an example, the 1886 Second Plenary Council of American Bishops recommended that parishes start Catholic industrial schools to stem the flow of Catholic youth into Protestant-controlled reformatories (McClusky, 1964, p. 82). By the turn of this century, industrial education was so common for incarcerated youth that the Reverend Hubbard of Auburn, New York, complained that a boy who was a criminal had a "free passport to board, clothing and the opportunity to become self-supporting." The honest boy had no such advantage

(NAM, 1907, p. 127). Industrial education was also disproportionately common among blacks.

Following the Civil War some writers suggest that industrial education and education for blacks became synonymous (Lazerson and Grubb, 1974). Samuel Chapman Armstrong of Hampton Institute pioneered the solution to the "Negro problem." Historian Donald Spivey (1978) charges that the solution was education designed to train blacks for their place; the curriculum was job training. Industrial training became a central theme of debates between conservative and liberal black leaders (Hall, 1973, p. 17). By the turn of this century, training schools were common throughout the South. It was only the Brown desegregation case that finally closed many of these schools that were often supported with Smith-Hughes funds. From the point of view of many black Americans, they have only recently escaped institutions for training. Blacks, however, are not the only ones who have grounds to suspect that training programs may have been designed to keep them in their place.

A Means of Social Control
The class specific nature of populations traditionally served by vocational programs is not the sole reason many shun them. Also operating is the suspicion that the covert objective of the programs is to track youth into lower status occupations. While historically this has been a hotly debated issue, evidence exists to support this belief. Early industrial education rhetoric frequently contained social control themes. James Kay, a leader in Britain's industrial school movement, wrote in 1839 that the objective was to turn out students who had habits that "shall afford the largest amount of security to the property and order of the community" (Bennett, 1926, p. 251). In America, there is evidence that many who promoted industrial education did so because it was socially efficient.

"Above all," wrote the influential educator Ellwood Cubberley (1909),
the new and intensive interest in industrial and vocational training is especially significant of the changing concept of the function of the school and the classes in society which the school is in the future expected to serve. (p. 53)
The new class were the children of the immigrant factory worker, the new function was social efficiency: training each individual for that occupation where he can make the greatest contribution to the national interest. President Theodore Roosevelt, in a letter of support to the NSPIE, put the issue in more concrete terms when he wrote: "Youth must get over the idea that making twenty dollars a week and calling it a salary is better than making twenty-five that is called wages" (NSPIE, *Bulletin No. 3*, 1907, pp. 6-7). Herbert Miles, chairman of the NAM Committee on Industrial Education, hoped industrial education would do something about factory children looking upon "a shop too much as a jail" (NAM, 1912, p. 154).

The social efficiency philosophy was a widely accepted mission of education during the formative years of the vocational education movement.

Perhaps as suggested by revisionist historian Paul Violas (1978), children were selected for industrial education not because of any particular expressed trade interest but because their parents were working people. Many then and now would agree with Cubberley (1934) when he wrote in his widely read *Public Education in the United States* that "vocational education is the most effective agency so far devised for the seventy percent who can not or will not continue in the regular course."

There is a message in this for those who will debate changes in vocational education terminology. First, traditional terms have definite socioeconomic connotations. Programs have traditionally served minorities and children of the working class. Second, traditional labels are closely associated with the doctrine of social efficiency, a doctrine that may still be popular with national policy-makers but is decidedly unpopular with parents and advocacy groups. Again to illustrate this point, by contrast, terms such as "industrial arts" and "career education" have none of these connotations. The implications would seem to be that any discussions regarding terminology cannot be separated from discussion of who is to be served and why.

POLITICS AND TERMINOLOGY

Melvin Barlow (1967) has observed that "one consistent trend from the beginning of the industrial education movement has been its struggle with terms and concepts, causing confusion in oral and written communications" (p. 267). The experiences of the National Society for the Promotion of Industrial Education (NSPIE) supports this view. In the tradition of the progressive era, the society was formed in 1906 to nationally promote programs to train the ever-growing numbers of factory workers. The name was mostly borrowed; there had already been a Society for the Promotion of Manual Labor in Literary Institutions in 1831 and a National Association for the Promotion of Technical and Secondary Education in 1887. The unique feature was the term "industrial education" and the society immediately found the vagueness of the word a source of trouble.

The introductory note to the *Proceedings of the Organizational Meeting* (1906, p. 7) of the NSPIE suggests an early awareness of confusion and coming problems surrounding the exact meaning of the term "industrial education." Industrial education was defined as being between manual training of the elementary school and the engineering colleges. It dealt "with training of direct vocational value to the industrial workers." The correspondence of the NSPIE reveals even this noncommital definition did not escape controversy. James Monroe, manufacturer and member of the organizational committee, wanted to include agriculture education within the definition of industrial education and thus the mission of the society (Library of Congress, 1906, Box 13). The organizational committee decided, however, that it was "not expedient and unwise to include agriculture education because it would dissipate its energy and overweigh its strength" (Library of Congress, 1907, Box 4). There was even some discussion as to whether industrial education should include training for women. To the credit of the NSPIE board of managers, it was decided that it did (Library of Congress, 1906, Box 7). A more revealing comment, however, was the disclaimer by the society that its intent was limited to the immediate establishment of the trade school.

Union-Manufacturer Conflict

The turn of this century was a period of intense conflict between labor unions and middle-level manufacturers, especially those who belonged to the National Association of Manufacturers (NAM). As an indication, the American Federation of Labor's (AFL) budget to organize new factories had grown from $6,400 in 1897 to $83,000 in 1904 (Livesay, 1978, pp. 111-114). This conflict extended beyond the factory gates to related issues, one of which was the trade school. As stated by Frank Duffy of the United Brotherhood of Carpenters and Joiners, unions had long ago decided that limiting the number of apprentices was the best way to raise wages (NAM, 1908, p. 31). Manufacturers looked to the trade schools, which turned out apprentices, as a way to break this "labor trust." David Parry, third president of the NAM, reasoned that the association should promote trade schools because "union restrictions as to apprentices must certainly be rendered ineffective" (NAM, 1903, p. 80). Thus in the early 1900s, battles were fought in many manufacturing cities over the establishment of trade schools. One such conflict indirectly caused the NSPIE considerable trouble.

In 1891 the unions in St. Louis were successful in blocking the efforts of a local brick manufacturer, Anthony Ittner, to establish a trade school. Ittner was not a good loser and became one of the era's most outspoken union baiters (NAM, 1904, pp. 132-133). Unfortunately for the NSPIE, Ittner was the chairman of the NAM standing committee on industrial education. Because much of the work for the NSPIE organizational meeting was done by two NAM members, Milton Higgens and M.W. Alexander, it is not surprising that Ittner was elected to the NSPIE executive committee. The brick manufacturer had a single purpose in his membership: to narrow the definition of industrial education, and therefore the purpose of the society, to the trade school.

By 1907 the term "industrial education" was causing the NSPIE serious recruitment problems. To the trade unions, industrial education connotated manufacturers; Philadelphia unionists automatically assumed the NSPIE was just another employer group organized to "throw arrows into the vitals of the labor unions" (Library of Congress, no date, Box 30). Manufacturers were no less suspicious; the NAM refused to supply the NSPIE with a copy of its membership list until it indicated what side of the "open shop" issue it stood. Ittner wrote C.R. Richards, then secretary of the NSPIE, regretting the absence of the "words trade school" from the society's constitution and suggesting that such a correction would "settle the question and place it beyond the power of anyone to divert the action of the society from what should be essentially its main purpose" (Library of Congress, 1906, Box 1). It was a recommendation of the efficiency expert, Frederick Taylor, that ultimately settled the issue.

A Committee of Ten Tackles the Problem

Never one to tolerate vagueness, Frederick Taylor, then a member of the NSPIE board of managers, sought to define "industrial education." It was popular among educators at this time to establish "committees of ten" to investigate major issues. Taylor recommended in January of 1908 that such a committee be established to investigate the relationship of industrial training to the general system of education (NSPIE, *Min.,* Jan. 1908). Ittner sensed the importance of the committee to his objectives and sought to preempt its activities by proposing a resolution to the board of managers. It called for efforts to promote "practical industrial education" that taught "finish skills" through regional trade schools (Library of Congress, 1908, Box 27). Ittner was facing an uphill battle; his resolution was referred to the committee of ten where it was conveniently lost (Library of Congress, 1908, Box 27).

By 1908 there was probably little doubt what the committee of ten report would contain. The NSPIE had realized that it would never succeed unless it could attract labor support (Library of Congress, 1908, Box 22). This objective required a definition of industrial education acceptable to the unions. Knowing this, it is not surprising that the committee's report stated that youth trained in industrial education programs "will not be a skilled journeyman in any field, but will have received a fundamental training in those things that will make him a skilled journeyman in a short time" (1907, p. 7). The committee found a clever way out of the trade school issue. Trade schools were recognized as important but only for those already in the trade.

Terminology and NSPIE Membership

The effect of defining industrial education on NSPIE membership is particularly instructive. It was not a coincidence that following the report of the committee of ten, manufacturers' membership in the NSPIE fell dramatically. The complexion of the society was forever changed. Again, Anthony Ittner had a part in this development.

During the committee of ten deliberations, Ittner kept in close contact with his personal friend John Kirby, who would become the fifth President of the NAM. In 1909, Ittner recommended to Kirby that should the society pursue an industrial education policy contrary to that of the NAM, relations should be severed (Library of Congress, 1909, Box 23). The relegation of the trade school to those already in the trade and thus to union members, as well as the endorsement of a more general definition, led Kirby to conclude that the society was in the hands of the labor unions. In 1911, Kirby ascended to the NAM presidency and did the NSPIE serious damage.

At the 1911 NAM convention, Kirby attacked the NSPIE in his opening remarks. He charged that any organization that sought to promote industrial education through the involvement of organized labor was following a policy as foolish as "associating with bums and drunks to cure the habit of drink." (NAM, 1911, p. 75). Kirby went on to make a pointed plea to the membership to disassociate itself from the NSPIE. In that year, the records of the society reveal that membership fell by one-third (NSPIE, *Min.,* Nov. 1911).

Manufacturers Desert NSPIE

Contrary to the interpretations of some analysts, manufacturers drifted away from the NSPIE following the committee of ten report. As indicated in the correspondence of Charles Prosser, then secretary of the society, those manufacturers who remained were a few wealthy and loyal supporters (Library of Congress, 1913, Box 23). By 1915, it was difficult to find a manufacturer who was willing to serve on the board of managers. Among a multitude of employers' groups, only the National Metal Trades Association supported the Society (NSPIE, *Min.,* June 1915). Manufacturers interpreted the failure to define industrial education in trade school terms as an indication that the movement was going the way of manual training; it would be of little use to them. Indicative is a letter from a manufacturer of machinery who in 1914 wrote Prosser that "we are disappointed in the outcome up to the present time, feeling that the National Society has swung largely into the hands of, and has been influenced by, those favoring the 'academic policy rather than the industrial' " (AVA, 1914).

In a way, this attitude by manufacturers was a self-fulfilling prophecy. By 1915, the society was in such financial difficulties that Prosser was compelled to turn to "groups whose interest we know beforehand" (NSPIE, *Min.,* Jan. 1915). Membership applications were sent to large numbers of school superintendents and by December of 1915, educators were in the majority (NSPIE, *Min.,* Feb. 1916).

The above episode from the history of the industrial education movement illustrates well the relationship between terminology and support. Two divergent constituencies, employers and employees, looked to the NSPIE's refinement of the term "industrial education" as an indication of whose side the society was on. Having decided that the support of labor was critical, the NSPIE defined industrial education in terms acceptable to unions. To those who would underestimate the importance of terminology, the dramatic effect on NSPIE membership and revenue should provide food for thought. It could be also argued that the seemingly unimportant report of the little known NSPIE committee of ten did much to assure that the vocational education movement would be dominated by educators.

The story just told is not typical however. Infrequently in the history of vocational education are definitions decided by small committees of supporters. More frequently they are decided by the legislative process and a multitude of actors and considerations. This reality is illustrated by the evolution of the term "vocational education" through the efforts to secure federal aid. It is to these developments we now turn our attention.

Terminology and the Drive for Federal Legislation

Rupert Evans (1981) suggests that "as long as there is major misunderstanding about what vocational education is, it is difficult to get legislation to make it better" (p. 31). In 1909, many within the NSPIE had reached the same conclusion regarding industrial education. The committee of ten recommended that a clarification of terminology would do much to help the movement. In the ensuing years, the political process would encourage the adoption of the term "vocational education" and refine its meaning.

The label "vocational education" begins to appear in the literature around 1909. For example, in that year *American Industries,* a manufacturers' trade publication, carried an article entitled "Trade Schools or Vocational Education." Undoubtedly an important figure in originating the term was David Snedden, commissioner of education in Massachusetts and active member of the NSPIE. In his widely published work, *The Problem of Vocational Education* (1910), Snedden chose "vocational education" as a useful term to contrast the difference between a liberal education and education for employment. Echoing others, Snedden wrote that "in this field great confusion of terminology still prevails" and went on to suggest five categories of vocational education: professional, industrial, commercial, agriculture and household. Not included was manual training. Snedden considered this field to be a prevocational and liberal education.

The nomenclature developed by the commissioner from Massachusetts gained rapid acceptance. The 1913 report of the NSPIE committee on terminology used the term "vocational education." By 1914 a survey of the National Education Association (NEA) committee on vocational education and vocational guidance (NEA, 1914, p. 577) found that the term "vocational education" was in general use. A major reason why the label "vocational education" suddenly became popular was its political acceptance. The politics of the drive for the Smith-Hughes Act both popularized and refined the term "vocational education."

Confusion over "Mechanical Arts"

The first effort to secure federal aid for training below the college level was a bill sponsored by Charles Davis, congressman from Minnesota. This 1907 bill was a pioneering effort and, as such, was the first to encounter opposition due to terminology. Correspondence in the National Archives (Senate Appendix, pp. 1163, 1227) reveals that Davis sought the support of the NAM through its president, James Van Cleave. Van Cleave, however, had an objection. The bill used the term "mechanical arts" instead of "industrial education." Davis responded that the bill "was encountering a problem due to differences of opinion regarding trade schools among manufacturers and labor." The term "mechanical arts" seemed the least objectionable but broad enough to be interpreted later.

True to form, Anthony Ittner was not satisfied. He liked the idea of correcting the injustice of spending $8 million from the Morrill Act (which established the land grant colleges) for 2 percent of the population, while 98 percent got nothing. He feared, however, that the term "mechanical arts," derived from the 1862 Morrill Act, would lead to programs similar to manual training and thus have no "substantial or practical" value (NAM, 1907, p. 36). This difference of opinion over terminology prevented the NAM from supporting the legislation, assuredly a factor in the bill's lack of success. It was the next legislative effort, namely the equally unsuccessful Dolliver-Davis Bill, that brought to the fore the term "vocational education."

The campaign to secure federal aid for vocational education is commonly viewed as an urban movement. The NSPIE members were an interesting collection of mostly urban reformers, educators, labor leaders, clergy and manufacturers. Despite this visibility of those from the cities, a strong argument can be made that agricultural interest played an equal role. Congressman Davis promoted his bill not only with the contention that it would provide training for the mushrooming urban working class but also as a way to "stem the desire to leave the land and go to the cities: by rural farm youth" (*Congressional Record,* 1907).

Several factors made support by rural interests imperative. While the country's wealth was increasingly concentrated in the cities, the majority of votes, particularly in the Senate, came from farming states. It is worth remembering that both Hoke Smith and Dudley Hughes were from a Southern rural state, Georgia. As important, the congressional committee that heard the Dolliver-Davis bill was the Committee on Agriculture and Forestry, a committee that could be predicted to have little interest in a bill benefiting only urban states.

Considering the political necessity of gaining rural support and avoiding conflict between unions and manufacturers, it is no wonder that politicians adopted the term "vocational education." The 1910 hearings on the Dolliver-Davis bill were entitled "Hearings on Vocational Education." The term, as defined by Snedden, was politically astute in that it included both industrial and agriculture education. In fact, with both the NSPIE and the NAM on the sidelines, these hearings were a joint effort by the AFL and various agricultural interests led by Henry Wallace, editor of the influential *Wallace Farm Journal* (U.S. Congress, 1910).

After 1910 vocational education became the widely used umbrella term for the training movement. Yet, this was not the end to controversy over terminology.

Clarifying "Vocational Education": 1910-1917

While the term "vocational education" became popular in legislative efforts by 1910, what it meant had yet to be decided. It was the politics of the campaign for federal funding that ultimately defined vocational education. At stake were such key issues as who would govern vocational education and what types of programs would receive funding.

Perhaps the most hotly debated issue of vocational education was the question of who would control the programs: general educators, manufacturers, labor leaders, existing or separate school boards. Charles Prosser agreed with manufacturers; if the new movement was to remain practical and not go the way of manual training, it must remain beyond the control of the general educator (Library of Congress, Aug. 1912, Box 25). Labor leaders supported this view but insisted the programs be controlled by the public. The issue quickly centered on whether vocational education meant control by existing or separate school boards. The idea of separate school boards, as was being tried in Wisconsin, was bitterly attacked by such educational gurus as John Dewey. Manufacturers, in turn, saw themselves in a holy battle with the "old fashion education priesthood" *(American Industries,* Nov. 1913). Politics, not debate, settled the issue.

The NSPIE's association with the separate school board concept brought the society increasing criticism from "school men." (Library of Congress, Dec. 1913, Box 23). It became evident that a bill which contained such a provision would not pass. Not surprising, the report of the Commission on National Aid to Vocational Education (1914), of which Prosser was a member, did not require separate local boards for vocational education. Yet the battle was not over. Manufacturers still held out for a representative federal board. Herbert Miles characterized the proposed federal board made up of cabinet officials as a collection of "dummies," headed by the commissioner of education whose only practical experience had been at a small college (NAM, 1916, p. 63). When Miles threatened to work to kill the Smith-Hughes bill, with the sympathy of both the AFL and the U.S. Chamber of Commerce, the NSPIE board of managers passed a resolution calling for a representative federal board (AVA, 1916). The issue of governance was thus decided by political realities, not by what was best for the movement. The same was the case in deciding what programs would be included in the federal definition of vocational education.

It will be remembered that Snedden's definition of vocational education included commercial education, now called business education. In 1913, however, the report of the NSPIE committee on terminology omitted commercial education as a field of vocational education. The issue was a sensitive one for the NSPIE. Several of the society's most generous supporters, including Lincoln Filene, a Boston retailer, wanted commercial education included (AVA, 1914), while manufacturers were of the opposite opinion.

Correspondence reveals that during the deliberations of the Commission on Vocational Education, manufacturers sought to prevent the inclusion of commercial education. Howell Cheney wrote Prosser that although the demand for classes in salesmanship was strong, it was better to "face the music" than let commercial high schools receive funding that would "result in relieving the states of a burden they had already assumed" (AVA, 1914). The influence of Cheney and those whose views he represented was greater than those of retailers—the Smith-Hughes Act did not provide funding for commercial education. Funding considerations and political clout decided what types of programs were included in the federal definition of the term "vocational education."

CONCLUSION

This chapter has attempted to provide an historical perspective for the current need to examine terminology. Overall, we have seen that debates over terminology are not new and that they should not be taken lightly.

Training programs have historically been for the wayward and the lower classes. The vocational education movement developed partly from the recognition that it was in the national interest to provide training to the "hand minded." These class specific and social efficiency connotations are strongly attached to the terminology developed at that time. This is basically the same terminology still in use today.

Changing or redefining terminology can have effects of unforeseen magnitude on supporters. The estrangement of manufacturers and the dramatic fall in NSPIE membership in 1911 can be traced to its refinement of the term "industrial education." To avoid devastating surprises such as these, the generic needs of sought-after groups must be understood. Predictably these needs will sometimes be in conflict and thus the issue of mission emerges.

Finally it was political considerations, not debates among educators, that led to the adoption of the term "vocational education" and its definition. It became popular because it was acceptable to both rural and urban interests within the Congress. As suggested by Rupert Evans (1981), it is still the Congress—not vocational educators—that is defining vocational education. The implication is that unless this situation changes, any proposed change in terminology must be tempered with the reality of federal politics.

REFERENCES

PRIMARY SOURCES

Manuscript Collections:
American Vocational Association. *Papers of the National Society for the Promotion of Industrial Education* (NSPIE). Includes minute books of the executive committee. Arlington, Va.

Library of Congress. *Papers of the National Society for the Promotion of Industrial Education.* Manuscript Division. Washington, D.C.

National Archives, U.S. Senate, 63A-F15, Washington, D.C.

Trade Journals:
American Industries (Journal of the National Association of Manufacturers.) 1902-1917.

Proceedings:
National Association of Manufacturers (NAM). *Proceedings of the annual convention.*

National Education Association (NEA). *Address and proceedings.* 1913-1914.

National Society for the Promotion of Industrial Education. *Bulletin no. 6, proceedings of the first annual meeting, part I.*

Government Documents:
Commission on National Aid to Vocational Education. *Report on the commission on national aid to vocational education.* House Doc. 1004, 63d

Cong., 2d Sess., June 1, 1914. Washington, D.C.: Government Printing Office, 1914.

Federal Board for Vocational Education. *Statement of policies No. 1.* Washington, D.C.: Government Printing Office, 1917.

U.S. Bureau of Education. *Report of the commissioner: 1883.*

U.S. Congress. *Vocational education.* Committee on Agricultural and Forestry, Hearings, 61st Cong., 2d Sess., April 1910. Washington, D.C.: Government Printing Office, 1910.

U.S. *Congressional Record.* Vol VXLI, Part IV, 1907, pp. 122-125.

Published Primary Sources:

Dewey, J. An undemocratic proposal. *Vocational Education,* March 1913, 374-377.

Miles, H., & Duffy, F. *How shall the obligation to provide industrial education be met?* New York: National Society for the Promotion of Industrial Education, 1911.

Snedden, D. The problem of vocational education. *Vocational education: Its theory, administration and practice.* Boston: Houghton Mifflin, 1910.

SECONDARY SOURCES

Barlow, M. *History of industrial education in the United States.* Peoria, Ill.: Chas. A. Bennett, 1967.

Cubberley, E. *Changing conceptions of education.* Cambridge, Mass.: Riverside Press, 1909.

_____. *Public education in the United States.* Cambridge, Mass.: Riverside Press, 1934.

David, H. On thinking about vocational education policy. Address at the National Conference on Public Policy, Austin, Tex., 1977.

Evans, R. Reauthorization and the redefinition of vocational education. *VocEd,* Jan./Feb. 1981.

Hall, C. *Black vocational technical and industrial arts education.* Chicago: American Technical Society, 1973.

Kotler, P., & Levy, S. Broadening the concept of marketing. *Journal of Marketing,* 1969.

Lazerson, M., & Grubb, N.W. *American education and vocationalism: 1870-1970.* New York: Teachers College Press, 1974.

Livesay, H. *Samuel Gompers and organized labor in America.* Boston: Little, Brown & Co., 1978.

McClusky, N. *Catholic education in America.* New York: Teachers College Press, 1964.

Spivey, D. *Schooling for the new slavery.* Westport, Conn.: Greenwood Press, 1978.

Violas, P. *The training of the urban working class.* Chicago: Rand McNally, 1978.

REDEFINING THE WORK ETHIC FOR THE 1980s

Paul Sultan

On a warm May evening in 1970, Abbie Hoffman spoke to a large campus gathering on the Yale Mall:

> We gotta redefine the — — language. Work—W-O-R-K—is a dirty four-letter word. We need a society in which work and play are not separate. We gotta destroy the Protestant ethic as well as capitalism, racism, imperialism—that's gotta go too. We want a society in which dancin' in the streets isn't separate from cuttin' sugar cane. (quoted in Giamatti, 1976, pp. 18-19).

SDS leader Carl Oglesby (1969) offered an even more imaginative prescription to deal with the evils of capitalism when he wrote that "individuals would be freed from the tyranny of work only when we have one hundred percent unemployment" (p. 12).

In the 1950s and 1960s, the work ethic was under assault from yet another source: the upward surge in labor productivity, the consequence of automation, which was bringing the American economy to the "edge of abundance." The creation of such abundance, one would think, would be an occasion for celebration. But capitalist structures are not calibrated to deal with the surfeit of goods and services. Under our system, scarcity is essential to maintain price, value and profits. With the productivity surge threatening the unprecedented cornucopia of goods, markets might be glutted quickly and industry demoralized. Because our consumption could not keep up with the increased production, the rate of productivity growth established the rate of job loss. The challenge to contemporary society was to convert oppressive and massive labor displacement to noble and creative leisure. But our capacity to deal with the issue of leisure was crippled by our commitment to the work ethic, or the biblical text that "in the sweat of thy face, thou shall eat bread" (Genesis 3:19). Historically, the work ethic has been seen as the solution to any society's problems of scarcity. But now that "solution" was the problem.

Low Productivity Growth Today

Today, in contrast, our concerns center on zero productivity growth. It seems paradoxical that only two to three decades ago we were concerned with the disruptive consequences of rapid productivity improvement. But

49

some of our most distinguished scientists gave credence for such concern. Norbert Wiener (1954) analogized the consequence of a small acceleration of labor productivity growth to taking strychnine: "The difference between a medicinal dose of Strychnine and a fatal one is also only one of degree" (p. 45). Rand scientist Richard Bellman speculated that in our lifetime, the foreseeable needs of society could be produced by only 3 percent of the work force. As if this were not startling enough, he later reduced the estimate to 0.9 percent.

Admittedly, a distinction should be drawn between the concerns of the new left and those of the scientific community. For the new left, the exploitive elements of capitalism foreclosed the opportunity for the individual to fashion life experiences that would provide for individual fulfillment. The press for new arrangements that would allow individuals *not* to work was hardly intended as a demand for complete idleness. It was to emphasize that occupation and vocation had the affect of usurping energy or attention to personal avocation. One's life design was not, then, the product of individual artistry, but bore the heavy stamp of oppressive market realities. Allusions to personal freedom under capitalism, then, were simply an appeal to illusion.

Scientists, in contrast, were concerned with the linkages between man and machine, with the speculation that improvements in the former through education and training could not pace the improvements in the latter, the product of research. As an extreme case in point, farm mechanization has proceeded apace, notwithstanding farm-sector access to undocumented workers with a fierce commitment to a work ethic and laboring for pitifully low wages. The enigma in all of this is not, as the new left contended, that individuals are confronted with the tyranny of work. It is rather that they are confronted with the tragedy of nonwork. In this context, labor may be acquiring the commodity status of potatoes in being an "inferior" good. In an increasingly opulent society, individuals forgo their consumption of potatoes for more elegant alternatives. And similarly, in factor markets, management's appetite or taste for labor may diminish as it is confronted with the menu (and modest prices) of its glittering high-technology options.

THE CONTEMPORARY POLICY SETTING

The central theme of this paper involves the linkages between self and society, the connections between self-fulfillment and societal growth. Today, conflicting views on how we trigger personal incentives and the opportunity and capacity to work is the anvil over which national policy changes are being forged.

Supply-Side Economics

The new supply-side economics emphasizes that:
1. The spur to achievement often involves the prospect of failure.
2. Such failure, when it occurs, is more likely to involve personal, rather than systemic, malperformance.

3. Social investments, in creating a safety net, have eroded the work ethic, creating a perverse form of bondage for minorities and indigents. Counting all forms of support payments, a considerable segment of those categorized as poor simply cannot afford to consider work as an option. Working involves the loss of support systems that have a higher value than take-home pay.
4. Egalitarian programs have dulled acquisitive labor force participation impulses at every level of our society.
5. The recent decline of labor productivity can be largely explained by lagging capital growth. Capital-labor ratios, the key to productivity, have not increased. Neither has labor productivity.
6. The Great Society attention to the social pathologies has led to an over-populated public sector and an overloaded private sector.
7. Investments in human capital may well have been pushed to the flat of the curve in labor's production function. Because educational exercises are not attuned to market needs, and because educational experiences lack disciplined attention to study, educational experiences are often dysfunctional. Education—the centerpiece for the improvement of the human condition in the last two decades—is now being replaced with its alternative spur to achievement, the tax reduction.

The Liberal View

The scattered and demoralized liberals have yet to redeploy their forces. Liberal idealogues have yet to assess what can be salvaged from the conservative blitz. But liberals insist their course has been essentially correct:
1. The strength of an opulent culture is measured by the dignity it affords its crippled and impaired constituencies. The cause of humanity cannot be subsumed to the market mechanism; it must remain above the fray.
2. Investments in people represent, in this stage of capitalism, a much more critical priority than investments in machinery. This is not to assert that the philosopher, reflecting on hypothesis construction while he prods the potato patch with a stick, is more productive than the traditional farm worker with his Caterpillar diesel. But the design of the production process, including the design of the diesel, is a product of human ingenuity.
3. The speculation that increased inequality will prove a spur to individual productivity has yet to be tested. It assumes that those who have the cake will not eat it. And those suffering the last of adversity will be moved, not to rioting or to the subterranean economy, but to accommodation of expectations to labor-market realities. While Lenin asserted that the power to tax is the power to destroy, we are required to believe its less certain opposite: the power *not* to tax is the power to create.

Even if the sweep of conservative economic policies should prove successful in reducing the level of consumption from its present 95 percent share of disposable income, can we be certain that the ensuing portfolio of private

51

investments will not endanger domestic growth and employment? Here again, the critics of capitalism have assembled their traditional criticisms with some new twists: American management is predisposed to self-enrichment rather than reinvestment, involving their purchase of vintage cars, paintings and speculative land holdings, rather than fresh capital formation. Multinationals are exporting United States capital to create global assembly lines making extensive use of low-wage Third World workers. In effect, jobs are being exported. The increase of profits will involve the raising of profit targets; this will encourage modest-profit plant closures in single-company towns. And there has been a conspicuous use of corporate energy and financial resources to effect mergers and divestitures. Even if corporate resources are targeted on corporate growth, investments take the form of product, rather than process, innovation. We end up, then, with new scents on our tissues and new wrinkles on our potato chips, not new configurations in technology to assure our competitive advantage and job growth.

Even if long-term benefits in the shift of the portfolio of investments proves a spur to growth, the short-term penalties can involve major dislocations, including serious job loss for up to one million persons. Nor is it instructive to preach about Horatio Alger and the work ethic to the very elderly, the frail, crippled, the institutionalized or infants yet to be born. Thus, while conservatives are persuaded of the high risks involved in creating a risk-free society, liberals have rejoined that any culture must give individuals a reasonable opportunity to behave the way society expects them to behave. We violate personal dignity at our peril. The issue, then, involves that of defining the origin of work opportunities and, with that, the role of the work ethic itself.

HISTORICAL PERSPECTIVES ON THE WORK ETHIC

The necessity for a culture to instill in its population the desire and ability to work is so obvious as to hardly require elaboration. Any culture must first produce that which it can consume. But beyond this level, the issue as to just who should be obligated to work and how its rewards should be distributed has been a topic for both tormented intellectual debate and overt internecine warfare. We offer below just a few highlights of this richly-textured doctrinal debate.

With the casting out of Adam and Eve from paradise for their original sin, the obligations for self-support became obvious. If man was to consume the forbidden fruit, he must subsequently plant his own orchard. Work, in this context, contains elements of expiating sin.

In the early status societies of the middle ages, life was rude and short. The stamp of position in society was dictated by birth and sanctioned by the weight of religious and political authority. The specialization of function between thinking and doing, between leisure and labor or between reflection and work were obvious necessities in the semi-autonomous self-sustaining economies that dotted the European landscape. But the unity of these functions was not to be expected within individuals but between individuals. And by some accounts, with the stamp of status dictated at birth, status systems provided some measure of tranquility. The peasant was relieved of the unsettling expectations to distinguish himself through career advancement.

Such status systems ultimately gave way to the force of new market systems, the restless spirit of capitalism or the unbounded energy of entrepreneurship. But before undivided attention could be given to materialism, and to treat the acquisition itch as something more than an aberrent affliction, it was necessary to find a conceptual and philosophical sanction for profits.

Self-Interest as Motivation

In Adam Smith's *Theory of Moral Sentiment* (1759), Smith had concluded that the excesses of self-interest could be moderated by each individual's need to enjoy the approbation of the larger society (Whittaker, 1960). The neutral observer, representing that public, would make explicit the tolerable limits to personal exploits. But meanwhile, Bernard de Mandeville, in his *Fable of the Bees,* offered the satirical view that "in reality, almost all private vices ultimately became public or collective virtues or benefits." Smith found this contention unanswerable. He became a convert to the view that self-interest, while not the highest motive, was certainly the human species' strongest motive.

In Smith's *Wealth of Nations* (1776), the harmony between self and society was made explicit. An invisible hand assured the transfer of benefits from the economic man to its unintended beneficiaries, the general public. Indeed, even conscious altruism was disparaged: "I have never known much good being done by those affecting trade for the general welfare" (p. 421). The uninhibited pursuit of personal material gain promised, as certainly as night follows day, enlarged benefits for the outside community. Economic interests were no longer avaricious, predatory assaults on the human condition. They were the mainspring for the creative expression of human energy.

Biology and Religion

This was, of course, pretty heady stuff for cultures infused for generations with the biblical scripture that it would be more difficult for the rich man to enter heaven than for a camel to pass through the eye of the needle. But help came from two highly different sources: Social Darwinists undertook the transfer from biology to economics of the biological paradigm found in the struggle between species. Once again, competition (conflict) was programmed within nature. And if the laws of biology were not persuasive enough in supporting Smith, we could find sanctions in religious authority itself. Calvin's doctrine of predestination again reflected original sin. At birth, man was either saved or condemned. In order to decode the diety's design for each of us—an issue of hardly trivial significance for those contemplating spending eternity in hell—one might seek clues through a life of hard work and frugality. In this way, the pursuit of wealth was not an exercise engineered by the devil to allow, in turn, an orgy of self-indulgence and dissipation. It was a virtuous pursuit equivalent to building a temple on earth, in which employees themselves might "worship" by displaying their fidelity to God and the work ethic.

Thomas Carlyle, probably more than anyone else, espoused the view that work involved a form of communion with God. The question posed in our lifetime should not center on what we have gained but on what we have accomplished. All honest labor was sacred. And the more strenuous the labor, the more certain its divineness. He was concerned, however, as he viewed the evidence of conflict and craven materialistic passions on all sides, that democratic societies would prove fragile under the assaults of greed. (LaValley, 1968). But he advanced, as though to reassure himself, the "indisputable" proposition that an individual would tend to secure a fair day's wage for a fair day's work. This connection was as incontrovertible as the Gospels or multiplication tables (Carlyle, 1843, chap. 3).

The case, then, for the individual's commitment to work seemed well cemented by the converging doctrines of Smith, Darwin and Calvin. The harmonization of ethical principle with economic analysis was firmly secured, with the comforting assurance that the drive for personal accumulation would serve both the economy's needs and God's will.

THE DISAFFECTION WITH WORK

But for some, the obligations to work were dictated by more simple realities, such as the need for survival. Why labor over an abstract rationale for an activity so obviously necessary? In *Candide,* Voltaire explained: "Let us work without theorizing; it is the only way to make life endurable." Charles Kingsley, in his *"The Three Fishers"* (1851), offered the classic lines: ". . .men must work and women must weep. . .for there's little to earn and many to keep." And in portraits drawn of our industrial history, there is little testimony about the euphoric state of the work force crawling into bed after 14 hours of difficult and dangerous work, enjoying the "high" of one's communion with God and harmony with the employer.

Marx: The Exploitation of Labor

It was Karl Marx who cast the status of labor in a context of capitalism and technology that was both formal and formidable. Marx borrowed from classical writers in asserting that labor produced all value and that capital forms were simply embodied forms of labor concealed in the creation of those capital instruments. Capital's labor power was "rubbed off" in the final product as the capital instruments depreciated with use. But capitalists could not "exploit" a machine, only the labor it used. And exploitation was the source of surplus value and profits.

The contradiction of capitalism involved the tendency for individual firms to attempt to gain a favored market position by adopting labor-saving technologies. While this would allow a temporary advantage, the diffusion of the technology throughout the industry would follow. This was associated with the widespread displacement of labor by the machine, adding to a reserve army of permanently unemployed workers. The futility in the process was further revealed when employers, with a narrowed labor base to exploit, would find the flow of surplus value insufficient to nourish their massive technologies. The "immiseration," or deprivation, of the working class would ultimately lead to revolution (Marx, 1915; see also Marx, 1933, 1935).

The helplessness of the individual worker emerged in this drama, represented by his sense of alienation. Alienation involved stripping from labor that source of leverage it had in negotiating a pay level by offering the employer both labor skills and supporting tools. With industrialization, the worker had only his services to sell. The second significant source of alienation involved the separation of the employee from the final product. He no longer had the psychic satisfaction of his craft. His influence on the final product was indistinguished and undistinguishable.

To those classic explanations for employee discontent, we can add more recent refinements. The employee may be demoralized because he sees little evidence that the value of his service is revealed in his paycheck. Second, work often involves mindless activity that might better be provided by robots. The job may not begin to tap the reservoir of skills acquired through extensive education and training. Third, work is often degrading, both in the way it wears down one's body and exhausts one's spirit. Fourth, work is often useless, involving activities that have neither discernible consequence for the production process nor benefit for society. Fifth, work may involve the production of commodities that are known to be hazardous to the health of the larger community. Sixth, work assignments might pose some unusual hazards to the worker, such as the risks of injury or death in underground mining, or its long-term risks of black-lung affliction.

THE HIGH RISKS OF LEISURE

If one is not persuaded that hard work provides its own rewards, one may be attracted to work in considering the high risks of its complement—leisure. Households seek happiness in the second home, the third car, the fourth television and the five-hour workday. Popularized portraits of contemporary culture center on our hedonism and narcissism, as we switch our affection from Horatio Alger to the Happy Hooker. For more Americans, the quest for pleasure is pursued with the same zeal and mechanical ingenuity as our quest for wealth. This involves a frantic search, a kind of juvenile race to the candy store. We are caught between "Bring on the clowns . . ." and "Is that all there is?" Simone de Beauvoir (1953) explains that this forlorn process can be attributed to the incapacity of Americans to believe or accept the transitory reality of their existence.

> Life must constantly be filled anew to dissemble the curse it carries within itself; that is why Americans like speed, alcohol, horror films and sensational views. Their demand for new things and ever newer things is feverish since they find no rest in anything.
> . . . As a result of losing themselves in pursuit of the object, they find themselves without any object.

The emptiness of the limits of the American culture is seen in its super-structure and in its scrap heaps, monuments to its search for life's meaning. Fulfillment involves the accumulation of the external trappings of success without its internal substance. Whether one can find happiness with one's videotape recorder remains an open question. A complementary theme is that our search for pleasure, however clumsy or childish, is characteristically extravagant. And this often means that we are quite literally consumed by the process of consumption or self-indulgence.

The visible evidence of our incapacity to moderate our hedonism is seen in the unscheduled absenteeism on Monday morning (reflecting the after-shocks of the exhaustive search for pleasure) and absenteeism again on Friday, as we plan fresh assaults in the quest for fulfillment. All of this ultimately takes its toll in our physical and mental capacity, or even our taste, for the discipline of the job. Note here that the stream of destruction flows, not from work to the home, but from home to work. Opulence, un-happily, carries with it the seeds for its own destruction.

EVIDENCE OF OUR ATTRACTION TO WORK

Portraits can easily distort our view. While it is fashionable to berate the labor force for its disinterest in work, considerable evidence exists that im-pulses to work are alive and well. In survey polls that ask individuals if they would forgo working should their incomes be such that work would no longer be necessary, consistently, some 75 percent of the respondents indicate they would continue to work. If this is too conjectural to be persuasive, note the "subtle revolution" of the sustained increase in the female labor-force par-ticipation rates. In the 1980s women will be deployed in two of every three jobs created. This remarkable shift in the female role can be explained in large part by the female desire to enjoy sanctions of worth found in the marketplace rather than in the home. They are willing, in large numbers, to accept discriminatory pay levels on the job in place of zero pay levels in the home.

It has also been estimated that there are today from 20 million to 30 mil-lion persons outside of the labor force poised for labor-force entry (Smith, 1979). Indeed, it is clear that we must create three jobs to reduce the pool of unemployed by one job because two of those jobs are taken by persons previously not defined as being "in" the labor force. We note, too, the reluc-tance of the United States worker to take reductions in the length of his work week in lieu of pay, the evidence of considerable moonlighting by those who already hold full-time jobs and the reluctance of most workers today to participate in job sharing programs that would divide the burden of work, along with its rewards (Kanter, 1978).

THE WORK ETHIC AND THE NEW BREED

All discussion of the decline of the work ethic inevitably turns to the values of the new generation, that substantial bulge in our population now being ingested into the work force. Much is now made in the shift of youth values from idealism to paganism and in its more recent version, from altruism to pragmatism. The youth problem, in the popular view, will solve itself with time as the metaphorical cobra swallows this goat. It is not likely, however, that the aging of the new breed will purge our culture of values generated in the 1960s and 1970s. They will be manifest in surprising and unanticipated ways, as youthful idealogues assume responsible positions in the court system, the academe and industry.

One cannot ignore the youth movement, for it was an eruption that challenged most elements held sacred by our society, including the work ethic. The assault was made on the hypocrisy of organized religion, the predatory implications of the industrial-military complex, the sterile irrelevance of the academic fare offered in higher education, the racism and discrimination of middle-class America and the brutality and futility of a Vietnam war.

Such protest was, in time, confronted with the full police force of the state. Youth turned, instead, to modified forms of passive resistance, hoping to defuse violence by placing flowers in the muzzles of the rifles of the national guard. The movement turned to mysticism, religions of the East, the sensual and the psychedelic.

In retrospect, higher education seems for the most part to have been untouched by all of this trauma. Senior faculty often viewed student protest as involving an ideology of irrationalism. It was the innocence of youth to hold that knowledge could be secured in the street, that wisdom could be secured through intuition or inspiration rather than through disciplined study. In the end, the movement began to realize the fragility of its own organization, the poverty of its resources and the necessity for social protest to consolidate around more commonly-perceived evils. Such protest movements were ultimately engulfed in reality, with youth belatedly realizing that they had survival needs that required some accommodation to the status quo.

Changes in the Family

While this thrust of social protest appears to have exhausted itself, other social currents have been at work to create unsettling circumstances for youth. One involves the shifting characteristics of the family unit. The divorce rate has increased to well over a million a year. The number of children growing up in less-than-complete families has been increasing at a rate of more than 250,000 per year. In 1970, the proportion of youth aged 16 to 18 living with "complete" families (husband and wife present) was 89 percent; this had decreased to less than 80 percent in 1980 and projections have been drawn for a 60 percent proportion by 1990. In some divorce settlements, neither parent has wanted to assume custody of the children. In Maryland alone, in 1978, some 6,000 parents went to court to surrender responsibility for a teenage child. It is estimated that currently there are about two million incidents of battered children annually. Such violence in the home might help explain the 1979 incidence of 110,000 cases of student assaults on teachers, an increase of some 40,000 of such episodes over 1978 levels.

Today in about one half of all families, both husband and wife are working. If both parents perceive the rewards for their work ethic are involving a multi-product outcome of the family unit—that is, if they see themselves as manufacturing both a joint income that allows access to the good things in life *and* the production of successful children—they may develop concerns about the product mix. More specifically, they may see their own children as being raised in a culture confronted with present shock and future uncertainty, with their chances of successful parenting forced beyond their control. And they may feel they have little capacity to endure failure in parenting. In Lance Morrow's (1979) colorful simile, "We see a nation recoiling from its young like W.C. Fields beset with Baby Leroy."

But from the viewpoint of many youth following their fathers' routes to happiness, as Gail Sheehy (1976) explains, life is seen as a fate marginally better than suicide: "They dread waking up at the age of fifty-five from the money, power, fame, success and grind they watched their fathers pursue, to find they have only a few years left to enjoy life between the first and final heart attack." There is some sense, in this, of a reciprocity of disdain. It may say something about the renewed interest of both working parents to find that "solace" on the job that will substitute for the lack of fulfillment in the home.

EDUCATION AND THE WORK ETHIC

Education has the mission of transmitting intergenerational values essential for the working of our culture. To what extent can we attribute the lapse of faith or commitment to the work ethic to the educational process itself? If the sentiment of popular accounts is a measure of public opinion, the academe has much to explain. And much to do.

The criticisms are now part of the steady drizzle that seems to have dampened spirits rather than to have generated an academic response. After all, in the traditional view, education is preparation for life, not for work. But if life *is* work, what are we left with? The drumbeats of criticisms are familiar. Over half of our unemployed youth aged 16 to 21 are functionally illiterate. Some 40 to 50 percent of children in urban schools are reading below grade level—in many cases, two grades below. Some 46 percent of Spanish-speaking persons and 44 percent of black persons are found to be functionally incompetent. At least 16 percent of the white adult population is equally incompetent. Indeed, depending on how one defines illiteracy, estimates of the adult population requiring some form of remedial education range from 20 million to 50 million. Other estimates (Jackson, 1979) note that functional illiteracy is 2.5 times higher among the unemployed than for the employed (36 percent vs. 15 percent); greater by a factor of three among non-white adults that white adults (50 percent vs. 20 percent); five times greater among adults earning less than $5,000 per year than those earning over $15,000 (40 percent vs. 8 percent) and six times greater among juvenile delinquents than among high school students (85 percent vs. 15 percent).

Are Teachers Teaching?
Much of this is attributed to the lack of discipline (including attention to the work ethic) as an element in preparing youth for both life and work. Most of it is ascribed to a softness of the academic exercise. As Chicago educationist Leroy Lovejoy makes the point to his colleagues: "You can't be any more kind on the kids than society is going to be on them" (Morrow, 1979). The evidence of ineffectual teaching is seen in the steady decline of SAT scores, the sharp increase in the real dollar costs of education concurrent with declining student enrollments, relaxed expectations for homework and classroom performance and the decline of mandated courses in the hard subjects of English, mathematics and science. Teachers, for their part, are suffering burnout, physical and verbal abuse and wavering or nonexistent administrative support when they attempt any discipline. But the popular allegations remain: teachers—for whatever reasons—are not teaching and students are not studying. Some 14 percent of the high school graduating class, to use the popularized charge, are unable to read their own high school diplomas.

CHALLENGE FOR THE FUTURE
The remarkable advances in the educational achievement of our work force is a vital force influencing the future definition of a work ethic. We now have 30 million employees who have either graduated from college or who have "some" college experience. Another 30 million workers have completed high school. Such educational attainment sets the stage for heightened expectations involving job autonomy, job challenge, job enrichment, job promotions and personal enrichment. It is not clear that the current configurations of our technology will support those expectations.

Nor is it clear that we have defined just how we can couple the coming age of robotized production with those needs. We have not yet perceived, in a sense, how we can effect a humane and enriching fusion of the human agent with its "million dollar" limbs. The problems is more interesting than those posed in the 1960s since the new generation of robots are being equipped with brains and new sensory capacities. They are available at an estimated operating cost of $8.00 per hour relative to estimated labor costs of $18.00 per hour. We cannot afford to succumb to a pessimism that we are once again involved in a zero sum game in the competition between the human agent and its non-human replications.

Labor: Our Richest Resource
The challenge is all the more significant when we appreciate that by 1990 the United States will have a work force of close to 120 million. This is double the level projected for Japan and greater by more than a factor of four for the work force anticipated in England, West Germany, France or Italy.

Labor, then, is our most abundant resource. It must remain our richest resource. The task is to define a work environment where fulfillment of labor's creative potential is possible.

There is some urgency in all of this. The urgency stems from the realities of international competition, and the most conspicuous example involves the capacity of the Japanese to colonize the United States economy in 20 years. We supply Japan, for the most part, with raw materials, unprocessed grains, uncut lumber and unprocessed scrap. With the marriage of contemporary technology and their own exquisite form of the work ethic, Japan's high-quality products find a ready market in the United States. We have, in effect, become hewers of wood and drawers of water. Our comparative advantage, even in this humble assignment, involves a unique sectoral linkage of thinking and doing, involving land-grant colleges, agronomy, research, farm technology, a farm extension service and a rural work ethic.

In truth, the recent decline of our labor productivity rate can be explained by many more elements than labor's faltering dedication to a work ethic. But at the bottom, the incentives and pride we have in creative production represent the energizing mechanisms for future growth and employment. We are confronted with the obvious reality that our gross national appetite has exceeded our gross national product. We recall, too, a simple-minded aphorism that one must first produce that which he would consume. Surely our society has not grown so preoccupied with "conceptual complexity" as to neglect the obvious realities. The challenge before us is to fuse a new union in working and thinking, a union between productivity and consumption, and we believe, a union between a work ethic and personal fulfillment. Perhaps even Abbie Hoffman would agree.

REFERENCES

Carlyle, T. *Past and present,* Book I. London: Chapman and Hall, 1843.

de Beauvoir, S. Adieu to America. In *American, day by day.* New York: Grove Press, 1953.

Giamatti, A.B. Sentimentality. *Yale Alumni Magazine,* January 1976, pp. 18-19.

Jackson, Rev. J. *Statement on basic skills.* Hearings before the Subcommittee on Education, Arts and Humanities of the Committee on Labor and Human Resources, U.S. Senate, 96th Congress, 1st Session. Washington, D.C.: Government Printing Office, 1979.

Kanter, R.M. Work in a new America. *Daedalus,* Winter 1978, pp. 47-78.

Kingsley, C. The three fishers (1851). In *The Kingsleys: A biographical anthology.* London: George Allen Urwin, Ltd., 1973.

LaValley, A. *Carlyle and the idea of the modern.* New Haven, Conn.: Yale University Press, 1968.

Marx, K. Capital. In F. Engels (Ed.) *A critique of political economy.* Chicago: Charles H. Kerr & Co., 1915.

Marx, K. *Wage-labour and capital.* New York: International Publishers Co., Inc. 1933.

Marx, K. *Value, price and profit.* New York: International Publishers Co., Inc., 1935

Morrow, L. Wondering if children are necessary. *Time,* March 5, 1979.

Oglesby, C. Break down the system? *The General Electric Forum,* Vol. 12, No. 1 (Spring), 1969.

Sheehy, G. *Passages.* New York: Dutton, 1976.

Smith, A. *Wealth of nations.* London: Methuen and Company, 1922. (Originally published 1776).

Smith, E. *The subtle revolution—Women at work.* Washington, D.C.: The Urban Institute, 1979.

Whittaker, E. *Schools and streams of economic thought.* Chicago: Rand McNally, 1960.

Wiener, N. *The human use of human beings: Cybernetics and society.* Garden City, N.J.: Doubleday & Co., Inc., 1954.

EARLY VALUES UNDERLYING VOCATIONAL EDUCATION

Melvin D. Miller

Values may generally be defined as social goals, principles or standards held or accepted by an individual, class, society or other group. Ultimately, however, values may also be thought of as what one is willing to settle for. In the ongoing debates over the purposes and effectiveness—as well as the future—of vocational education, a helpful first step might be to look to the past to determine what were the values underlying the early development of vocational education. In the United States, the years between 1906, when the National Society for the Promotion of Industrial Education (NSPIE) was founded, and 1917, when the Smith-Hughes Act became law, constitute those foundation years. As Barlow (1976, p. 1) has written, " . . . nearly everything discussed during the past forty to fifty years in vocational education can be traced to our historical beginnings, particularly the period between 1906-1917."

An important document of that period is the *Report of the Commission on National Aid to Vocational Education* (1914), the work of a commission established by joint resolution of Congress and, which in the final analysis, set the tone and direction for vocational education for the first half of this century. It was the recommendations of this commission that essentially became the Smith-Hughes Act. And although neither the commission's report nor the Smith-Hughes Act represented exactly what early advocates of vocational education sought, it does represent compromise and what these advocates were willing to settle for.

A major figure in the work of the commission was Charles A. Prosser, who at the time of his appointment to the commission, was secretary of the NSPIE. Prosser's seemingly tireless efforts to promote vocational education have left us with a good source of information about those early years and what was valued. In addition to Prosser, David Snedden, mentor to Prosser, is generally accepted as one of the educators of influence in shaping vocational education.

EARLY VALUES

Education for All
Democratizing the schools was an early value underlying the development of vocational education. While schools at the early part of the twentieth century were open to all, the intended outcome of schooling was preparation for college, not preparation for work. Any outcomes related to this latter

area were indirect rather than intended (Snedden, 1910). Since working was more attractive than schooling to the youth of the 1890s, these youth left the public schools by the average age of 14, with less than half of the 14-year-olds having completed the sixth grade. By today's standards, 90 percent of the population was in the category of high-school dropout. Obviously, schools were not adequately serving the needs of youth.

Advocates of vocational education believed that vocational education would make the public schools more democratic. Prosser claimed that, "The American school will become truly democratic when we learn to train all kinds of men, in all kinds of ways, for all kinds of things" (Prosser, 1914, p. 406). Since schools at that time were serving only the needs of a small percentage of the population, the majority of youth were not able to secure at public expense preparation for their work in life. Vocational education as an alternative for those leaving school at 14 years of age would provide a reason for continuing in school, extend general education, and thus democratize education. In short, vocational education would be open to all.

Female and Male. The failure of the schools was related to all youth. While 60 percent of all high school graduates in 1910 were women (U.S. Department of Labor, 1968), schools were failing to serve the needs of females. In this era, 30 percent of all women between the ages of 15 and 24 were gainfully employed (NSPIE, 1907) and according to the Federal Board for Vocational Education (1920), 40 percent of all women in the 16-to-20-year group were employed. Clearly, women were employed outside of the home yet lacked suitable preparation for entering the work force.

Jobs for women were limited in variety and scope. Most were low-level factory and manufacturing positions with limited opportunity for advancement. Working conditions were generally poor and frequently deplorable. Women usually were not encouraged nor prepared to seek or advance into challenging and rewarding positions.

These conditions led early leaders of vocational education to see the need for education as twofold—education for wage earning and education for the work of the home. Early departure from high school, coupled with a lack of preparation for work, left most women inadequately prepared to cope with the roles they would fill. As Snedden (1910) said, "Society will undoubtedly require that the two functions become harmonized, to the end that the welfare of the individual and the soundness of society may at the same time be concerned" (p. 52). The dual preparation for women was in the forefront as vocational education was being planned.

Additional Benefits. Several additional benefits were envisioned from establishing vocational education in the public schools. As education for employment extended the years of schooling, the level of citizenship would likely increase. Training in the scientific principles of farming and the household occupations would contribute to greater efficiency in farming and to strengthening the American home (Marshall, 1907). The Commission on National Aid to Vocational Education anticipated that vocational education would have an indirect but positive effect on the aims and methods of general education. As an outcome, better teaching methods would emerge for children who did not readily respond to book instruction, and an education based on utility could take a place with dignity, side by side with the liberal, connecting education with life by making it more purposeful and useful.

Preparation for Work

Preparation for job entry clearly stands out among the early values of vocational education. Preparation for work has been continually associated with vocational education in this country and is, in fact, a distinguishing feature of vocational education as compared to general education.

Prosser (1913) put the matter quite well when he answered his own questions of "What is vocational education? How does it differ from general education?" with the response that "General education prepares us to live well. Vocational education prepares us to work well" (p. 401).

The Commission on National Aid to Vocational Education held that the controlling purpose of vocational education should be to prepare persons for useful employment in a trade or industrial pursuit or on the farm or in the farm home *(Report of the Commission,* Vol. 1, 1914).

Needs of People and of Industry. There were several reasons for pursuing this goal of preparing people for work, one of which was to increase the wage-earning capacity of boys and girls by helping them move from areas of unskilled labor to being the skilled workers sought by industry. At the same time, by fulfilling the needs of people, the creation of a well-trained work force could serve the needs of industry.

As part of its work, the Commission on National Aid to Vocational Education held extensive hearings and conducted surveys to determine the need for, and the public's sentiment concerning, federal grants for vocational education. The commission surveyed each chief state officer, over 800 superintendents, 104 national organizations of labor and 70 representative employers, five of whom were selected by each of 14 associations of manufacturers.

The commission's final report (Vol. 1) stressed the human needs issues in several ways. The commission found that vocational education was a way to prevent a waste of human labor, to increase earning power, to offset the increased cost of living and to achieve higher standards of living as a result of better education.

Among those testifying before the commission was the U.S. Secretary of Commerce, W.C. Redfield. According to Redfield, factories throughout the country were cursed with untaught and untrained people. His concern was that these workers lacked self-respect and although willing to work, these persons did not know how to work and were ashamed (*Report of the Commission,* Vol. II, 1914).

Samuel Gompers, President of the American Federation of Labor, also expressed a concern for people. His concern was that a proper balance be maintained between the supply side of labor and the demand for workers.

Otherwise, according to Gompers (1914), injury to labor and the worker would result. H.H. Rice, president of the National Metal Trades Association, concurred with Gomper's position. He saw that a system of vocational education would tremendously advance the welfare of workers *(Report of the Commission,* Vol. II).

At the time the commission began its work there was a constantly increasing demand upon industries for more and better goods, and at the same time, a diminishing supply of trained workers. Factories were producing fewer goods that were costing more and were of lower quality. Inefficient labor was viewed as a primary cause of higher prices and lower profits. To fail to promote vocational education, according to the commission, would lead to a general backwardness in industry *(Report of the Commission, Vol. I).*

A Continuing Relationship

The early relationship established with the marketplace has strongly influenced vocational education. Curriculum for vocational education is shaped by work place demands. Advice is sought from those knowledgeable about the needs of agriculture, business, government, industry and the trades. Followup is used in part to measure how well vocational education is doing in preparing individuals for work. Placement in a work role has been accepted as a reasonable outcome for vocational education. In many ways, each of these preferred practices are a direct result of the job preparation goal upheld by early proponents and practitioners of vocational education.

PREFERRED PRACTICES

In making the determination that two early values of vocational education were education for all and preparation for work, the early leaders in the field needed to decide what practices were necessary to help achieve these goals. Among the most important issues considered were the use of qualified teachers, practical supervised experience and research in vocational education.

Teacher Qualifications

A concern for qualified teachers was signified by diverse statements early in the development of vocational education. Snedden (1910), in discussing problems concerning vocational education, pointed out that the pedagogy of vocational education would differ widely from that used in liberal education, especially with respect to making practice, or participation in productive work, a fundamental element.

Occupational experience was considered a primary requisite for vocational teachers. The Commission on National Aid to Vocational Education recommended that vocational-teacher training be given only to persons who had adequate vocational experience in the line of work for which they were preparing to teach (*Report of the Commission,* Vol. 1).

Early Values Underlying Vocational Education

While occupational experience was foremost among teacher qualifications, it was not the only issue. The teaching function also was emphasized strongly. NSPIE discussed this issue in its meetings and published a bulletin in 1917 on the subject. The bulletin addressed the qualifications of industrial school teachers and urged that readers keep in mind the controlling purpose of vocational education — to prepare students for useful employment. While the bulletin stressed that industrial teachers needed industrial experience or training adequate for their particular task, it was also emphasized that the industrial school was not just a place for teaching a trade; it was, as well, a school dealing with the education of adolescent children. As such, the industrial school had responsibilities similar to those of any secondary school. Like other public schools, it should require its teachers to meet certain qualifications as to personality, educational background and teaching ability.

Supervised Experience

Practical experience was considered an integral aspect of early vocational instruction. Learning by doing was a theme that recurred in numerous discussions and eventually appeared in the Smith-Hughes Act.

Snedden (1910), was among those who gave prominence to the need of students to have occupational experience.

> Between the experience of the worker and the studies in the schools, there have been too few points of contact to serve true pedagogical effect.
>
> From this point of view, for example, in the making of the true agriculturalist of middle rank, we should expect the boy to participate for a part of each day, or week, or month, or year, in the actual productive work of the home or school farm. (pp. 36-37).

Snedden believed that no matter what line of work students were preparing for, they ought to receive actual work experience. He pointed to instances of students alternating schooling with working in actual shops and suggested that the most effective vocational education might be achieved through the systematic cooperation of schools with other agencies.

Prosser shared much the same point of view as Snedden. He believed that successful vocational education required the combining of two elements: practice and thinking about practice; doing and thinking about doing. According to Prosser (1913, p. 407), practice and theory had to go hand in hand in vocational education. The more intimately practice and theory went hand in hand, the more the school would contribute to the learner's immediate success and equip the person for the requirements of one's calling. Prosser, as a member of the Commission on National Aid to Vocational Education, eventually saw his position represented in the report of the commission.

The commission recommended that practical experience be required in agriculture and in trades and industrial education. In agriculture, teaching was to be accompanied by directed or supervised practice for at least six months to a year. In the trades and industry area, it was recommended that a minimum of 30 hours of instruction per week for nine months be given, with at least half of the instruction devoted to practical work on a useful or productive basis.

An interesting sidelight in the area of occupational experience relates to distributive occupations and the Federal Board for Vocational Education. The Federal Board, established by the Smith-Hughes Act, was authorized to undertake studies in the area of commerce. While distributive occupations were not identified as a specific area for funding in the Smith-Hughes Act, one of the Federal Board's early publications (1918) dealt with the retail occupations. The bulletin pointed out how schools and business may cooperate in preparing young people for retail selling.

Administration

The decision as to who was to administer vocational education resulted from compromise. Though it was clear that vocational education was being promoted as a part of public education, the early advocates believed that the administration of such programs should be kept separate from the bookish and impractical education typical at the turn of the century. Snedden (1910) argued for a separate administrative structure, but in the end was willing to concede that "in time it will undoubtedly prove true that men of capacity as school administrators will come to understand the philosophy of vocational education, after which they will become competent as directors of the same" (p. 58).

Prosser's views were parallel to Snedden's, and in the final analysis, Prosser saw no fundamental reason why local school boards, which believed in vocational education, which were willing to provide the competent teaching staff necessary and which were able to secure adequate funds, could not conduct effective vocational training as well as any special or independent board. Those most adamant in their belief that vocational education should begin as a separate part of the public education system were willing to settle for a single administration in order to achieve the goal of having vocational education in the public schools.

Research

Research has been a part of the dynamics of vocational education from the very beginning. The data-collection process and the 11 years of study that preceded the passage of the Smith-Hughes Act underscore the role of research in establishing vocational education.

The Commission on National Aid to Vocational Education concluded in its final report (Vol. I) that one of the most valuable ways the federal government could aid the states would be through national grants for research studies. It further recommended that annual appropriations be established for the Federal Board for Vocational Education to undertake such studies. Agriculture, home economics, trades and industries, commerce and commercial processes, as well as methods of teaching and development of courses for the foregoing areas, were all indicated as research topics. The

Smith-Hughes Act implemented this recommendation and thereby formalized the importance of research in early vocational education.

CONCLUSION

In this brief review, we have looked at what were considered some of the primary values for vocational education in its developmental years, as well as some of the practices chosen to help achieve those goals.

Those early values appear to be as valid today as they were at their initial formulation. As we look to the future, what is important for us as vocational educators is the need to constantly reexamine whether the practices being used are serving to fulfill those underlying values, and if not, to determine what changes are needed or what new practices might be implemented.

REFERENCES

Barlow, M.L. *Implications from the history of vocational education.* Columbus, Ohio: The National Center for Vocational Education, 1976.

Federal Board for Vocational Education. *Retail selling. Bulletin no. 22, commercial education series no. 1.* Washington, D.C.: Government Printing Office, 1918.

Federal Board for Vocational Education. *Trade and industrial education for girls and women. Bulletin no. 58.* Washington, D.C.: Government Printing Office, 1920.

Gompers, S. *The attitude of the American Federation of Labor toward industrial education.* New York: National Society for the Promotion of Industrial Education, 1914.

Marshall, F.M. *Industrial training for women. Bulletin no. 4.* New York: National Society for the Promotion of Industrial Education, 1907.

National Society for the Promotion of Industrial Education. *The selection and training of teachers for state-audit industrial schools. Bulletin no. 19.* New York: Author, 1917.

Prosser, C.A. The meaning of industrial education. *Vocational Education,* 1913, 401-410.

Snedden, D. *The problem of vocational education.* Boston: Houghton Mifflin Co., 1910.

_____. *Vocational education.* New York: MacMillan Co., 1920.

U.S. Commission on National Aid to Vocational Education. *Report of the commission on national aid to vocational education, 2 vols.* Washington, D.C.: Government Printing Office, 1914.

U.S. Department of Labor. *Trends in educational attainment of women.* Washington, D.C.: Government Printing Office, 1968.

CULTURAL FOUNDATIONS OF BLACK LEADERSHIP

Sonja H. Stone

INTRODUCTION

This is a study of the cultural foundations of black leadership in vocational education. According to Gavins (1977, p. vii), Ralph Bunche defined black leadership as "individual and collective contributions to Black uplift, including Black spokesmen, community organizations, protest movements, and race relations." Because vocational education is considered one vehicle of black uplift and because the most outstanding black figures in vocational education have also been identified with the overriding goal of black uplift, their leadership may be examined within the context of the cultural foundations of the black community. It is axiomatic that the ability of black leaders to attract followers is proportionate to the degree of consensus between them and their constituencies on racial goals and cultural values.

The central question addressed in this paper is: what can we learn from a study of black leaders in vocational education about the cultural foundations of their leadership? Underlying the question are the following assumptions: that the historical process of socialization and discrimination of black people in the United States has produced a range of cultural characteristics which may be ascribed to black leadership; that these characteristics are embedded in goals, values, beliefs and traits transmitted through such formal and informal agencies as the family, church, press, historically black colleges and the civil rights movement.

In addition to the general role expectations assigned and/or assumed by all leaders, black leaders are also expected to devote their energies to black uplift. This cultural expectation imposes on black leaders a phenomenon that closely approximates Du Bois' (1903, p. 16) concept of "double-consciousness." Double-consciousness, or biculturalism, requires black leaders to further the aspirations of the black community, while simultaneously meeting the standards of their profession. Finally, it is assumed that the recurrence of certain themes in the biographies of selected leaders is one index to the cultural foundations of the Afro-American community.

Focus on Two Themes

According to Thorpe (1969), the dominant themes in black history are the quest for freedom and the struggle for manhood. In view of the extensive treatment of freedom and manhood in scholarly and popular literature, this paper focuses on two themes— altruism and optimism—which may be

71

somewhat less dominant but nonetheless vital to the cultural foundations of black leadership.

In the field of vocational education, black people have performed limited though significant leader/trainer roles both in the South and the North for several hundred years. Booker T. Washington once stated that at the close of the Civil War, black people were "in possession of nearly all the common and skilled labor in the South" (Washington, 1976, pp. 364-365). In the antebellum North, vocational education for blacks went beyond informal and apprenticeship training and became incorporated into such institutions as Avery College in Pittsburgh (Hall, 1973). During the post-bellum period, black people emerged as leaders of an impressive number of Negro institutions devoted to vocational education. Among the leading black advocates of vocational education during the period 1879 to 1955 were Fanny Jackson Coppin, Booker T. Washington and Mary McLeod Bethune.

Since 1964 a contemporary figure, Leon Howard Sullivan, has joined their ranks. An examination of the careers of these four figures sheds light on the ways in which cultural values, such as altruism and optimism, are crystallized in black leadership behavior.

Four Who Pioneered in Vocational Education

Fanny Jackson Coppin, an ex-slave who received the baccalaureate degree from Oberlin College in 1865, was the first black woman in the United States to head an institution of higher education. From 1869 to 1902, Ms. Coppin served as principal of Philadelphia's Institute for Colored Youth (ICY). During her tenure at ICY, she launched an industrial education crusade which evolved into the institution known today as Cheyney State Teachers' College. Perkins (1977) describes Coppin as a classical scholar and teacher-trainer par excellence who viewed industrial education as one option for black people, not exluding academic pursuits. She believed that black people ought to have equal access to all fields of employment, including the trades. From the triple vantage point of a teacher, administrator and community leader in Philadelphia, Coppin earned an international reputation as an educator, churchwoman and advocate of women's rights.

By far the most influential black advocate of vocational education was Booker Taliafero Washington. Unlike Coppin, Washington's ideas on education were an integral component of a larger ideology of racial accommodation. Washington graduated from Hampton Institute where he was trained by Samuel Chapman Armstrong, a white New Englander and former union officer, who recommended him to become the first principal of Tuskegee Institute. Washington started Tuskegee in a chicken house in 1881 and developed it into a teacher training and industrial arts institute of international acclaim. As the leading black spokesman, favorite son of white philanthropists and convener of the "Black Cabinet" (a group of political appointees, elected officials and leaders who served in an informal advisory capacity to the White House), Washington profoundly affected the political and educational conditions of black people until his death in 1915.

Considered by many to be the successor to Booker T. Washington as the leading spokesperson of the race, Mary McLeod Bethune founded the Daytona Literary and Industrial School for Training Negro Girls on the site of a garbage dump in 1904. After a merger with Cookman Institute at Jacksonville, Florida, she became President of the Bethune-Cookman College. In her several capacities as officer of the National Association of Colored Women, founder of the National Council of Negro Women, key member of the "Black Cabinet," Director of the Division of Negro Affairs of the National Youth Administration (NYA), Bethune, like Booker T. Washington, wielded phenomenal influence among blacks and whites (Ross, 1975).

The Reverend Leon Howard Sullivan created in 1964 the Opportunities Industrialization Centers of America (OIC), a community-based employment training agency. OIC was started in an abandoned jailhouse in Philadelphia but has since spread to more than 150 cities throughout the United States and abroad. A protege of the preacher-politician Adam Clayton Powell, Jr., a disciple of the civil rights and labor leader A. Philip Randolph, an admirer of the self-reliance programs of Father Divine and Elijah Muhammed, Sullivan is deeply rooted in the tradition of black leadership and well-connected with industry and government. He is the first and only black man to be elected to the board of directors of General Motors. As his predecessors used their educational institutions as a sphere of influence, so Sullivan has used his church—the 5,000-member Zion Baptist—as a base for vocational education and community development (Anderson, 1976).

Significantly, all four visionaries were driven by a creative force that empowered them to transform the fecal matter of society—chicken house, garbage dump, jailhouse—into viable cultural institutions. Sullivan (1969), for one, recognized the renovated jailhouse as a symbol of OIC's power to transform human untouchables into proud, productive members of society. Above and beyond their own creative genius, Coppin, Washington, Bethune and Sullivan were adhering to at least two of the cultural imperatives of black leadership—altruism and optimism.

ALTRUISM

"Lifting as we climb," the motto of the National Association of Colored Women, is one index to the spirit of altruism which permeates the tradition of black leadership. The African sense of community found continuity in the mutual comfort and aid that black people extended to each other during slavery. The Underground Railroad was founded by free blacks of the North who risked severe reprisals to help fugitive slaves escape to freedom. The antebellum free black communities organized charities, vigilance societies and educational activities to protect and elevate their less fortunate brothers and sisters. The principles of service and elevation dominated the rhetoric of the nineteenth-century black conventions and newspapers. During the Civil War, northern black churches dispatched missionaries to the South and collected money, clothing, medical and other supplies for the contrabands who were swelling the union camps and border towns. The post-bellum black agenda was initially hammered out in the conventions, newspapers and churches of wartime northern black communities. Cain (1864) reported that one of the most pressing priorities was the recruitment and relocation of educated blacks "to guide the rising generation of the Southern states." Bullock (1967) quoted Booker T. Washington as crediting Hampton with "the great and prevailing idea that seemed to take possession of everyone was to prepare himself to lift up the people at his home." But this idea was thoroughly entrenched in the tradition of responsible black leadership long before the Civil War.

The story of post-bellum black education can almost be summed up in the adage, "Charity begins at home and spreads abroad." The selfless, tireless efforts of Northern missionaries—black and white—were matched only by the supreme sacrifices that black people made to educate themselves and their people.

Fanny Jackson Coppin

Despite her heavy course load, teaching duties, and extracurricular activities as a student at Oberlin, Fanny Jackson Coppin (1913) started an evening school for the freedmen who settled in the town of Oberlin during the Civil War. Perkins (1977) declares that Coppin directed the Institute of Colored Youth for 20 years without a salary increase. She consistently depleted her personal resources to assist needy students. When ICY's board of managers refused to build a dormitory to accommodate black students from the South, Coppin raised money for a multipurpose dormitory called the Women's Exchange and Girls' Home, which was located next door to her own residence. Moreover, she and her husband provided lodging for as many as 15 students per year in their home.

By involving herself in her students' health, employment, living conditions and future careers, Coppin not only ministered to their "whole person" but also extended her ministry to the whole of Philadelphia's black community. She saw herself as the teacher of two schools—the Institute of Colored Youth and the black community. No class or institution in black Philadelphia escaped Coppin's concerned and vigilant attention. She was the driving force behind a home for the elderly. She spearheaded the campaign to save the *AME Christian Recorder*. As a columnist for the *Recorder,* she attempted to influence women and children who could not be reached through ICY.

Coppin was acutely conscious of both racial and sexual discrimination. Though declining in health, she was among the first officers of the National Association of Colored Women. Upon retiring from ICY in 1902, she accompanied her husband to South Africa where she organized missions among the women. Owing to her own previous condition of servitude, she was especially empathic with black domestic workers. A signal triumph in Coppin's career was her eloquent and successful plea before the Working Women's Guild of the New Century Club to admit black women. This was a significant breakthrough insofar as discrimination in trade unions was one of the most stubborn barriers to equal employment (Perkins, 1977).

Booker T. Washington

Upon graduating from Hampton, Booker T. Washington strained his meagre resources to help send his brother, his adopted brother and his sweetheart to Hampton. This same kind of familial concern was typically extended by teachers and administrators to poor students at Tuskegee and all black colleges.

Booker T. Washington's outreach, however, extended far beyond the confines of the campus. He insisted that the routine work of the classroom was not enough, that a teacher must be a social worker. He helped to organize the Alabama State Teachers Association, the Farmers' Conference, the Workers' Conference and the National Negro Business League. Hence, Washington's altruistic efforts enabled him to lay hands on, and make a difference in, the lives of a wide cross section of the black community.

A concrete example of how Washington's service orientation figured into his success formula is the National Business League (NBL). Founded by Washington in 1900 as the Negro Business League, the organization preceded the United States Chamber of Commerce by 12 years. Originally conceived by Du Bois in 1899 as an outgrowth of his Atlanta University Conference on the Negro in Business, Harlan (1972) claims that the NBL "provided Washington with an organized body of loyal, conservative followers in every city with a substantial black population" (p. 266). The League has since evolved into a significant national lobby and has greatly affected federal policies and programs designed to assist and develop minority businesses ("National Business League: Forerunner of Black Solidarity," 1980).

Mary McLeod Bethune

Mary McLeod Bethune also made extreme sacrifices to assist immediate and extended, as well as non-family, members to obtain an education. Newsome (1981) relates the story of how she exhausted her savings to subsidize the education of Kwame Nkrumah, the first president of Independent Ghana. Like Coppin and Washington, Bethune also used her school as a social service agency. She started a community hospital because black people were denied equal treatment at the local white hospital. In the face of threats by the Ku Klux Klan, she sponsored voter education workshops on her campus for the black community of Daytona Beach, Florida.

Blackwell (1978) summarizes the work of the National Council of Negro Women (NCNW) under Bethune's leadership. The NCNW concentrated largely on equal educational opportunity but also was instrumental in establishing such outreach programs as day-care centers, hospitals, homes for delinquent youths, consumer education clubs, citizenship classes and economic self-help projects.

Bethune's outreach activities were also interracial and international. During her tenure with the National Youth Administration, she unofficially extended her services to American Indians. Among other involvements, she touched bases with the international community through her association with Moral Re-Armament (Newsome, 1981).

Leon Howard Sullivan

In 1943 Sullivan went to New York where he became involved in the most progressive civil rights and political movements in the country. Notwithstanding these demands and the rigors of graduate school, Sullivan became immersed in the problems of urban juvenile delinquency. He mediated gang dissension, organized a police support system and provided wholesome recreational outlets for young people in Harlem. Undoubtedly, these early experiences in youth work ultimately contributed to the establishment of OIC.

Shortly after assuming the pastorate of Philadelphia's Zion Baptist Church, Sullivan's concern for the plight of black youth led him to organize the Philadelphia Citizens Committee Against Juvenile Delinquency and its Causes. Despite the committee's lack of resources and its eventual decentralization, it was sufficiently effective to earn Sullivan the honor of being chosen by the National Junior Chamber of Commerce as one of the 10 outstanding young men in the United States in 1953. The key to the Citizens Committee was broad citizen participation and police cooperation.

Sullivan's experience with the Citizens Committee led to a tactical assault on a root cause of delinquency—poverty. Accordingly, he established a Youth Employment Service which, reputed to be the most effective program of its kind, ran head-on into racist employment policies. After unsuccessfully appealing to corporate heads and government officials to intervene, Sullivan organized the Selective Patronage Campaign.

The Selective Patronage Campaign was carried out by 400 black ministers who persuaded their congregations to boycott certain firms until they agreed to negotiate the question of hiring black people on the ministers' terms. One by one, Tasty Baking Company, Sun Oil, Gulf Oil and Atlantic-Richfield were boycotted and forced to negotiate with the very leaders whom they had earlier rebuffed. Esso was among the firms who agreed to negotiate before they were hit (Sullivan, 1969).

The success of the Selective Patronage Campaign led to requests from employers for persons with skills that were sometimes scarce in the black community. It was then that Sullivan recognized the need for a community-based employment training facility and conceived of the Opportunities Industrialization Centers of America. OIC is the peculiar synthesis of Sullivan's outreach ministry over a period of two decades—1943 to 1963. His lessons and experiences in community organization, civil rights, direct nonviolent action, youth development, adversarial and coalitional politics all culminated in the formation of OIC, which Sullivan views as an extension of his ministry.

Through his sermons, speeches and writings, Sullivan (1972) explains the theological basis of his outreach ministry. Among other scriptures, Mark 6: 34-44—the story of Jesus' miraculous multiplication of the loaves and fishes—provides the Biblical foundation of his altruism. Faith in the miracle of sharing is one of Sullivan's cardinal alternatives to despair.

Because technical and vocational education for blacks has, historically, been something less than that for whites, black people have vigorously objected to higher education for manual labor. Accordingly, a perennial problem of black leaders in vocational education has been the dual burden of convincing black people of the value of vocational education while pressuring the vocational education establishment for greater training and employment opportunities for blacks (Nichols, 1980; Moody, 1980). The reality of racial discrimination in education and employment impelled Coppin, Washington, Bethune and Sullivan to assume an altruistic/advocacy posture toward vocational education and a means of black uplift.

OPTIMISM

Deeply embedded in the black psyche is the West African quality of optimistic fatalism, known in its Christian context as eternal hope or undying faith. It was a dominant theme in the spirituals of the slaves.

> You may bury me in de Eas'
> You may bury me in de Wes'
> But I'll hear de Trumpet
> Soun' in dat mornin'.

Among the Senegalese, this trait has been described by Davidson (1969, p. 173) as:

> a principle of *solide optimisme,* a "philosophical optimism," deriving from the life force which, product of Being and Becoming, projects the Past into the Future and assures both identity and continuity to the group.

Needless to say, the experience of slavery shook optimism, identity and continuity to their very foundations. Still, black people continued to perceive value and purpose in life. Throughout the writings of the black vanguard and the oral literature of the masses, the faith of Afro-Americans in ultimate liberation is pervasive. "We Shall Overcome" was the anthem of the civil rights movement. Even in the blues idiom, "the sun is gonna shine in my back door some day" is a familiar theme.

Missionaries

With the exception of Booker T. Washington, all of the figures were deeply religious. Above and beyond their chosen professions, they were missionaries. Although Washington had been trained by missionaries at Hampton, he nevertheless developed a degree of skepticism about conventional religion. Still, Washington maintained a strong sense of optimism about the future of black people. His optimism derived from his confidence in himself, his faith in black people and his belief in the good will of "quality" whites. To a greater or lesser extent, Coppin, Bethune and Sullivan shared Washington's sentiments but anchored them to a divine faith.

Throughout her career, Coppin was closely associated with liberal and philanthropic whites, but she preferred to concentrate her fund-raising efforts in the black community. She frequently addressed black audiences on

77

the topic, "The Power There is in Us to Help Ourselves." She demonstrated her faith in the intellectual equality of black people by making the Institute for Colored Youth an international showcase of academic excellence. Coppin delighted in the challenge of transforming black children from the most deprived circumstances into competent scholars, professionals and tradespersons. A statement of her confidence in black intelligence is found in Perkins (1977): "In 99 cases out of 100, the reason that pupils do not learn is not because they haven't brains enough, but there has been unskilled teaching and difficulties have been allowed to accumulate" (p. 154).

Given the scarcity of Coppin's extant writings and speeches, her optimism must be measured primarily by her teacher-leader behavior. At a time when both scientific and popular opinion held that blacks and women were inferior breeds, Coppin proved otherwise, not only through her own dazzling accomplishments but also through the thousands of students who emulated her.

A Constructionist Optimist

Booker T. Washington's optimism, though at times bordering on a pathological denial of white racism, nonetheless appeared consistent with the cultural value of optimistic fatalism. Kelly Miller (1908) correctly capsuled Washington's constructionist-optimist bent: "He founded his creed upon construction rather than criticism. He urged his race to do the things possible rather than whine and pine over things prohibited" (pp. 18-19). What is "possible" is, of course, a philosophical question, open to innumerable interpretations. Washington's interpretation of what was possible rested on a theory of interdependence which, according to Anderson (1973), linked "an indispensable Black labor force with interested white capitalists" (p. 178). Throughout his career, Washington espoused the belief that the economic indispensability of black workers would lead to economic independence, which in turn would gain the respect and acceptance of white people who would then admit blacks to the ranks of first-class citizenship. Washington (1911) expressed complete confidence in the conviction that black people could and should prove their worth to white people: " . . . I had faith in the good common sense of the masses of my own race" (p. 24).

In her last will and testament, Bethune wrote:

> I LEAVE YOU FAITH. Faith is the first factor in a life devoted to service. Without faith, nothing is possible. With it, nothing is impossible. Faith in God is the greatest power, but great faith too is faith in oneself. The faith of the American Negro in himself has grown immensely, and is still increasing. The measure of our progress as a race is in precise relation to the depth of the faith in our people held by our leaders. (Holt, 1964, p. 288)

Mary McLeod Bethune's self-image was that of a woman of destiny whose "impossible" dreams were realized through the power of faith. Number 15 of 17 children, she was the first to attend school. Commissioned by "no

78

employer but God," Bethune (1954, p. 15) started a school on the site of a garbage dump. She secured the financial support and cultivated the friendship of many of the wealthiest families in America. She served as advisor to four presidents of the United States. Her ability to circumvent the barriers of caste, race and sex in a classist, racist and sexist society lends further credence to the transcendental nature of her faith.

From Struggle to Success

Leon Sullivan's account of his early struggles with OIC is an eloquent testimony of his faith, notwithstanding his claim (1977) that "I am not a pessimist, the nation knows that I am not an optimist. I am a pragmatist." Lacking either funds or experience in the employment training business, Sullivan returned to Philadelphia from the 1963 March on Washington for Jobs and Freedom determined to launch another offensive against poverty. With an abandoned jailhouse as a training site, Sullivan borrowed large sums of money from his church and mortgaged his home to get the OIC program going. He recounts (1969, p. 96) the time he had exhausted all of his resources and desperately needed $13,000 to keep the door open. He got down on his knees and prayed. Within five minutes he received a phone call from Fidelity Bank, advising him that they were in the process of dissolving a trust and were sending him a check for $13,000.

Sullivan's religion tells him, "I can do all things in Him who strengthens me"—Philippians 4:13. He, therefore, does not view the power elite as the permanent enemy of poor minorities. "My experience on the Board of General Motors showed me how a huge multi-billion dollar giant of the free enterprise system could be turned around on the issue of racial injustice and equal opportunities" (Sullivan, 1977). The Reverend Thomas Ritter, Sullivan's longtime associate and board chairman of the Philadelphia OIC, was quoted by Ditzen (1980) as describing their role as that of "industrial missionaries."

Sullivan's faith is pragmatic insofar as it is active in the day-to-day process of solving the problems of survival and economic equity. It is militant insofar as it undergirds his assault on social and economic injustices. It is the very antithesis of despair, to which he proposes the alternative of positive people power. Sullivan (1977) espouses the faith that a coalition of poor minorities and community-based organizations can enter into a working relationship with government, industry and labor to:

attack the twin evils of disastrous unemployment rates and dangerous inflation rates in a manner that will take Americans out of the darkness of hopelessness and despair and lead them into the light of new hope and renewed confidence.

To the extent that Sullivan is a change agent who activates his faith in protest and program, he may be excepted from Kelly Miller's charge that optimistic fatalism is little more than fatal optimism (Eisenberg, 1960, p. 185).

Black Intelligence

Any system of education is predicated upon assumptions regarding the nature of the learner as well as the subject matter. Whether and to what extent educators perceive of blacks as heathen, subhuman, inferior, docile, stupid, etc., naturally reflects an underlying philosophy of black education and inevitably affects the nature of the curriculum. A fundamental difference between black educators and many of their white counterparts lies in their perception of black intelligence. Booker T. Washington is a case in point. Despite his allegiance to his white mentor and benefactor, General Armstrong, Washington sharply departed from Armstrong on the question of black intelligence. Whereas Armstrong (Bullock, 1967, p. 76) declared that black people lacked the power to "assimilate and digest" knowledge, Washington (1969 [1911]) insisted that "human life and human society are so complicated that no one can determine what latent possibilities any individual or any race may possess" (p. 238). Clearly, Washington could not have consummately internalized Armstrong's concept of black intelligence without severely damaging his own self-concept. Hence, faith in the intellectual capacity of black people is, at one level, an extension of the faith of black educators in themselves. Thus, black people have been able to adopt white educational programs without necessarily accepting their premises and objectives, particularly the negative white view of the nature and potential of the black learner.

To be sure, the educators' vision or perception of their students is a major determinant of the quality of education. If, as is so often the case in compensatory or remedial programs, the staff has limited expectations of the students, then there will be limited outcomes. Compounding the challenge of defending black intelligence has been the problem of extending vocational education to the most deprived sectors of the black community. This is Sullivan's charge to the Opportunities Industrialization Centers. Underlying this charge is an implicit if not explicit faith in 1) the capacity and right of people to change and 2) the power of human relationships to effect change. The optimism of these four black vocational educators—Coppin, Washington, Bethune and Sullivan—has been a mighty force in the struggle to defend black intelligence and to increase educational and economic opportunities for black people.

CONCLUSION

Black leadership is an ethno-socio-historical phenomenon which is inextricably linked with the oppression and aspirations of African-Americans in the United States. Black leadership emerges to articulate, advocate and activate the concerns of black people. Irrespective of ideological or occupational differences, the common denominator of black leadership is its commitment to the elevation of black people. Black leadership is rooted in the Afro-Christian cultural tradition which, among other things, values the attributes of altruism and optimism. That these values are both pervasive and persistent is reflected in their appearance as recurring themes in the biographies of four black leaders over a period of nearly 150 years. Related themes that surfaced during the course of this study, and which warrant further treatment, include survivalism, self-help, resistance, collectivism and regeneration. Among black women leaders, women's rights is a prevailing preoccupation.

With the exception of Booker T. Washington, the subjects were not vocational educators, per se. Coppin was a classical scholar and teacher-trainer; Bethune, a missionary; Sullivan, a minister. Yet all promoted vocational education as one means of alleviating economic deprivation in the black community. That they managed to eclipse many trained vocational educators attests not only to their individual talents and fortunes but also to their cultural roots in the black community. The significance of ethnic values needs to be addressed in the context of leadership development programs. Further inquiry into the foundations of black leadership in vocational education is expected to yield implications for leadership theory, black studies, ethnic studies and vocational education.

REFERENCES

Anderson, B.E. *The opportunities industrialization centers: A decade of community-based manpower services.* Philadelphia: University of Pennsylvania, The Wharton School Industrial Research Unit, 1976.

Anderson, J.D. *Education for servitude: The social purposes of schooling in the black south, 1870-1930.* Unpublished doctoral dissertation. University of Illinois at Urbana-Champaign, 1973.

Bethune, M.M. What my faith means to me. *The Church Woman,* 1954, 14-17.

Blackwell, B.G. *The advocacies and ideological commitments of a black educator: Mary McLeod Bethune, 1875-1955.* Unpublished doctoral dissertation. The University of Connecticut, 1979.

Bullock, H.A. *A history of Negro education in the south: From 1619 to the present.* Cambridge, Mass.: Harvard University Press, 1967.

Cain, R.H. *AME Christian Recorder,* July 9, 1864.

Coppin, F.J. *Reminiscences of school life, and hints on teaching.* Philadelphia: AME Book Concern, 1913.

Davidson, B. *The African genius.* Boston: Little Brown & Co., 1969.

Ditzen, L.S. Ritter: We were missionaries. *The Philadelphia Bulletin,* November 19, 1980, p. A8.

Du Bois, W.E.B. *The souls of black folk.* New York: Fawcett Publications, Inc., 1961 (Originally published, 1903).

Eisenberg, B. Kelly Miller: The Negro leader as a marginal man. *The Journal of Negro History,* 1960, *45,* 182-197.

Gavins, R. *The perils and prospects of southern black leadership: Gordon Blaine Hancock, 1884-1970.* Durham: Duke University Press, 1977.

Hall, C.W. *Black vocational technical and industrial arts education.* Chicago: American Technical Society, 1973.

Harlan, L.R. *Booker T. Washington: The making of a black leader, 1856-1901.* New York: Oxford University Press, 1972.

Holt, R. *Mary McLeod Bethune: A biography.* Garden City, N.Y.: Doubleday & Co., Inc., 1964.

Miller, K. *Race adjustment.* New York: Neale Publishing Co., 1908.

Moody, F.B. The history of blacks in vocational education. *VocEd,* January 1980, pp. 30-34.

National Business League: Forerunner of black solidarity and architect of economic emancipation. *National Black Monitor,* June 1980, pp. 26-35.

Newsome, C.G. Mary McLeod Bethune as religionist. Unpublished paper to be included in a forth-coming volume by the Commission on Archives and History of The United Methodist Church, Lake Junalaska, N.C.

Nichols, C.F., Sr. How well are we serving black America? *VocEd,* January 1980, pp. 22-24.

Perkins, L.M. *Fanny Jackson Coppin and the institute for colored youth: A model of nineteenth century black female educational and community leadership, 1837-1902.* Unpublished doctoral dissertation. University of Illinois at Urbana-Champaign, 1977.

Ross, B.J. Mary McLeod Bethune and the National Youth Administration: A case study of power relationships in the black cabinet of Franklin D. Roosevelt. *The Journal of Negro History,* 1975, *60,* 1-20.

Sullivan, L.H. *Alternatives to despair.* Valley Forge: Judson Press, 1972.

_____. *Build brother build.* Philadelphia: Macrae Smith Co., 1969.

_____. Positive people power: An alternative to despair. Speech delivered at A Conference on the Role of Community Based Organizations in Manpower Programs and Policy, Washington, D.C., The National Commission for Manpower Policy, October, 1977.

Thorpe, E.E. *The central theme of black history.* Durham: The Seeman Printery, 1969.

Washington, B.T. Industrial education for the Negro. In L.H. Fishel and B. Quarles (Eds.), *The black American: A documentary history* (3d ed.). Glenview, Ill.: Scott, Foresman and Company, 1976.

Washington, B.T. *My larger education: Being chapters from my experience.* Miami: Mnemosyne Publishing, Inc., 1969. (Originally published, 1911.)

SECTION III

A GROWING NETWORK OF VOCATIONAL EDUCATORS

This section identifies three alternative delivery systems that can help vocational education extend its services to new clientele through various approaches to education for work.

William Mirengoff provides an assessment of programs under the Comprehensive Employment and Training Act (CETA) and offers a policy perspective from which linkage with CETA might be utilized. Robert W. Glover reminds the field of vocational education that apprenticeship is a growing and contemporary force that provides a useful alternative in job training. Because of the integral way that apprenticeship is linked to the private sector, this chapter furnishes a basis for planning vocational education-apprenticeship partnerships that will be appropriate for the future.

Richard Swanson and Brian Murphy give an overview of private sector training. The growth and utilization of private sector training is a contemporary phenomenon, which promises to continue in the future. It poses one of the challenges for vocational education for finding ways to bolster, assist and collaborate with this alternative method of obtaining work skills and competencies.

THE CHANGING FORTUNES OF CETA

William Mirengoff

Enacted in 1973, the Comprehensive Employment and Training Act (CETA) has recently undergone considerable scrutiny by the Reagan administration and is due for reauthorization in 1982. These two events suggest that a review and assessment of the law and its evolution are particularly timely. In this chapter we trace the genesis and development of CETA, placing the act in its political and social context, examining its outcomes with particular emphasis on public service employment programs and assessing its current status.

Our discussion of CETA's evolution and its assessment is based primarily on data obtained from a series of evaluation studies conducted in a sample of 28 prime sponsor jurisdictions from 1974 to 1980.[1] The sample was drawn from a universe of prime sponsors, stratified by type of sponsor (six cities, nine counties, nine consortia and four states), by size and by unemployment rate. The studies were supported by grants from the Ford Foundation and, more recently, the Employment and Training Administration of the U.S. Department of Labor.

ANTECEDENTS AND BEGINNINGS

The immediate antecedents of CETA were the Manpower Development and Training Act of 1962 (MDTA), the Economic Opportunity Act of 1964 (EOA) and the Emergency Employment Act of 1971 (EEA). MDTA and EOA were aimed at improving the employability of the *structurally* unemployed—persons who lack the skills, education or other qualifications to compete successfully in the job market. EEA, in contrast, was a *countercyclical* program for persons whose joblessness was due to downturns in the business cycle.

This legislation was enacted in a decade marked by a proliferation of Great Society programs. From these three acts some 20 separate and uncoordinated programs were spawned, each with its own statutory basis, funding and regulations. All were designed and controlled at the federal level and operated locally by the office of the U.S. Employment Service (ES), local educational agencies and various community-based organizations. Local elected officials, however, figured very little in this scenario.

Disenchantment with the duplication and confusion surrounding these programs soon developed and set the stage for CETA, the next phase in the evolution of the nation's employment and training design.

CETA was shaped by the confluence of two major forces: one pragmatic, the other ideological. First, Congress and the federal manpower administrators were dissatisfied with the patchwork of uncoordinated programs and sought reforms. Second, the Nixon administration had embraced the philosophy of the New Federalism and sought to decentralize a number of federal programs through block grant funding—an approach the present administration has renewed.

CETA assumed control over a multi-billion dollar system encompassing numerous categorical programs, shifted authority from federal to state and local entities and consolidated these separate programs into block grants designed to provide flexibility in meeting local needs.

Decentralization and Decategorization

The two key concepts of CETA were "decentralization" and "decategorization." Decentralization simply meant the transfer of authority for manpower programs from the federal government to state and local governmental units. Decategorization provided prime sponsors with flexibility to use block grant funds over an array of generic services.

Supporters of the CETA legislation included both ideologues and pragmatists. The former believed that decentralization would permit a better expression of the popular will and ensure greater community involvement. The latter maintained that, under local control, ineffective programs would be weeded out, coordinated programs would replace fragmented ones and that local officials, familiar with their jurisdictions, would introduce new employment and training designs and programs.

CETA received bipartisan support in the Congress, but there were two major differences to be bridged. The first concerned the incorporation of a public service employment (PSE) component in CETA. The Democratic Congress insisted upon a significant PSE program and the Republican administration opposed it. This difference has recently resurfaced, albeit in a fiscal rather than an ideological form. The second difference was over the federal role in CETA. The administration wanted the federal presence to be minimal, but Congress insisted on a watchdog role for the federal sector.

The PSE issue was resolved by compromising on a modest PSE program, Title II (CETA Titles are summarized in Figure 1), limited to areas with substantial unemployment, a kind of miniature EEA program. The differences over the federal role were papered over by endorsing both positions. *Yes,* local programs should be operated by autonomous prime sponsors, and *yes,* there should be strong federal oversight.

An astute observer of the political scene has expressed the situation very well: "If you want legislation enacted, keep its purposes vague." However, the effect of saying yes to such contradictory positions was to create a large gray area in which the reach of the "feds" contended with the grasp of the "locals."

Figure 1
SUMMARY OF CETA TITLES

Title	Provision
I	Contains the basic administrative provisions. • Cities and counties of 100,000 or more and consortion are designated as prime sponsors. State governments are prime sponsors for balance-of-state areas. • Other provisions cover establishment of advisory councils, planning documents, limitation on enrollment and payment of allowances.
II	Authorizes prime sponsors to provide training, work experience and supportive services to improve employability of economically disadvantaged.
III	Authorizes nationally administered program for Indians, migrants, seasonal farm workers, older workers and special groups. Also authorizes research evaluation and demonstration projects.
IV	Authorizes Job Corps, summer youth programs and extends Youth Employment Demonstration Project Act (YEDPA).
V	Establishes National Commission for Employment Policy.
VI	Authorizes temporary public service jobs for low income, long-term employed and welfare recipients. Fixes average wage rate.
VII	Authorizes two-year demonstration program to test methods for increasing participation of private business in CETA programs.
VIII	Authorizes employment of youth in conservation and other public projects.

OUTCOMES

To determine whether the objectives of the original CETA were realized, we need to look at both strategic and programmatic objectives.

The Early Period

The central strategic objective of CETA—decentralization—was achieved in large measure during the early CETA period. For the first time, manpower programs in each community were built into the local government structure under the authority of the elected official. But the federal oversight responsibility was not abdicated. The degree of federal presence was, and continues to be, a controversial issue.

The accomplishment of CETA's second strategic objective—decategorization—has been sidetracked. In response to new developments, Congress loaded CETA with new categorical programs. As these special programs increased to meet the needs of particular groups, their purposes became more narrowly defined, regulations proliferated, the federal presence was extended and the flexibility of local officials diminished. In short, CETA has never been completely decentralized, nor has it been entirely decategorized.

With respect to the early programmatic goals of CETA, our survey found:

- In terms of management, delivery of services and local participation, CETA was a better way of handling the nation's manpower programs than the earlier centralized, categorical design.
- Although there was more local participation in the decision-making process, local planning councils tended to be passive, and the CETA plans largely became an exercise for obtaining federal funds.
- Contrary to expectations, there were no significant changes in the kinds of employment and training programs. Prime sponsors tended to continue the activities they inherited.
- There was a shift in the distribution of employment and training resources—from the South to the Northeast and from large cities to suburban areas.
- With decentralization, the earlier institutional relationships were scrambled, and this led to a vigorous struggle for turf among the agencies that participated in manpower programs. The pre-CETA roles of the Employment Service, vocational education agencies and community-based organizations diminished. They lost their direct association with the federal establishment and were now beholden to local officials.
- As to the persons being served, there was a weakening of commitment to the disadvantaged population. This was attributed to a loosening of the eligibility requirements; the spread of employment and training programs into suburban areas that generally have a lower proportion of disadvantaged persons; and the inclination of program managers to select persons most likely to succeed rather than those most in need.

Having sketched the early CETA period when attention was centered on

Figure 2
PSE OUTLAYS, 1975-1980

Fiscal Years

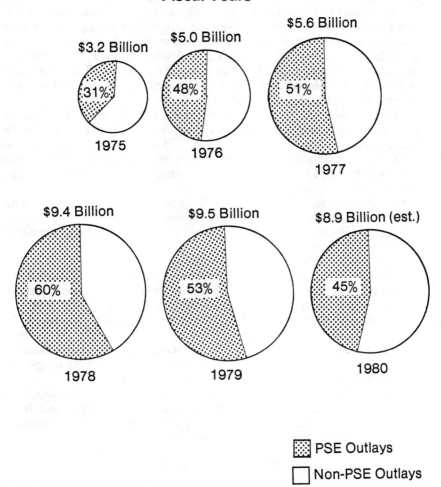

PSE Outlays

Non-PSE Outlays

Outlays for Public Service Employment Rose from 30 to 60 percent of all CETA expenditures by 1978 and then declined.

Source: Based on data from the Office of Management and Budget.

the structural problems of its clientele, we now turn to the second phase in CETA's development—the Public Service Employment (PSE), or countercyclical, period.

The Countercyclical Period

CETA was barely launched when it was overtaken by the recession of 1974 and harnessed to the countercyclical wagon. Congress enacted Title VI, which authorized CETA funds to create jobs for the unemployed in state and local governments and in nonprofit organizations. As Figure 2 indicates, between 1975 and 1978, PSE more than doubled (300,000 to 750,000) and accounted for 60 percent of all CETA expenditures in 1978. This countercyclical program elbowed aside the original structural objective and has now become the centerpiece of CETA.

PSE programs appealed particularly to elected officials. Indeed, in the view of many of them, PSE was *the* CETA program. The reasons for this attraction were not hard to discern. In 1978, CETA accounted for 6 percent of the 12.7 million state and local government workers, and in some locations it was much higher. PSE provided visible and useful services to communities and fiscal relief to hard-pressed cities.

With the increasing prominence of PSE came three intractable problems that would prove to be the nemesis of the program:

- *Creaming*—inadequate participation by persons on the lower rungs of the socioeconomic ladder.
- *Substitution*—the use of PSE to supplant rather than supplement local resources. Estimates of substitution range from 17 to 90 percent.
- *Program abuses*—in the hasty pursuit of numbers, ineligible persons were enrolled, programs were approved on the basis of expediency rather than usefulness, and they were not adequately monitored. Allegations of program abuse were widespread. The media, always more industrious in highlighting horror stories than in reporting successful outcomes, kept CETA on the front pages and the negative image that resulted eroded Congressional and public support.

Some of these problems reflect the inherent difficulty in a decentralized program: achieving congruence between the national objectives and the interests of local officials who administer the program. The difficulty is further aggravated by ambiguous legislation.

CONGRESSIONAL RESPONSES

Program Extension Act of 1976

The first response of Congress to the drift of CETA away from its intended purposes was the passage of the Emergency Jobs Program Extension Act of 1976, which extended the life of Title VI and attempted to get the program back on the track originally charted. The 1976 act sought to increase the proportion of disadvantaged persons in PSE programs and to constrain substitution. Its efforts, however, were only partially successful. In the drive to reach very ambitious enrollment levels, program objectives and program quality were sacrificed to the tyranny of time and numbers.

Another Effort: The Reauthorization Act of 1978

The most recent and most successful effort to address the shortcomings of the PSE programs was the Comprehensive Employment and Training Act Amendments of 1978. CETA came up for reauthorization in 1978 and immediately ran into a barrage of Congressional criticism:
- Program abuses were rife;
- The wrong people were getting into the program;
- There was no liability for enrolling ineligible persons or effective monitoring; and
- Substitution was widespread.

Most of the criticisms were leveled against Title VI and almost resulted in the elimination of the program. It was saved only by the adoption of several very far reaching amendments.

The objectives of the 1978 amendments are not very different from the aims of earlier attempts to reform the program. However, the means used to achieve these ends are radically different. The new legislation relies less on rhetoric and vaguely worded provisions that merely nibble at the edges of the problems and more on stringent requirements and self-enforcing devices that drive the program in the direction Congress intended.

The reauthorization amendments modified PSE in a number of ways:
- It tightened the requirements for entry into the program;
- Restricted the wage levels that could be paid to PSE workers (they have since been raised);
- Limited the length of time a person could remain in PSE to 18 months;
- Required that employability development plans (EDPs) be prepared for all Title II participants and that a training component be added to PSE jobs;
- Stipulated rigorous procedures for determining and verifying the eligibility of CETA applicants and held prime sponsors liable for improper enrollments; and
- Imposed stronger monitoring measures and required that every prime sponsor establish an independent monitoring unit.

The amendments also attempted to simplify the planning and grant application processes, added a new private sector initiative program (Title VII) and folded in the new youth programs.

In short, Congress sought to design a "clean" program that would enroll only the "right" people, assign them to meaningful work that otherwise would not be done and move them quickly into unsubsidized employment.

Effects of the Amendments

Our reports indicate that the overriding objective of the amendments—to serve more fully those whose needs are greatest—is being achieved. This is

91

the first time that we have seen such a sudden and sharp change in the characteristics of the new PSE enrollees. Compared to their 1978 counterparts, for example, more recent enrollees (1980) are younger, have had less schooling, include more women, contain a higher proportion of public assistance recipients and are more likely to be minorities. More significantly, the participation of low-income participants rose from 75 to 92 percent of new enrollees. Table 1 summarizes these findings.

Table 1
CHARACTERISTICS OF NEW ENROLLEES IN PSE
FISCAL YEARS 1978 & 1980

	Percent of Total PSE Enrollment	
Participant Characteristics	1978	1980
Women	38	46
Youth 16-21	23	28
Less than high school education	25	35
Member of minority group	39	48
Family receives public assistance	22	31
Family income less than 70 percent of lower level standard budget	75	92

Other post-amendment program improvements include greater protection of the program's integrity and a decline in competition between disadvantaged and nondisadvantaged workers. The former improvement has been achieved through fixing the liability for program abuses on the prime sponsor and prescribing strict monitoring procedures. The latter has been accomplished through reduced wage levels, which have discouraged better qualified persons from competing with more disadvantaged applicants for PSE jobs. Further, with the shift to less qualified enrollees, fewer opportunities to fill professional and skilled positions and the limited tenure of PSE participants, incentives for substituting PSE participants for regular workers have been weakened.

Costs of the Amendments
Such programmatic improvements have not been achieved without cost. Many of the changes have added a host of administrative tasks to a system already badly strained and have reduced local flexibility. No provision of the reauthorization act has caused as much consternation among prime sponsors as the wage restrictions. Wage rates have been lowered in four out of five

areas by an average of 10 percent. As a consequence, almost all sponsors have dropped or restructured some of their PSE positions. All areas reduced their share of professional jobs, and there was a clear shift from high-skill positions to laborer, low-level clerical jobs and service jobs. Where jobs were "restructured," it was sometimes accomplished by creating "trainee" or "aide" positions, in which little changed but the salary and title. When substantive changes in job content did occur, the diluted jobs were often of limited value to either the participant or the community.

Despite the changes in the occupational profile of the PSE jobs, CETA administrators still perceive them to be useful, although three out of four of them feel that their usefulness has been reduced. The challenge to policy-makers is to set PSE wage rates at a level that maximizes client targeting and minimizes the adverse effects on services.

The eligibility verification procedures and the liability provisions have reduced the number of ineligibles in PSE and made prime sponsors more sensitive to problems of program abuse. Yet the cost may not be trivial. For example, there is duplication in checking eligibility, resulting in enrollment delays. Further, sponsors increasingly are handling the eligibility function themselves rather than relying on the Employment Service and other agencies. The effect of these restrictive measures was to weaken the prime sponsor support for PSE. Some government agencies, in fact, viewed the problems as outweighing the benefits and withdrew from the program.

In sum, the reauthorization changes appear to be moving the program in the direction that Congress had charted with respect to persons to be served, containment of substitution and program integrity. The driving forces behind these changes are the restrictive wage provisions and the stringent eligibility requirements, supplemented by tighter monitoring, enforcement and liability provisions. But the price paid for these achievements was high.

ONGOING POLICY ISSUES

Since its inception, and throughout its several iterations, CETA has been wrestling with four broad policy issues: the inherent limits of PSE, the lack of congruence between national and local goals, the internal inconsistency among its multiple goals and the absence of any protracted period of stability.

PSE has been a workhorse driven in all directions: to create public sector jobs for the cyclically unemployed, to assist the structurally unemployed, to furnish essential community services and to provide fiscal relief to hard-pressed communities. At issue is whether PSE can be a program for all seasons. Should local and state governments, which account for only one-eighth of total employment, be expected to carry most of the burden of providing temporary employment for the unemployed and the disadvantaged? Alternatively, what role should the private sector play in job creation programs?

A Problem of Congruence

The underlying premise of decentralized block grant programs is that local objectives and practices are congruent with national objectives. In fact, however, there are significant divergencies. CETA is a meld of national, state and local aspirations implemented by an array of federal, state and local institutions. Each partner in the triad is motivated by its own interest and attempts to shape the program to those ends. However, local deviations from national objectives invite restrictive legislation and tighter compliance which, in turn, erode local autonomy. Sorely needed is an equilibrium that can balance federal and local interests and relationships.

The congruence problem is compounded by the fact that CETA is liberally sprinkled with goals, some of which are competitive or contradictory. The pursuit of one may preclude the attainment of another. For example, sponsors are urged to emphasize the placement of CETA participants in unsubsidized jobs, while being restricted to enrolling persons who are hardest to place. Again, PSE is expected to provide essential services to communities. Yet, the wage and eligibility provisions preclude the kinds of jobs necessary to perform these services.

Finally, if there is one need that surpasses all others, it is the necessity for a period of stability. CETA has, from its inception, been buffeted by a succession of legislative, regulatory and procedural changes. Moreover, the size and timing of its funding have been uncertain. Sponsors have been strapped to a roller-coaster; first urged to expand PSE enrollments, then to reduce them, only to be pressed to expand again. Responsible planning and management are difficult to achieve under these conditions.

FUTURE PROSPECTS

As part of its effort to reduce federal expenditures, the Reagan administration proposed to cut the CETA budget from the 1980 authorized level of $8.1 billion to $3.6 billion in fiscal year 1982. In March, 1981, the administration announced its intention to phase out Titles 11D and VI and to complete the phase-down in the remaining seven months of the fiscal year. The phase-down in the last half of 1981 is being accomplished by freezing new hirees and by ordering early layoffs for those on board. The Department of Labor instructions to prime sponsors require them to arrange for the transfer of laid-off enrollees to other CETA titles, where possible; to assist in the placement of participants in unsubsidized employment; and where necessary, to apply for temporary waivers of terminations. The rapid time schedule for the phase-down may pose major administrative problems. The complexity of the task is reflected in the instructions that authorize exceptions from the average wage, training and project requirements.

The administration's proposal for the termination of PSE is based on five main perceptions: the PSE programs are not well managed; PSE cost and benefits compare unfavorably with other CETA programs, particularly on-the-job training; PSE is not an effective countercyclical device because of substitution and its inability to respond to changes in unemployment levels in a timely fashion; the private sector should play a larger role in job creation programs; and, finally, the elimination of PSE would return CETA to its original purpose of improving the employability of the structurally unemployed by providing them with skills that are marketable in the private sector.

These explanations are best understood in the context of the administration's fiscal policy and its plans to reduce federal expenditures. In such an environment, PSE is especially vulnerable; it requires a large budgetary expenditure and it has a poor image, as well as a weakened constituency.

Charles Harris assisted in the preparation of this chapter.

Footnotes

1. William Mirengoff and Lester Rindler, *The Comprehensive Employment and Training Act: Impact on People, Places and Programs,* National Academy of Sciences, Washington, D.C., 1976; William Mirengoff and Lester Rindler, *CETA: Manpower Programs Under Local Control,* National Academy of Sciences, Washington, D.C., 1978; William Mirengoff, Lester Rindler, Harry Greenspan, and Scott Seablom, *CETA: Assessment of Public Service Employment Programs,* National Academy of Sciences, Washington, D.C., 1980; William Mirengoff, Lester Rindler, Harry Greenspan, Scott Seablom and Lois Black, *The New CETA: Effect on Public Service Employment Programs,* National Academy Press, Washington, D.C., 1980.

APPRENTICESHIP TRAINING AND VOCATIONAL EDUCATION AS PARTNERS

Robert W. Glover

Despite decades of effort by the U.S. Department of Labor and various state agencies to promote apprenticeship, a pervasive ignorance exists among the general public in America regarding apprenticeship. Even those who have heard of apprenticeship have major misconceptions about it.

Some think apprenticeship is an obsolete form of training no longer practiced. In fact, the apprenticeship system currently has more than 300,000 American workers in training. Although apprenticeship in America dates back to colonial days, it has evolved considerably from the residential indenture system between master and apprentice. Today's apprenticeship is a structured system of formal training leading to careers in high-paying craft occupations. In some trades, apprenticeship offers the most modern and best quality training available in America.

Some consider apprenticeship to be an informal or loose mode of training in which a young person learns on the job under the guidance of a master craft worker. Actually, today's apprentices work under formal training programs that specify work processes and rotation schedules so that apprentices learn all facets of the trade. Almost all apprenticeships also require related instruction in a classroom to supplement learning that occurs on the job.

Perhaps the most pervasive misconception is that apprenticeship programs are union programs. The truth is that over 80 percent of apprenticeship programs are sponsored unilaterally by employers. Not a single apprenticeship program is sponsored exclusively by a union. Certainly several unions have been strong supporters of apprenticeship, but whenever they are involved as sponsors of apprenticeship, unions work jointly with employers.

Some view apprenticeship to be a closed system that is reserved largely for sons and nephews of current craft workers and discriminates against minority applicants. Yet today, fewer sons are following in their fathers' footsteps in the trades, and the proportion of relatives working in most apprenticeable crafts is probably no larger than that found in many occupations. Further, over the past dozen years, in response to affirmative action pressures and with the help of special outreach efforts, apprenticeship has made great strides in including members of minorities. By the end of 1978, 18.2 percent of apprentices were from minority groups.

Public ignorance regarding apprenticeship is compounded by inadequate career counseling in school. Few school counselors have any familiarity

97

with apprenticeship, and information on apprenticeship is not a part of any regular curriculum for training school counselors. Further, the attitudes of school counselors tend to reflect our society's bias against manual work and in favor of college education. Thus, better students who could make excellent apprentices are steered away from working apprenticeable trades and toward college.

AMERICAN APPRENTICESHIP: AN OVERVIEW

American apprenticeship is a highly diverse and largely decentralized institution. Any candid attempt to describe apprenticeship must start with a warning, namely: there is as much variation among apprenticeship programs as there is among programs of vocational education. Each apprenticeship program has its own jurisdictional area, selection methods and criteria, starting wages, techniques of job dispatching, credit provisions for prior education or experience and so on. Considerable variation also exists in the quality of training offered through apprenticeship. Moreover, some programs attract huge numbers of applicants, while others have difficulty finding sufficient numbers of qualified candidates. Some programs show high dropout rates, yet others are known for their exceptionally high rates of completion.

This chapter will serve as an introduction to a few common features of American apprenticeship. Readers who plan to work effectively with apprenticeship programs in this country are encouraged to consult further references on the topic.

Common Features of Apprenticeship

Perhaps the most sensible way to begin is to define the term "apprenticeship." Beatrice Reubens (1980), in a review of apprenticeship practices in several nations, concludes that:

> Apprentices are those who participate in an industry-based initial training system under a contractual employment relationship in which the firm promises to make available a broad and structured practical and theoretical training of some length in a recognized occupational skill category. Completion of the apprenticeship establishes skilled worker status and transferable qualifications, although it may not be the only route to skilled employment. (p. 7)

Apprenticeship is one form among many of alternating work-study training schemes. Two other examples of common work-study schemes are cooperative education and clinical education. At least four features distinguish apprenticeship from other forms of work-study arrangements: (1) apprenticeship is conducted in occupations recognized as apprenticeable; (2) apprenticeships are jobs rather than just training positions; (3) most of the training occurs on the job; and (4) most importantly, apprenticeship is industry based rather than school based. It is designed to train for the industry rather than for a single employer. Let us review each of these in turn.

Occupations Deemed Apprenticeable

Apprenticeship training is conducted in an occupation recognized as "apprenticeable" by the Bureau of Apprenticeship and Training of the Employment and Training Administration, U.S. Department of Labor, or one of 32 other apprenticeship agencies in the states and territories that can interpret the federal criteria for apprenticeability.

According to Department of Labor regulations, an apprenticeable occupation is a skilled trade that possesses all of the following characteristics:

1. It is customarily learned in a practical way through a structured systematic program of on-the-job supervised training.
2. It is clearly identified and commonly recognized throughout an industry.
3. It involves manual, mechanical or technical skills and knowledge which require a minimum of 2,000 hours of on-the-job work experience.
4. It requires related instruction to supplement the on-the-job training. *(Federal Register,* 1977, p. 10141)

As one can see, these 1977 criteria are quite broad and represent a substantial broadening of the definition of apprenticeship used in previous years.

The issues of what occupations are apprenticeable and how apprenticeability is determined are matters of some confusion, controversy and disagreement. Officially, the Bureau of Apprenticeship and Training (BAT) recognizes approximately 450 occupations as apprenticeable. However, a consolidated list compiled in March, 1980, of the occupations recognized as apprenticeable by the BAT or by state apprenticeship agencies revealed 723 occupational titles. The occupations ranged from accordion maker to X-ray equipment tester.

In practice, apprenticeship training is concentrated within a few occupations and industries. For the March, 1980, list, there was not a single apprentice registered nationwide for nearly half of the apprenticeable occupations. Indeed, 10 occupations accounted for more than 60 percent of all the 290,224 apprentices registered at the end of 1978. These were carpenter, electrician, plumber, pipefitter, machinist, tool and die maker, sheet metal worker, automotive and related mechanic, bricklayer and structural steelworker. Of these 10, seven were building trades. This is due, in part, to the fact that apprenticeship institutions—such as joint sponsorship by a group of employers and a union and the apprenticeship trust fund concept—are especially suitable to unionized construction labor markets. The construction industry has been a major user of apprenticeship in the United States and, in turn, apprenticeship has been influenced significantly by construction industry perspectives.

A second area of concentration is among metal workers and craft workers in the maintenance departments of large-scale manufacturing firms. Such firms suffer little turnover among their employees. Also, their operations are so large that they can enjoy economies of scale in establishing training workshops.

With the exception of cosmetology, apprenticeship is concentrated in jobs traditionally held by men. Because of this, it became a target for women's activists during the 1970s. In 1978, under pressure from a court suit, the U.S. Department of Labor applied affirmative action goals and timetables for women to apprenticeship. According to these goals, approximately 20 percent of all new apprentices were to be women. Various outreach groups also increased recruiting activities for women in apprenticeship. In 1973, only .8 percent of all newly indentured apprentices were women. Five years later, the figure was 4.3 percent. Today, it is a little more than 6 percent. Progress has been made, but there is a long way to go, and simply getting women to enter into apprenticeships may not be sufficient to integrate the skilled crafts. Concern has been raised recently over the fact that women in apprenticeship have higher attrition rates than men.

Apprenticeships as Jobs

An apprenticeship is a *regular* job—not just a training position. The apprentice is paid progressively increasing wages according to a predetermined agreement, and assuming satisfactory performance, the apprentice will be retained beyond the duration of apprenticeship. Since employers often consider apprenticeship training an expensive investment, it is in their interest to keep apprentices after training. An important point here is that since apprenticeships are jobs, the number of positions available is limited by *present* labor market conditions even though future labor market conditions ideally should be considered in determining the number of craft workers to be trained.

Because apprenticeships are jobs, they offer a special opportunity to apprentices of earning while they are learning. This reduces the opportunity cost of training and makes skill training affordable to those who might not otherwise be able to consider it. This feature also lengthens the term of apprenticeship since apprentices are involved in regular production work rather than only concentrated training.

The Balance between Classroom and On-the-Job Training

The bulk of the time in apprenticeship is spent learning on the job rather than in school. Federal apprenticeship regulations specify that apprenticeships should involve a minimum of 2,000 hours of on-the-job work experience, whereas a minimum of only 144 hours per year is required for related training. In practice, most American apprenticeships run about four years, and apprentices spend less than one hour in the classroom for every 10 spent on the job.

Apprenticeship Training

Apprenticeship as Industry-Based Training

In America, apprenticeship programs may be sponsored by single employers, by groups of employers, by single employers working jointly with a union or by groups of employers working jointly with a union.

The government plays a limited role in promoting, supporting and regulating apprenticeship through registering apprenticeship programs and certifying that they comply with minimum standards. Government apprenticeship agencies recognize occupations deemed apprenticeable, provide technical assistance to program sponsors, keep records and grant certificates of completion to those who successfully pass their apprenticeships. Since the mid-1960s, the government also has promulgated a series of measures to assure that apprenticeship is open to everyone on an equal opportunity basis regardless of race, sex or ethnic background. Through vocational education, the government has partially funded the institutional or classroom portion of the training for many programs.

Apprenticeship in the United States remains almost entirely privately sponsored and funded. Further, the apprenticeship sponsors are committed to retaining the essentially private character of the system, and they resist any effort that they view as government intervention. Partly because of this suspicion of public sector involvement and partly because of the failure of public schools to understand apprenticeship and reach out to industry in the past, meaningful alliances between vocational-technical schools and apprenticeship programs are sensitive and difficult to build, despite the fact that related classroom instruction is often provided to apprentices by local school systems or community colleges.

Apprenticeship is *industry based* rather than school based. In practice this means that industry generally has primary influence over decisions regarding training. Key areas of concern to industry include the following:
1. The number of applicants admitted to training, what their qualifications should be and selection of those to be trained.
2. The length, coverage and organization of the curriculum.
3. The qualifications of the instructors and who should teach.
4. Determination of progress (and thus wage rates) through the apprenticeship.
5. The design of the training facilities.
6. The equipment used in training.

There are several advantages to leaving such decisions regarding the training program to industry officials. First, the training is likely to be more job relevant and more up to date with the latest technological changes than could be provided in a school setting. Second, the training is more likely to be geared to the labor market, in that those who complete the program have greater assurance of continued employment.

On the other hand, there are potential shortcomings to industry decision-making in these matters. For example, left unchecked, an individual employer may train the individual narrowly and specifically to fit the needs of the employer's firm, so that few transferable skills are taught.

Apprenticeship provides an important counterbalance to such a tendency since, by design, it is aimed at producing broad and transferable skills applicable across industry. Another shortcoming is that due to adverse economic conditions in the present or because of a lack of accurate long-range forecasting, conservative outlook or general reluctance to invest in training, industry may undertrain for a given occupation. Although those who do complete apprenticeship have high assurance of continued employment related to their training, there are often too few trained to meet full labor market needs.

INDUSTRY-SCHOOL COOPERATION IN APPRENTICESHIP

Decision-making in the six areas of concern to industry *can* be made jointly by industries and schools. But joint decision-making can only be effective if industry is at least an equal partner with schools. Due to fundamental differences in perspective, reaching agreement between schools and industry may not be easy. For example, take the issue of instructor selection. Industry officials will generally seek out master craft workers who may have no teaching background but do have good practical and technical knowledge. School officials, on the other hand, tend to choose those who are trained and hold credentials to teach but do not necessarily have in-depth experience at the trade.

Reasonable people will see that the best apprenticeship instructors are those with *both* technical background and teacher training. Apprenticeship instructors may have a masterful knowledge of their crafts, but be unable to communicate this knowledge effectively in the classroom. As apprenticeship sponsors increasingly recognize, in addition to technical proficiency at the trade, apprentice instructors need to know how to teach. As some educators are coming to realize, it is often easier to train skilled craft workers to teach than it is to train teachers to be craft workers. Many apprenticeship programs have found public vocational institutions to be of significant assistance in providing instructor preparation. Perhaps some of the best apprentice instructor training is being conducted at Purdue University and The Ohio State University under contracts with various national industry apprenticeship training trust funds. All parties report that they have gained and learned much from the experience.

A Trend toward Separate Training Facilities

One result of this difficulty of industry-based apprenticeship programs and schools working together can be found in the trend among the better-financed apprenticeship programs to build their own training facilities. In a few areas, several trades are pooling their resources to construct multi-trade training facilities. Although there are many factors involved in this movement away from public schools, a primary ingredient is dissatisfaction with the treatment that programs receive in public vocational education facilities. Whether correct or not, many program sponsors feel that they have received low priority in the allocation of public facilities.

The advantages of having one's own facility are numerous and include:
- Full access to facilities at convenient times.
- Access to space adequate for "hands-on" practice with tools and materials.
- Greater control over the use of proprietary curriculum materials.
- Greater identity for the program (i.e., a building).
- Less concern about minimum class size.
- Ability to leave standing mock-ups and equipment out and undisturbed between instructional periods.
- Access to expensive and technologically current equipment not available in public schools.

What the future will bring is unclear, but certainly most apprenticeship sponsors and coordinators look with envy on those programs that have their own facilities. At the same time, some public vocational education officials and apprenticeship officials are asking, "What is the need for such duplication?" (Glover, 1980, p. 12).

In some places, schools and industry have pooled their resources to build and equip facilities for apprenticeship training. This sort of cooperation upgrades school facilities beyond what they might have hoped to achieve on their own, while reducing the cost of training for industry.

An Alternative to Vocational Education

Some observers view apprenticeship and vocational education as parallel and competitive training systems for occupational preparation. Although it must be acknowledged that there is often antipathy between the two systems, this need not be the case. We have many fine examples of cooperation between apprenticeship and public vocational education. Further, there is extensive interaction between the two. A 1979 survey of apprenticeship in Texas revealed that approximately 12,000 of the 17,000 registered apprentices in Texas were receiving some form of assistance in related training through public vocational education. The most common form of assistance was partial subsidization of apprentice instructors' salaries. If these data were to hold true nationally, public vocational education may provide assistance in some form to over two out of three apprentices across the country, or as many as 200,000 apprentices.

There is much to be gained by fostering better working relationships and by improving cooperation between local programs of apprenticeship and public vocational education. Two areas that offer much room for immediate cooperation come to mind. First, vocational education can help to channel well-prepared and well-informed candidates into apprenticeship. For example, a series of seven pilot school-to-work apprenticeship linkage projects, funded by the Department of Labor, have shown that apprenticeship can be piggy-backed onto high school cooperative education programs, allowing high school graduates to move right into apprenticeship at an advanced stage.

Second, public vocational education can serve as a resource for providing the related training portion in apprenticeship. By training apprentice instructors in teaching methods, helping to develop curricular materials, providing technical assistance in such innovations as performance-based training and helping to defray the cost of related instruction, public vocational education can be an excellent resource to apprenticeship.

It is time to ask: Are apprenticeship and public vocational education really alternatives or partners?

REFERENCES

Apprenticeship programs: Labor standards for registration. Title 29, Code of Federal Regulations, Part 29, as published in the *Federal Register,* Vol. 42, No. 34, February 18, 1977, pp. 10138-10144.

Glover, R.W. *Apprenticeship in the United States: Implications for vocational education research and development.* Columbus, Ohio: National Center for Research in Vocational Education, Ohio State University, Occasional Paper No. 66, 1980.

Reubens, B.G. with Harrisson, J.A.C. *Apprenticeship in foreign countries.* Washington, D.C.: U.S. Department of Labor, Employment and Training Administration, R&D Monograph 77, 1980.

THE GROWING TREND OF INDUSTRY AND BUSINESS TRAINING

Richard A. Swanson and Brian P. Murphy

The core goal of vocational education in the United States is to prepare learners for jobs that are available in the labor market. Yet even with the years of vast funding for vocational education at the federal, state and local levels, most of the knowledge and skills held by the American work force have been developed through on-the-job training—not by vocational education. This should not be particularly disturbing to vocational educators. It would be unreasonable to think that vocational education could either compete with the richness of the country's work places and the rewards for learning that exist there or to be able to respond to all of the unique demands of individual companies.

Recently private sector training and development has been receiving a fair amount of attention from the public educational system (*Phi Delta Kappan,* 1980; *Journal of Industrial Teacher Education,* 1978). This is not a result of significant shifts in job training from the public to private sectors. Rather, the attention is based on an increase in the number of structured training programs being offered by industry and business, as compared to unstructured programs. Unstructured training may be characterized as "on-the-job" or "buddy-system" training; structured training is more formal and more closely parallels practices found in vocational education (Cullen, Sawzin, Sisson & Swanson, 1976).

The concerns for performance and accountability that have been a part of vocational education are often valued at an even higher level in the private sector training profession. The following definition of training, utilized by a major manufacturer's corporate training department, illustrates this point.

> Training is the presentation of controlled information and practice resulting in performance of criterion behavior by the learner in a manner which allows evaluation. The definition implies both effectiveness and efficiency (Johns-Manville, 1976).

TRAINING IN INDUSTRY AND BUSINESS

While it may be impossible to determine precisely the numbers of trainees, training hours and dollars committed to training in industry and business, estimates are available. A 1977 survey by the New York Conference Board of 610 firms having 500 or more employees found that these firms spent

105

over $2 million on employee training in just one year (Lusterman, 1977). Tables 1 and 2 illustrate a breakdown of the training within the firms surveyed by the Conference Board. Beyond training their own employees, major employers are providing on-the-job work experiences for approximately 400,000 college and high school students annually (Lusterman & Gorlin, 1980).

A revealing comparison may be found by looking at expenditures for audiovisual training aids and materials. In 1978 educational institutions spent $1.69 billion for audiovisual materials as compared to business and industry's outlay of $2.5 billion (Ruark, 1979). The time and financial investment being made in industry and business training constitutes an impressive effort that has been referred to as this nation's shadow educational system (Goldstein, 1980).

A Many-Faceted Profession

Given the diversity of industry and business, the fact that training is a secondary objective of the organization and the range of human resource development concerns that each firm encounters, training must take on many faces in order to be responsive. Figure 1 illustrates the field of training in terms of types of training and the job roles within the profession. Any single cell or combination of cells within the matrix could constitute an individual trainer's total job.

Table 1
PREVALENCE OF EDUCATION/TRAINING PROGRAMS BY COMPANY SIZE

	Percent of Companies Reporting Program			
Company Size By No. of Employees	Tuition Aid After Hours	Other Outside Courses	Company Courses After Hours	During Hours
10,000 or More	97	90	56	96
5,000-9,999	95	83	51	96
2,500-4,999	91	79	52	91
1,000-2,499	94	77	45	86
500-999	82	66	25	71
All Companies	89	94	39	55

Source: Lusterman, 1977

Table 2
TYPES OF COURSES GIVEN IN
DURING-HOURS COMPANY PROGRAMS

Type of Course	Percent of Companies Providing Courses	Employees Involved Number (000)	Percent of Total	Expenditures Millions of Dollars	Percent of Total
Management Development/ Supervisory	60	1,400	37	430	24
Functional/ Technical	54	2,300	61	1,340	74
Basic Remedial	8	30	1	15	1
Other	11	30	1	15	1
All Courses	70	3,760	100	1,800	100

Source: Lusterman, 1977

Figure 1
TRAINING IN INDUSTRY

		TYPES OF TRAINING		
		A Skills and Technical	B Management and Subject Matter	C Motivational
Job Roles in Training	1 Instructor	1.A	1.B	1.C
	2 Media Producer	2.A	2.B	2.C
	3 Designer	3.A	3.B	3.C
	4 Manager	4.A	4.B	4.C

Three types of training are identified in Figure 1. Skills and technical training deals with worker-machine interactions and most typically is given to hourly workers. Management and subject matter training deals with worker-worker or worker-idea interactions and most typically is provided to salaried employees. Motivational training deals with worker attitudes and is most widely used in sales, safety and team-building training.

Table 3
VOCATIONAL EDUCATION AND TRAINING PROFESSION: COMPARISON OF EXPERTISE ON R&D ISSUES

Dimensions of Training	Selected R&D Issues	Available Expertise		
		Training	Equal	Vocational
Overall Training Issues	1. Cost-Benefit of Training	X		
	2. Goal Analysis of Total Organization		X	
Types of Training • Skills and Technical Training	3. Analysis of Processes and Troubleshooting Behavior	X		
• Management and Subject Matter Training	4. Analysis and Synthesis of Subject Matter		X	
• Motivational Training	5. Ethics of Attitudinal Training		X	
Job Roles • Instructor	6. Development and Evaluation Instructional Skills			X
• Media Producer	7. New High Technology Media-Communications	X		
• Designer	8. Understanding the Training Design Process		X	
• Manager	9. Training Needs Assessment	X		
	10. Computer Managed Training		X	

The job roles provide another view of the profession and the training specializations. The titles of instructor, media producer, designer and manager are not alien to vocational educators, but when pursued as jobs in themselves, a profession quite different from vocational education emerges.

Within the model of training in industry and business a recent analysis presented several major research and development issues facing the profession (Swanson, 1981). These issues provide one means of comparing the relative emphases and professional strengths of vocational education and private sector training. Table 3 lists the 10 research and development issues and an estimation of the present expertise of vocational education and private sector training in each.

At surface inspection, Table 3 contains several terms and issues uncommon to vocational educators. A more thoughtful inspection allows one to integrate private sector training and public sector vocational education into a larger conceptual structure of "education for work." Yet, several of the issues noted in Table 3 suggest different levels of concern. These include financial investment/return, learning efficiency/effectiveness and appropriate training. These issues and the resulting private sector organizational demands for responsiveness often make it difficult and/or impossible for trainers to work with traditional vocational programming methods.

All indications are that training in industry and business will continue to expand. If vocational education wishes to become a partner, it will need to analyze the issues facing private sector training and respond in new ways.

RECOMMENDATIONS FOR VOCATIONAL EDUCATION

The goals of vocational education and training are the same—to meet the labor needs of industry and business. The issue is not so much to debate differences, but to identify how to achieve this common purpose. Communication and understanding are required in order to meet needs through cooperative efforts. In this regard, private sector recommendations to vocational education focus on two issues: (1) the behavioral attributes of vocational graduates and (2) the establishment of training services in vocational schools.

Fully prepared individuals entering the labor market are rare. By and large, most companies require minimal, functioning persons who can be trained and then later developed for occupational career paths within the organization. Candidate screening and selection presently rely on rather subjective assessments or require a heavy investment in the development and administration of defensible employment tests. Instances where efforts must be undertaken to minimally qualify candidates or prepare them for on-the-job training are viewed as an unwanted burden on the organization's resources. The growth of the training profession, as discussed earlier in this chapter, is evidence that the private sector will generally invest whatever resources are necessary to compensate for ill-prepared employees.

Determine Behavioral Attributes

The success of an employee working in any company is dependent on behavioral attributes suited to the work place. Minimum industry and business expectations are that all employees have sufficient general work attitudes and skills to function in their environment. The private sector considers it grossly inefficient to provide specific job skill training for persons who lack even the basic work attitudes and skills. Therefore, it is fundamental that vocational education clearly define, validate and include in its programs those general behavioral attributes that lead to success in the work place.

Dismal reading and math achievement levels have been reported within our nation. As a result, employers would be happy if their newly hired employees simply could read and write the English language and perform mathematics at the junior high level (Berman, 1979). Vocational education should first of all be aware of the need to support and reinforce basic education in all of its programs. Without basic skills, students have little chance of success in achieving behavioral attributes demanded in the work place.

Behavioral attributes that fall within vocational education are those that predict successful job performance. They may include such characteristics as good attendance, productivity while on the job, loyalty, honesty and freedom from debilitating personal problems like drug and alcohol abuse. Other aspects might relate to sufficient interpersonal skills necessary to get along with fellow workers. The base-line response for vocational education should be to identify and define general behavioral attributes. Their validity must be established from the perspective of the work place and internalized as a part of all vocational education programs.

Reliable records and valid assessments identifying individuals' general job behavioral attributes would lead many employers to vocational education in search of candidates, regardless of the students' specific skill preparation. For example: take two graduates from a welding program, the first a highly proficient welder, the second only moderately skilled but possessing the previously mentioned attributes to a greater degree than the first. The second candidate is preferable simply because chances are that neither will remain a welder during the entire course of his or her employment.

Other Training Services

Literally thousands of private sector training programs are locally developed and delivered each year. Many duplicate existing work in the field. Generic training packages are regularly purchased at premium prices from producers throughout the country. As demand has grown, so has the business. Because its response time is often too slow, vocational education has captured little of this activity. Many industry and business manpower needs develop and disappear in shorter time frames than can be accommodated through traditional programming methods. Vocational education could expand its role by providing training services that would meet the more immediate requirements of the private sector. Specific changes or additions would be required in organization, staffing and facility utilization.

The first step would be to add a training coordinator or a small department with the specific responsibility of meeting the training needs of local companies. Job roles of the training instructor, media producer, designer and manager are largely transferable from educational disciplines such as teacher, audiovisual specialist and curriculum developer. Completely separate staffs and facilities are, however, neither necessary nor likely to be efficient.

This service function would be organized to coordinate vocational education resources and expertise with the identified training objectives of individual companies. Much of what exists in an area vocational school could be accessed and utilized on an as-needed basis to meet various project objectives. Vocational trainers would basically analyze needs, design programs, coordinate development and delivery resources and control (evaluate) projects. These services would have to be delivered in a cost-effective manner to satisfy the private sector.

Success of vocational training services would depend on the type of staffing employed. Vocational trainers would need to be open to constant interactions with private organizations, be geared to rapid changes in program content and offerings and be aware of their responsibility to satisfy project clients. Such trainers could not afford to insulate themselves from the work place. They would have to demonstrate their ability to produce cost-effective results, synthesize the needs of several companies and maintain long-term working relationships with the local community.

Utilize Facilities Effectively

An aggravation for most companies is producing the right skills, in the right people, at the right time and in a convenient place. Private sector instructional space is expensive and its efficient utilization is a constant problem, especially for smaller companies. Empty rooms or two groups contending for one space at the same time opens training to criticism. Vocational training services could attenuate much of the problem by simply offering the physical space at the right time to deliver training. Classroom, seminar and laboratory space for groups and individuals already exists. Opening the doors, upgrading some instructional environments and charging for services could produce attractive returns on present vocational education facilities.

CONCLUSION

Training in industry and business and vocational education share common goals. An analysis of the current trends indicates that private sector training will be growing at a significantly higher rate than vocational education. Even so, it is reasonable to assume that together they still will not meet the true work place knowledge and skill demands in our nation. Within the mix, society will increasingly rely on private sector training to meet its manpower demands. In doing so training in industry and business will gain a greater portion of the recognition that vocational education has coveted over the years.

REFERENCES

Berman, B.H. Training the hard to train: the functional illiterate. *NSPI Journal,* 1979, *18*(7), 7-10.

Cullen, J.G., Sawzin, S.A., Sisson, G.R., & Swanson, R.A. Training, what's it worth? *Training and Development Journal,* 1976, *30*(8), 12-20.

Goldstein, H. *Training and education by industry.* Washington, D.C.: National Institute for Work and Learning, 1980.

Johns-Manville Corporation. *Definition of training.* Denver, Colo.: Author, Corporate Training Department, 1976.

Journal of Industrial Teacher Education. 1978, *15*(4).

Lusterman, S. *Education in industry.* New York: The Conference Board, 1977.

Lusterman, S. & Gorlin, H. *Educating students for work: some business roles.* New York: The Conference Board, 1980.

Phi Delta Kappan. 1980, *61*(5).

Ruark, H. *Technical photography.* September, 1979.

Swanson, R.A. Industrial training. In W.H. Mitzel (Ed)., *5th Encyclopedia of Educational Research.* New York: MacMillan Company, 1981.

SECTION IV

REFLECTING ON PAST EFFECTIVENESS

This section responds to previous challenges to the effectiveness of the field of vocational education. W. Norton Grubb and Marvin Lazerson have updated their research base on preparing youth for employment, and have come to the same conclusions they posited in their 1975 indictment of vocational and career education, as published in the *Harvard Educational Review*.

Another researcher, Paul Ringel, responds not only to Grubb and Lazerson, but to the practices and methods utilized by revisionist historians in analyzing the effectiveness and impact of vocational education. His interviews with graduates from vocational training that occurred between 1908 and 1923 provide interesting and dynamic information for responding to the effectiveness question of vocational education over time.

Eli Ginzberg was asked to give a personal assessment of the effectiveness of vocational education. His impressions of how the field has changed and is trying to change offer some caveats for viewing effectiveness.

In a more formal research sense, Morgan V. Lewis and Donna M. Mertens provide a synthesis and analysis of several studies undertaken in recent years. The conclusions on the effects of training at the secondary and postsecondary levels that they present are organized into employment, educational and ancillary effects.

These four chapters together form a broad and varied perspective about what kind of impact vocational education has had over time and offer a basis for discussing what kinds of criteria can be utilized to judge effectiveness in the future.

THE PERSISTENT FRUSTRATIONS OF VOCATIONAL SOLUTIONS TO YOUTH PROBLEMS

W. Norton Grubb and Marvin Lazerson

For much of the post-World War II period, American education enjoyed sustained growth. Expanding enrollments increased the size of the educational sector, and economic expansion absorbed the higher numbers of college graduates. Against this background, the contractions of the 1970s and 1980s seem especially severe. Taxpayer revolts, problems placing college graduates in "suitable" jobs and the rise of youth unemployment have reversed the experiences of the 1950s and 1960s. While demographic shifts are partly to blame, the abysmal economic conditions of the last decade—high rates of unemployment, high rates of inflation and low-growth rates—have been the potent forces in the tribulations of schooling, forces that have been at work on both sides of the Atlantic.

In the frantic search to improve macroeconomic conditions, the relationship between schooling and work has come under investigation. Concern that schools do not instill skills but simply "credential" or "signal" in inefficient and inequitable ways and that too many youth are "over-educated" relative to labor market demands have coexisted with political demands centered in the middle class to expand subsidies to higher education. For working-class youth, the dominant issue has become the high levels of unemployment, with the explicit charge that conventional schooling has failed to give working-class adolescents "employability skills." In almost every case, the urge to bring some semblance of rationality to the relationship between schooling and work has been dominant.

This concern is not new. Proposals to resolve youth unemployment and the other problems of youth through the schools stretch back almost a century. In particular, various forms of vocational education and training have been consistently offered as the appropriate solutions for those youth not continuing to college. Although these proposals are part of a more general trend within American education toward emphasizing vocational purposes, their application to secondary education and to youth problems has been distinctive. In this chapter we will review the vocational developments in American education, explain the persistence of this particular "solution" and examine its limits in coping with youth unemployment.

RECYCLING VOCATIONAL EDUCATION

The core assumptions of vocational education have emerged in slightly different forms during the past 100 years, from the manual training movement of the 1880s to the career education movement of the 1970s. Despite some differences, the similarities in the goals that have been promoted for vocational education and in the criticisms that have emerged are what have given vocational solutions their powerful political appeal.

The vocational education movement was the panacea of the Progressive Era. In the period between 1890 and 1920, a wide variety of individuals supported it, all for somewhat different reasons. For businessmen, extraordinarily active in the movement, vocational training promised to increase the supply of skilled workers and to instill appropriate attitudes toward work, including anti-union sentiments. For educators, vocational education could attract students and reestablish the legitimacy and purpose of schooling. This would eliminate dropouts and provide training suited to the background and "evident or probable destinies" of lower class and immigrant youth.

Social reformers joined educators in their enthusiasm for vocational education: it would reestablish the moral component of public schooling, provide training and thus employment, and thereby reduce poverty, shiftlessness and moral decay. By preparing pupils for employment, it would eliminate the "wasted years" syndrome, the period between age 14 (the usual limit of compulsory attendance) and age 16 when jobs were generally available, and thereby reduce the problems of truancy, delinquency and crime.

In the flush of enthusiasm, dissent went almost unnoticed, partly because the dissenters were not very powerful politically and partly because the conflicts were local rather than national. The most intense conflicts involved capital and labor over the control of vocational education. Organized labor feared most of all the possibility of extreme specialization in vocational courses. In seeking public rather than private sponsorship and the participation of labor in all decisions, labor hoped to avoid seeing vocational education develop into training for specific jobs, which might then become obsolete. Labor wanted to prevent the business community's interest in more and cheaper skilled labor from dominating the workers' interest in training beneficial to workers instead of employers. Organized labor thus joined the vocational education movement rather than be left completely out of power. But a suspicion persisted that vocational education was simply a second-class education in the interests of class stratification, and local conflicts were sometimes protracted and bitter (Lazerson & Grubb, 1974).

The Russell Report: Reaffirmation Despite Failures

The depression of the 1930s focused attention on vocational education as a solution to unemployment. Various New Deal programs—the Civilian Conservative Corps, the National Youth Administration and the Works Progress Administration—offered non-school vocational training. The George-Ellzey Act (1934) and the George-Dean Act (1936) increased federal funding. But controversy over the George-Dean Act prompted the formation of a national committee to review vocational education. The report of that committee—the Russell report—had almost nothing good to say about vocational education (Lazerson & Grubb, 1974, pp. 148-158). By promoting an overly narrow concept of education and by creating a dual schooling system, vocational education was guilty of training students in ways that were too specific, denying them flexibility in employment and creating a "caste system" in which social class and curriculum were related. There was substantial evidence that trade and industrial training had no economic payoff, since training generally failed to correspond to the available jobs.

Notwithstanding these indictments, the Russell report went on to reaffirm the principles of vocationalism, though it recommended that vocational education be made more general and flexible. The report itself had little impact, as vocational education was caught up in specific skill training for World War II production. But it was significant as an indication of the failings of vocational education in its first two decades and (unintentionally) as a model that later reports followed.

During the late 1940s and the 1950s, vocational education took a more generalized form as an aspect of "life adjustment education." Declaring that the schools were failing to educate 60 percent of youth who were neither going to college nor being trained for skilled trades in existing vocational programs, life adjustment proponents stated that the schools could correct this deplorable situation by redirecting all of schooling toward practical ends, making all of schooling stand the test of relevance to daily problem solving ("life adjustment needs"). Despite the seriousness of its premises, life adjustment was too general in its scope and offered little that was new; it soon became a caricature of anti-intellectualism in American life and of the status quo in American society.

Vocational Education Act of 1963

Vocational education again emerged as an issue in the 1960s. With high unemployment rates among unskilled workers and the specter of technological unemployment, President Kennedy appointed a national commission to review vocational education. The new committee's report sharply criticized vocational education for its narrowness and its insensitivity to labor market conditions (Panel of Consultants on Vocational Education, 1963). Like the Russell report, it went on to affirm the value of vocational education, particularly in addressing technological unemployment, the problems of minorities and the relevance of schooling. The resulting Vocational Education Act of 1963 attempted to make training more flexible and general and to focus its efforts on those—minorities in particular—who had been left on the fringes of the labor market.

Although most vocational educators viewed the 1963 Act as a significant shift, it failed to have much impact. A major report of the Advisory Council on Vocational Education (1968) reported that the major objectives of the 1963 Act had largely been ignored. The issues stressed in the 1968 report were all too familiar: the problems that technological advancement

117

caused in the form of unemployment and the failure of vocational education to serve the hard-core unemployed. Those criticisms again led to new legislation, the 1968 Vocational Educational Amendments, designed once more to make vocational education flexible and committed to the disadvantaged.

The cycle of criticism and reform has been reported once more in the 1970s. Among other criticisms of vocational education's administration and lack of responsiveness, a 1974 review by the Comptroller General repeated the familiar charges that programs train individuals for nonexistent jobs and fail to address changing manpower requirements; despite the 1963 Act and the 1968 Amendments, disadvantaged and handicapped students had not been given appropriate attention. With the development since 1968 of a more extensive literature evaluating vocational education, doubts about its effectiveness in preparing students for jobs have been increasingly well documented (Reubens, 1974; Grasso & Shea, 1979). But the Comptroller General's report, like its predecessors, stressed that vocational education should be revised, revitalized and extended.

The 1976 Amendments to the Vocational Education Act made new efforts to extend vocational retraining. To earlier fears that vocational education had neglected minorities were added the charges that it perpetuated sexual stereotypes and sex-based stratification and that it neglected the special problems of bilingual pupils. In response, the amendments gave special attention to eliminating sex stereotyping and to providing bilingual training, and in order to address once more the criticism that vocational programs provided training for nonexistent jobs, they also established detailed requirements for evaluation.

Career Education and Vocationalism
Around the developments of vocational education itself has come a new form of vocationalism—career education (Grubb & Lazerson, 1975). Career educators have attacked the schools for their continued irrelevance, urging them to measure every effort against the canon of usefulness. Self-consciously subsuming vocational education, career education at its most grandiose tackles every kind of economic, educational and social ill that has ever been mentioned in the past two decades.

Yet these claims are familiar from vocational education and most of them date back to the Progressive Era. The same insistence that career education can solve the "mismatch of workers and jobs" and thereby reduce unemployment and employment bottlenecks, that it can motivate workers by giving them a better understanding of their jobs and that it can upgrade the status of manual labor is found in various stages of the vocational educational movement. The claims that career education can solve some of the pressing problems of education—irrelevance, dropouts, "under-educated" and "over-educated" youth—were commonly made by previous generations of educators who espoused vocational education. And the advocacy of career education—or some program that integrates school and work—by a variety of groups worried about the "youth problem" of alienation from school, poor mental health and increasing rates of juvenile delinquency recalls the promise that vocational education could eliminate the "wasted years" syndrome and ease the transition from adolescence to adulthood.

There are, of course, some important differences between the two. The most important is the tendency for career education to make the most general and inflated claims, beyond even those made for its predecessor, leading to a notable slipperiness of definition. The goals of career education have thereby become a catalogue of all-purpose educational reforms (U.S. Office of Career Education, 1975). The likely outcome, as occurred with the life adjustment movement, is that career education will be unable to distinguish itself from more general reform impulses on the one hand or from vocational education on the other. Already there are signs that career education has degenerated into a renaming of traditional school activities— for example, calling plant tours and classroom talks by visiting firemen "career exploration"—and into traditionally taught classroom courses on occupation (McGowan & Cohen, 1977).

Employment and Training Programs

The school-based programs to provide vocational training and education "relevant" to occupations have constituted one important strand of American policies towards youth. A second strand emerged during the 1970s with the expansion of training programs outside the schools, as part of a larger package of employment and training programs provided under the Comprehensive Employment and Training Act of 1973 (CETA). The historical origins of these programs lie in the employment programs of the Great Depression, like the Works Progress Administration and the Civilian Conservation Corps, which were desperate responses to a crisis situation.

More recently, the manpower programs of the 1960s provided other non-school work training to cope with technological unemployment and the terrible unemployment rates among blacks. The real innovation of the CETA program is that it provides public employment as well as training. However, most public employment goes to adults, and so for youth CETA is again a training program. Although 43 percent of the individuals in general CETA programs are in public service employment positions, only 24 percent of youth are in these programs; the other 76 percent are enrolled in CETA Title I programs, which largely provide training and counseling but little employment. Only about 230,000 public service employment positions are open to those under 22, a small fraction of all youth who are in some kind of program and less than 10 percent of those who might be unemployed at any particular time (National Commission for Manpower Policy, 1978). About 80 percent of employment positions available to youth are summer jobs, so temporary that they are neither serious employment or training.

Although largely outside of the schools, CETA training programs share many of the assumptions of school-based programs. They assume that skill training will be sufficient to insure later employment. They also represent, even more clearly than school vocational programs, efforts to cope with unskilled young people who have no real place and are thus likely to engage in anti-social behavior; if they do nothing else, these programs at least keep adolescents off the streets and engaged in activities considered worthwhile. Yet the burgeoning of CETA programs for youth implicitly represents a recognition that the American public schools have by and large failed in their vocational purposes. Programs outside the schools present an alternative to school-based training not usually very different in their goals, in the kinds of youth they enroll or in the jobs they prepare youth for. The advantage of CETA programs has been their freedom from the rigidity of public school bureaucracies and from the traditions of ineffective school-based programs.

By now, the dual strands of the implicit American "youth policy" seem to have become institutionalized. The Vice President's Commission on Youth Employment, convened in 1977 to coordinate governmental attempts to reduce youth unemployment, generated intense battles between educators promoting school-based vocational education and those based in the Department of Labor advocating expansion of CETA programs. The final recommendations were a classic compromise, advocating expansion of both vocational education and CETA programs, along with vague mechanisms to link the two different approaches (Vice President's Commission on Youth Employment, 1980). The only remarkable element in these recommendations is their predictability: whether in or out of the schools, vocational training as a solution to youth problems is so well-established that it is promoted at every opportunity. The question remains why this approach has been so consistently promoted despite evidence of its failure.

EXPLAINING THE PERSISTENT APPEAL

The evaluations of vocational and training programs have consistently attacked their failings, often quite harshly. Three criticisms have dominated the periodic reevaluations. First and foremost has been the contention that vocational education and training are used to stratify the school system, to separate lower-class and minority youth from their white, middle-class peers, and to keep them separate if they have dropped out of school. Second has been the continuing suspicion that training programs have no real economic value, that they provide no long-term advantage in the labor market. As formal evaluations have cumulated, the evidence has mounted that vocational education fails to prepare students for existing jobs, so that—with a few exceptions, primarily among girls in secretarial courses— vocational education yields no returns in either earnings or employment rates (Reubens, 1974; Grasso & Shea, 1979). Similarly, evaluations of CETA programs have failed to establish the value of out-of-school programs and have confirmed that whatever earnings and employment advantages are created tend to dissipate after a few years (Schiller, 1978).

Finally, there has been a constant battle over the skills that should be taught in vocational curricula, whether these should be relatively specific or relatively general. The conventional wisdom has been to espouse more general training, to provide skills that can be readily transferred among occupations in a changing economy. The constant reaffirmation of the need for more general training—in the 1963 Act, the 1968 Vocational Education Amendments and the career education movement—indicates that in practice training tends more to the specific.

Despite this litany of failure, an equally consistent affirmation of the value of training has led to the political and legislative renewal of vocational education, the rise of career education and the expansion of CETA. There has been no serious consideration of the obvious implication of the evaluations: because of the assumptions and structure of vocationalism it cannot avoid becoming economically useless and sorting students by class and race. Why, then, is vocational education still proposed as a solution to a variety of social and educational problems?

Looking to the Schools for Solutions

The first and easiest answer to the question of resilience is that, in periods of apparent crisis, Americans tend to turn to the schools for solutions, and vocational education has been a consistent element in this approach to reform. This strategy is essentially conservative: by promising solutions through the schools, more fundamental reforms—particularly in basic economic and political institutions—can be effectively postponed. In an economy characterized by high and apparently insoluble unemployment, the promise that vocational education (like the manpower programs that proliferated in the 1960s) can help correct the mismatch between workers and jobs direct attention away from the structural inability of corporate capitalism to provide enough employment (DuBoff, 1977).

A second answer is that because vocationalism has always promised to help resolve a variety of economic, social and educational problems, all at the same time, its appeal has been widespread, and this has obviously helped provide a strong political base. Ever since labor decided to support vocational education, its opponents have been few and relatively weak. At most, politically powerful groups appear to be indifferent to vocational programs rather than actively opposed to them (McGowan & Cohen, 1977).

Third, the basic appeal obviously extends far beyond vocational educators themselves. In a society where work and productivity are so critical to an individual's sense of worth and accomplishment, turning to work and work experiences as the appropriate way to socialize the young is a seductive path. This aspect of vocational education invokes our most positive images of work, including the assumption that work is a fundamental expression of human need (U.S. Department of HEW, 1973, Ch.1). The contradiction between work in the abstract and work as it is actually available to most Americans is rarely discussed. This has been particularly true for

121

vocational education, which has prepared individuals almost exclusively for working-class jobs, rather than for professional and managerial jobs, which are the most rewarding (in terms of both earnings and working conditions).

Alleviating Tensions Within the School Systems

Vocational movements have also been responses to contradictions within the public schools. The most basic of these is that the schools have tried, on the one hand, to provide a mass educational system and promote equality (or equality of opportunity) and, on the other, have acted as a sorting mechanism, reproducing class and racial divisions from one generation to the next and preparing students for a labor market characterized by gross inequality in the status and rewards of different jobs.

For example, when the growth of higher education after World War II threatened to make postsecondary education more heterogeneous, the development of two-year colleges, particularly with a vocational focus, provided a mechanism for retaining the stratification desired by elitists (Karabel, 1972; Pincus, 1980). The tension between these two functions has taken rather obvious and increasingly strident forms in the past two decades, in battles over integration and busing, community control, school financing, compensatory education, open enrollment and preferential admissions. Vocational education (along with career education) has pledged in some measure to alleviate these tensions, offering greater opportunity through a substantial payoff while still training individuals for a wide variety of jobs.

Finally, in arguing that schooling should be "relevant," vocational education has posited a particular criterion of relevance: schools should be useful in terms of the cognitive skills and personal characteristics that are required in the labor market. To be sure, the image of work embodied in vocational education has often become outmoded and has required periodic refurbishing. But despite some confusion about what work is like, the goals of vocational education are clear enough—and they are distinctly different from the view that education should develop every aspect of human potential, including the critical facilities and capacities for self-motivated activity. That vision of education, associated particularly with John Dewey, has often been suspected of creating dissatisfied, unruly workers who are disrespectful of authority and of encouraging educational "frills" like art and music. In contrast, during those periods when the schools have threatened to become "useless," vocationalism has been ready to reassert that all of schooling should be evaluated by its contributions to the economic system—and to an economic system that itself is beyond criticism.

LIMITATIONS OF VOCATIONALISM

The persistent criticisms of vocational and training programs and the mounting evidence that their economic advantages are evanescent raise another question: are the failures of vocational solutions inevitable, or are they merely due to the poor implementation and inadequate planning of programs? Evidently, those who have participated in the cycles of criticism and reaffirmation of vocational training have held the second view and urged that American education and manpower programs try *one more time* to revise their failings. However, the persistence of similar criticisms suggests that we consider the alternative—that vocational solutions to the problems of youth unemployment ignore the fundamental causes of the problem and so cannot possibly work.

The Problem of "Credentialing"

One reason for the failure of vocational solutions has been common to the entire schooling system in the United States. The process of reorienting American education around primarily vocational purposes in the Progressive Era began a search for ever-higher levels of schooling, which has exploded recently as the problem of "credentialing." As schooling came to be the mechanism of social and economic advancement, the incentive for each individual was to gain as much schooling as possible. This process has in turn led to increasing rates of high school and then college attendance.

Yet the growth in the skill requirements of jobs has not kept pace with the educational attainments of the available work force, except for accidents of changing sectoral composition (like the expansion of professional and technical jobs in the post-World War II period). The consequence is the tendency for jobs of relatively low skill to be filled by individuals with higher levels of schooling, a process variously referred to as educational upgrading or (more pejoratively) educational inflation (e.g. Berg, 1970). The decisions of students, individually rational, have led to a situation that is in the aggregate irrational and where the relation between schooling and work is degraded and problematic.

For teenagers, who by definition cannot have high levels of schooling, the process of credentialing has placed most jobs—especially most decent jobs—beyond their ability to compete for these jobs, crowding youth into unskilled, poorly-paid positions with no incentives to be stable workers. The fastest growing occupations in the post-war period have been professional and government positions, most of which require high levels of education. The other category of rapidly growing occupations, service workers, include a large number of jobs that are conventionally open to teenagers but which are precisely the kinds of jobs that contain no career paths and which encourage unstable work—jobs in fast-food restaurants and service stations, as busboys, waitresses and babysitters.

A growing number of positions are therefore closed off to youth because of educational requirements, while the available jobs are increasingly the "dead-end" jobs in the secondary labor market, jobs that have always been criticized for contributing to the instability of youth. No amount of training, and especially no amount of skill-specific training, can make teenagers eligible for jobs that require some college education, and training programs cannot reverse the growth of secondary labor market jobs, which provide some employment for teenagers but induce them to be unsatisfied and unstable workers. To the extent that credentialing is responsible for youth unemployment, then, training programs cannot resolve the problem.

The Youth Market: Structurally Different

The most powerful reason for the failures of vocational solutions, however, is their inability to address the structural conditions of the labor markets for youth. In the United States, the "crisis" of youth unemployment during the 1970s represented a deterioration of chronically high rates of youth unemployment; throughout the post-World War II period, the unemployment rates for teenagers have been between 2.5 and 4.5 times as high as adult unemployment rates. This implies that the youth labor market is structurally different from the rest of the labor market. Employers prefer to hire older workers, and for most jobs—especially jobs with career potential—they will not seriously consider teenagers except in periods of labor shortage (Barton, 1975; Diamond & Bedrosian, 1970).

The reasons given vary: some employers cite child labor laws as barriers to hiring young people; others blame the minimum wage and other costs of employment, including Social Security, fringe benefits, occupational health and safety regulations, which thereby induce employers to hire individuals whom they consider to be more reliable and less willing to leave. These costs reinforce one of the dominant reasons given for not hiring young people—the feeling that they are unreliable and erratic workers. In an economy with a chronically high level of unemployment, where it is usually possible to hire a slightly older worker, there is no reason for an employer to run the risks associated with younger workers, and the youth employment rates suffer. Since training programs do nothing about the distaste for young workers, they cannot reduce this component of youth unemployment.

Minority Youth Suffer Highest Unemployment Rates

In the United States, there is also a large racial component to youth unemployment. In March, 1970, when the unemployment rate for white youth (16-21) was 14.1 percent, the rate was 19.4 percent for Hispanics and 28.1 percent for blacks. Despite the gains that blacks have made in the post-war period—in narrowing educational differences with whites and in the increased returns to schooling—these gains appear to have benefited experienced and well-educated blacks more than adolescents. While the efforts of the federal government to reduce employment discrimination have not yet had any clear effect in labor markets, even these efforts have been targeted on older workers and have almost completely bypassed youth.

The result is that unemployment among minority youth remains one of the most persistent social problems, as apparently intractable as it is threatening to white America. The problem of youth unemployment in America will never be resolved until patterns of racial discrimination are corrected. But since vocational programs leave racial discrimination untouched, they are of little help in correcting this dimension of youth unemployment.

The Persistent Frustrations

Finally, and affecting all other dimensions of youth unemployment, the generally high levels of unemployment in the United States have affected all other dimensions of youth unemployment. A central issue in the postwar period has been the increasing level of overall unemployment, from an average of 4.5 percent in the 1950s and 4.8 percent in the 1960s to more than 6 percent in the 1970s; older conceptions of "full employment"—3 percent in the 1950s, 4 percent in the 1960s—now seem unattainable (DuBoff, 1977). Youth have obviously been caught up in the escalating unemployment rates, especially since their unemployment rates have always been several times as high as adult rates. Since they do not confront the overall level of employment, the vocational and training programs that have dominated the American approach to youth problems have thus been doomed to ineffectiveness.

Problems Apply to Out-of-School Programs

The creation of training programs outside the schools, in CETA programs, has not altered the basic dilemmas of vocational solutions. The dismal American experience with manpower programs in the 1960s suggests again that structural problems will continue to be as serious for out-of-school training programs as for school-based programs. Two problems in particular seem especially threatening. The first is the tendency to generate training programs uncoordinated with the labor market and with the requirements of available jobs, a problem that has long plagued vocational education as well. The result has consistently been to "train for unemployment."

The second problem is more fundamental: the possibility that the task set for training programs is well-nigh impossible. These programs take lower-class youth, whom the schools have failed to train, and they attempt to do in relatively short periods of time what the schools have failed to do over a period of at least 10 years. Their supposed advantage is that, by being more closely connected to work and with the threat of unemployment more tangible, the incentive to learn is greater. Yet each of these assumptions is uncertain.

Training programs uncoordinated with specific and permanent jobs may be no more relevant to jobs than are school-based programs. The threat of unemployment may be palpable enough, but the threat may be irrelevant if a training program cannot guarantee a meaningful position upon successful completion. With an increasing number of decent jobs requiring formal educational credentials to enter them, dropping out of school and entering a training program may itself be destructive of future employment opportunities. Moreover, since the training programs are explicitly directed at lower-class youth and are based on the assumptions of personal failure, the labelling associated with this kind of state intervention may serve to undercut employment possibilities. In general, it is difficult to see why training programs should work where schools have failed.

Alternatives Are Available

It is hard to be optimistic about vocational approaches. Over the long run, vocationalism has generated the problems of credentialing, exacerbated the problems of equalizing opportunity, heightened conflict within the schools, and—through these various problems—contributed to the pervasive and recurring criticism of the irrelevance of schooling. As a consequence, vocationalism is so contradictory in its effects that it cannot resolve the problems it set out to solve: rather than making school-based training consistent with occupational requirements, it has made them increasingly irrelevant.

None of this was inevitable, since alternatives have always been available. One is to emphasize employment programs and institute training programs (in the schools or in some other institutional setting) geared to the jobs created, rather than continuing the present situation in which training programs are uncoordinated with job opportunities and public employment. Similarly, if youth unemployment is to be considered a serious problem, then expansion of employment programs as distinct from training programs seems an obvious prerequisite. For the problems that minority youth face in particular, there can be no substitute for efforts to reduce labor market discrimination; otherwise education and training programs simply fail to have as much payoff for them as for white students, and therefore fail to give them the intended advantage.

Other efforts to reduce credentialing might be undertaken. So too might efforts to eliminate training programs that have no payoff in terms of earnings or employment. The elimination of such worthless programs might transform the image of the schools, with high school and college reserved for "academic" programs and all skill-specific courses outside the school— either under public auspices, as in the short courses now part of community colleges, or in private hands as in proprietary training schools and firm-based programs. Such an arrangement would also eliminate one of the mechanisms of tracking within the high schools and community colleges— though of course it would not eliminate the pressure for stratification in the schooling system.

While a number of alternatives have been possible, they are not likely to be implemented. In the past, evidence of the irrationality of educational solutions has been ignored, particularly in the constant affirmation of vocational education, in the search during the 1960s for solutions through manpower programs and in the efforts in the 1970s to resurrect manpower approaches in "employment and training programs." The educational solution is too deeply embedded in our institutions; the alternatives are too politically embattled.

Alternatives to conventional educational resolutions have in fact been possible only as adjuncts to programs for adults. The youth programs of the Depression were part of employment programs for adults; the development of CETA and the Youth Employment and Demonstration Projects Act (YEDPA) programs for youth depended on prior demands for public employment programs for adults suffering high unemployment rates. Efforts to combat discrimination, rarely invoked for youth, began with efforts to reduce discrimination for adults. To be sure, the advent of public employment programs, antidiscrimination efforts, and the Occupational Health and Safety Administration during the 1960s and 1970s have slowly changed the conception of what the state might do with respect to personnel policies and labor markets. Still the historical record indicates that there can be no real change in programs for youth until there are corresponding changes in programs for adults, and youth are generally the last group to enjoy the benefits of these efforts. That conclusion reveals how unsatisfactory the resolution of the "youth problem" has been.

REFERENCES

Advisory Council on Vocational Education. *Vocational education: The bridge between man and his work.* Washington, D.C.: Government Printing Office, 1968.

Barton, P. Youth unemployment and career entry. In S. Wolfbein (Ed.), *Labor market information for youth.* Philadelphia: Temple University Press, 1975.

Berg, I. *Education and jobs.* New York: Praeger, 1970.

Diamond, D., & Bedrosian, H. *Hiring standards and job performance.* (U.S. Department of Labor Research Monograph No. 19.) Washington, D.C.: DOL, 1970.

DuBoff, R. Full employment: The history of a receding target. *Politics and Society,* 1977, *7,* 1-25.

Grasso, J., & Shea, J. *Vocational education and training: Impact on youth.* Berkeley: Carnegie Council on Policy Studies in Higher Education, 1979.

Grubb, W., & Lazerson, M. Rally 'round the workplace: Continuities and fallacies in career education. *Harvard Educational Review,* 1975, *45.*

Karabel, J. Community colleges and social stratification. *Harvard Educational Review,* 1972, *42.*

Lazerson, M., & Grubb, W.N. *American education and vocationalism: A documentary history.* New York: Teachers' College Press, 1974.

McGowan, E., & Cohen, D.K. Career education—reforming school through work. *The Public Interest,* 1977 (winter).

National Commission for Manpower Policy. *CETA: An analysis of the issues.* (Special Report No. 23, May 1978.) Washington, D.C.: Author, 1978.

Organization for Economic and Cooperative Development. *Youth unemployment, Vol. I.* Paris: Author, 1978.

O'Toole, J. (Ed.) *Work in America.* Cambridge, Mass.: M.I.T. Press, 1973.

Panel of Consultants on Vocational Education. *Education for a changing world of work.* Washington, D.C.: Government Printing Office, 1963.

Pincus, F.L. The false promises of community colleges: Class conflict and vocational education. *Harvard Educational Review,* 1980, *50.*

Reubens, B. Vocational education for *all* in high school? In J. O'Toole (Ed.), *Work and the quality of life.* Cambridge, Mass.: M.I.T. Press, 1975.

Schiller, B. Program outcomes. In *CETA: An analysis of the issues.* (Special Report No. 23, May, 1978.) Washington, D.C.: National Commission for Manpower Policy, 1978.

U.S. Office of Career Education. *An introduction to career education.* Washington, D.C.: Government Printing Office, 1975.

Vice President's Task Force on Youth Employment. *A review of youth employment problems, programs, and policies.* 3 Vols. Washington, D.C.: Government Printing Office, 1980.

This article has been reprinted from a special issue on "Schools, Youth and Work" in *Educational Analysis,* 1981, *3*(3), published by The Falmer Press, Lewes, England.

A RESPONSE TO THE CRITICISMS OF JOB TRAINING BY REVISIONIST HISTORIANS

Paul Joseph Ringel

> Some men are uncommon to extraordinary degree, some to lesser. And perhaps most uncommon of all is the common man whose achievements are exalted beyond the expectation of his circumstances. From Crawford H. Greenewalt, *The Uncommon Man* (1959).

Between 1870 and 1920 America became the world's leading industrial power and her citizens were "virtually transformed from a rural into a predominantly urban people" (Curti, 1974, p. 204). American society experienced dynamic changes in both population and industrial growth. The century after 1830 witnessed the most dramatic demographic migration the world had ever seen. The number of immigrants landing on America's shores totaled almost 37,000,000; the nation's institutions attempted to meet the unimagined demands necessitated by their arrival, and the very fabric of American culture changed, reflecting the heterogeneous quality of the new population.

HISTORICAL BACKGROUND

In the 1870s the United States was basically an agrarian country, with less than one-fifth of the people living in cities. By 1910 the urban proportion had increased to two-fifths, as the nation's population grew from 39,000,000 to 92,000,000 (Perkinson, 1968, p. 62). As wave upon wave of immigrants arrived on America's shores, they tended to settle in the already heavily populated urban centers. "By 1900 immigrants constituted 40 percent of the population of the twelve largest cities in the country, [with] another 20 percent ... second generation" (Hays, 1957, p. 95).

As American industry expanded, so did the demand for labor. Cities already crowded attempted to absorb the newest arrivals. Conditions in the urban centers deteriorated, the plight of the immigrants worsened and for many, the promise of the American dream faded. In the face of this dismal situation, Perkinson argued that "Americans [did as they had always done] looked to the schools to solve their social, economic, and political problems" (p. 12).

Between 1875 and 1900 manual training and industrial education were proposed as the "educational panaceas" that would meet the requirements of a new and differentiated curriculum. Herschback (1973), looking at the

129

last quarter of the nineteenth century wrote, "By the 1880's the industrial-urban forces of change sweeping across America had created a social environment receptive to industrial education" (p. 16). Education itself was undergoing a fundamental change because of attempts to make the course of study more practical. According to Cohen (1968), "few movements in the history of American education have taken so sudden and powerful hold on the minds of American school reformers" (p. 96); and yet,

> No subject elicited more controversy in the first decades of the twentieth century than vocational [industrial] training. Both its critics and advocates correctly understood that integrating programs directly applicable to the job market would transform public education. (Lazerson, 1971, p. 265)

Vocational/industrial education was an important and integral part of American education. To see it in the context in which it occurred is to understand not only the impact it made on its time but the influence it has on the present, and perhaps, the future as well. Vocational/industrial education was closely tied to the vast changes and pressures, ideas and ideologies that were present in American society. As a curricular innovation, industrial education was widely accepted because of changes that were taking place in American industry.

The decades preceding World War I witnessed the emergence of modern American industry. The roots of the new factory system can be discerned in the years after 1880 when, according to Nelson (1975), "the size and sophistication of factory operations gradually transformed the relationships between manufacturers, the shop managers, and the workers" (p. 163).

Shortage of Skilled Labor

At the end of the nineteenth century, with the ranks of the industrial work force swelled by the infusion of foreign labor, American industry continued to be plagued with the problem of obtaining properly trained workers. The problem, although complex, stemmed principally from the changed nature of industrial technology and the inability of traditional apprenticeship systems to meet the needs of modern production.

In an attempt to meet their demands for skilled labor, many large manufacturers modified their existing apprenticeship programs in order "to provide a steady supply of thoroughly trained employees, many of whom, it was understood would ultimately assume managerial positions" (Nelson, p. 97). The smaller companies, unable to develop large-scale apprenticeship programs, "joined reformers and educators in promoting government-subsidized industrial education" (Nelson, p. 97).

During the first decade of the twentieth century, many manufacturers and industrialists turned their attention to industrial education. Unlike its precursor, manual training, industrial education would be "education for specific trades." It was a workable curricular reform because "back of many groups of trades or factory processes [were] found certain elements of likeness" (NEA, 1910, p. 64). Certainly there was a demonstrated need for trained industrial workers (NEA, pp. 65-68). Although industrial education took many forms, cooperative education was one of the most innovative (U.S. Congress, 1912, pp. 50-59).

THE REVISIONIST VIEW

During the last decade and a half, a new revisionist historiography has been written in the field of educational history. According to Cohen (1968), "historians of education have begun to study the political and social conditions of the school's existence and the presuppositions concerning it. They have begun to ask new sorts of questions, questions having to do with power and control" (p. 96).

A Rejection of Liberal Values

Ravitch (1978) identified the *radical revisionists* "by their thorough rejection of liberal values and liberal society and their shared belief that schools are *consciously* designed by liberal reformers as undemocratic instruments of manipulation and social control" (pp. 30-31).

The revisionist historian Spring (1973) saw the school as becoming "increasingly important as the primary instrument for social control. It became the agency charged with the responsibility of maintaining social order" (p. 30). Karier (1975) concurred and wrote that "one of the central myths of the twentieth century is that schooling will result in social mobility" (p. 2). Greer (1973) rejected completely the "American school legend" which held that "America became great because of its public schools" (p. 3) and found "the assumption that extended schooling promotes greater . . . social mobility . . . fallacious" (p. 109). For Bowles and Gintis (1976), "Education over the years has never been a potent force for economic equality" (p. 8), and "the school . . . is [just] one of several institutions which serve to perpetuate . . . economic inequality" (p. 85).

Michael Katz, one of the earliest of the revisionist educational historians, has indeed looked at the past through a different lens and subjected the data to different kinds of questions, questions which have generated new and different kinds of interpretations. Throwing down the gauntlet to the liberal-progressive historians, Katz declared, "the burden of proof no longer lies with those who argue that education is and has been unequal. It lies, rather, with those who would defend the system" (1973, p. 435).

Who Controls Interpretations

Susman (1964) was correct in identifying the importance of history in understanding ideology; and, it thus appears that "the question which has really been posed by the radical revisionists is who shall have control over the interpretation of the educational past of the United States" (Cohen, 1978, p. 129).

By the beginning of the twentieth century, with the nation's ethnic population changing concomitantly with the growth in industrialization and urbanization, the introduction of a "differentiated curriculum" gained wide acceptance. One of the best known and universally debated curricular innovations was "industrial education." Although much has been written about it, Ravitch has pointed out that "far more is known about the stated intentions of its proponents than about its implementation and effects" (p. 46). In any event, the revisionists have looked at industrial education and concluded that it

> appeared to be a handy solution to the problems of catering to large numbers of less able or less academic students. It was also a solution fit for poor children; it would permit them to attend secondary school without imbibing aspirations beyond their class. It would continue to instill in them the attitudes and skills appropriate to manual working-class status. Regardless of the rhetoric of its sponsors, industrial education has proved to be an ingenious way of providing universal secondary schooling without disturbing the shape of the social structure and without permitting excessive amounts of social mobility. (Katz, 1971, p. 121)

Karier (1975) saw that "the business of the school was business" and that job "training took on the characteristics necessary to serve mass-production industries" (pp. 2-3).

A Class Stratification System

Bowles and Gintis (1976) also saw job training develop as "educational reformers began to propose a system of [social class] stratification within secondary education" (p. 191). For them, the industrial

> education movement was less a response to the specific job training needs of the rapidly expanding corporate sector than an accommodation of a previously elite educational institution—the high school—to the changing needs of reproducing the class structure. Particularly important in this respect was the use of the ideology of vocationalism to justify a tracking system which would separate and stratify young people loosely according to race, ethnic origins, and class backgrounds. (p. 194)

Tyack (1974) attempted to explain "how the schools shaped and were shaped by the transformation of the United States into an urban-industrial nation" (p. 3). The school system that emerged operated in a "predictable and systematic way," and in spite of the "stated intentions" of school officials, the educational system was rarely effective in educating the children of the poor and disenfranchised. In their search for "the one best system" to run the nation's urban schools, educational leaders played a systematic part in perpetuating the injustices of American urban life (p. 12).

Tyack, in agreement with Lazerson and Grubb (1974), feels that "the vocational [industrial] education movement was significant . . . because it represented an increasing conviction 'that the primary goal of schooling was to prepare youth for the job market' " (pp. 189-190). Although in many instances educational leaders were able to incorporate most vocational programs into their comprehensive educational systems, they were not as successful with the "question of social class stratification" because "the vocational program often became a dead-end side track for lower-class youth" (p. 190).

A Reflection of the American Factory

One of the latest criticisms of vocational education and job training appears in a long essay by Violas (1978). In it he studied "the socialization of urban working-class children by the American public school as the institution attempted to adjust those children to their inevitable industrial futures" (p. xii). The argument he makes is similar to the one suggested by Katz (1971), Spring (1972) and others in that the public school was conceived, constructed, and administered in such a way as to mirror, as closely as possible, the American factory. The school would inculcate those values and internal controls that would produce a willing and docile work force that would take its destined place in the industrial army "with as little pain and alienation as possible" (Violas, 1978, p. xii).

Violas saw job training as another means by which "the states through the public schools, officially sanctioned the emerging class structure of corporate industrialism" (p. 138). And like Karier (1975), he also saw

> the public schools in the business of not only training the industrial proletariat, but also of selecting it from the poor segments of society. Schools were asked not to facilitate intellectual development and social mobility, but to replicate the class structure. (p. 140)

Although many of the revisionist historians write from different perspectives, "they all see the schools maintaining order, harmony, and conformity in a technological society marked by immigration, industrialization, and urbanization" (R. Cohen, 1974, p. 428). Furthermore, they all seem to share the belief that schools in no way fostered social or economic mobility. In discussing historical methodology, Katz (1971) wrote, "Our concerns shape the questions we ask and, as a consequence, determine what we select from the virtually unlimited supply of 'fact' " (p. xxv). The authors of *Roots of Crisis* noted that the historian's work must be "validated by reason, logic, and empirical analysis. Context, internal consistency, cross-referencing, authenticity of documentation—all are tools with which the historian shapes and colors his picture of the past" (pp. 1-2). In his "Comment" for *History of Education Quarterly,* Katz (1969) noted the need for "case studies" of urban school systems in order to test the conclusions of the educational historians. Tyack (1974) introduced his work as "exploratory and tentative" while scholars continue to direct their "attention to monographic studies of urban schooling which will enrich our knowledge of how schools actually operated" (p. 3).

Revisionists Not All in Accord

Because the revisionists do not write with one pen, they are often at odds with each other (Katz, 1973; Tyack, 1974). Urban (1975) demonstrated that when some of the revisionists' work is tested by the very standards they set (Karier, Violas, and Spring, pp. 1-2), it is often found to be methodologically deficient. It was Katz who originally called for more case studies in order to better understand the history of public education. Ironically, as those case studies are being concluded, many of the revisionists' assertions are being found inaccurate and incorrect. In his study of the Gary public schools, Ronald Cohen (1974) concluded "it is easy to assert that urban education was designed to accomplish certain purposes, but *generalizations* break down when individual schools are examined" (p. 432, emphasis added). Looking at the other side of the coin, however, Cohen asked,

> if we accept the thesis of Katz, Spring, and Lazerson that the schools never intended to secure mobility for the disadvantaged, but were designed to enforce conformity and docility, then we should not criticize them for failing to do something they were never intended to do. (p. 435)

Although Cohen's question is, in the least, thought provoking, a more important question to consider is whether the schools actually did foster both economic and social mobility.

Did Schools Promote Mobility?

Kessner (1977), in his study of the Jews and Italians of New York City found that "the local schools . . . aided the immigrant to assimilate and to acquire essential [job] skills" (p. 174) so that in Manhattan as early as 1880 "they rose out of the manual class at a rate of 37 percent," and in Brooklyn by an "even more striking 57 percent" (p. ix). Kessner concluded,

> Whatever the methodology and whichever generation it is applied to, immigrant mobility was far more than a literary device or an ideological weapon; it was a fair interpretation of the American reality. (p. 126)

Blau and Duncan (1967) concluded that years of schooling accounted for nearly all of the direct effects of parental occupational status and education on son's occupational standing. Featherman and Hauser (1978), continuing and augmenting the research of Blau and Duncan found that

> Over the full range of the educational distribution, the role
> of schools as instruments of social stratification . . . has
> given even more ground to its dominant role as a vehicle
> for social mobility. (p. 311)

If the revisionists are correct, then the data being generated by contemporary social stratification and mobility studies will demonstrate that American society has been neither dynamic nor fluid. According to Featherman and Hauser (1978), "the measurement of occupational mobility across or within generations may provide insights into the openness or rigidity of society" (p. 19). As part of their conclusion they wrote,

> our analysis of social mobility among American men has
> detected . . . [that] the benefits of schooling—in the forms
> of occupational and economic returns—have increased;
> and the mobility-inducing effects of education are mani-
> festly stronger than in the recent past. (p. 19)

Blau and Duncan (1967) conceived of social mobility as a lifelong, dynamic process. "The seeds of such a process are sown within families of orientation, *nurtured and developed within the schools,* and harvested within the domestic and market economies of adulthood" (Featherman & Hauser, 1978, p. 10, emphasis added).

Violas (1978), on the other hand, presented a counter argument. He suggests that industrial education programs were *consciously designed* "to instill habits, values, and psychological traits" (p. 159) that would "produce the right sort of person" who would fit neatly into the existing industrial machine.

> The fact that children headed for the industrial proletariat
> would receive less than half as much work in academic
> subjects as upper-class children inhibited their social and
> intellectual development. Even more significant than
> restricted academic or cultural study, though, was the
> major disfigurement these restrictions caused. Children in
> vocational training curricula did not study the same kinds
> of [subjects] . . . as did students from upper class families
> who, at least theoretically, were educated to make inde-
> pendent decisions and assume leadership positions in the
> industrial army. (p. 184)

CASE STUDY: FITCHBURG HIGH SCHOOL

Like McBride (1974), Violas has also suggested that particular textbooks were chosen in order "to organize the academic subjects around the needs of industry" (p. 185). In this way, by manipulating the curricular materials, students in job training programs would be tracked for their industrial roles. To substantiate his argument, Violas referred to a list of textbooks used in the vocational program at Fitchburg (Massachusetts) High School. He then declared,

> Any resemblance between the following list and readings designed for standard English classes was clearly unintentional. The list suggest [sic] how vocational training might help fit the boy into his intended slot in the industrial labor force. (p. 186)

As to the other subjects, he said

> A mathematics course that used *Machine Shop Calculations* as its basic text, and a history course devoted to the rise of industry, *would encourage the child to believe that reality was limited to the factory and the machine that he was destined to tend.* (p. 187, emphasis added)

However, a closer look at Violas' source (McCann, 1913) indicates that the list he referred to was only "collateral reading" (p. 17) and that, in fact, required reading included *Lady of the Lake, Treasure Island* and *Ivanhoe*. Had Professor Violas read further (p. 18) he would have known that the following works were also required: Franklin's *Autobiography,* Burke's *Conciliation,* Shakespeare's *Julius Caesar* and *The Twelfth Night.* Furthermore, Violas was incorrect when he claimed that the basic text of the mathematics course was *Machine Shop Calculations;* in fact, the first year mathematics text was Stone & Mill's *First Year Algebra*—a text that emphasized "fundamental operations, manipulation of formulae; [and] quadratics" (p. 14).[1] Ringel (Note 1) has pointed out,

> The academic program developed by the [Fitchburg] School Department was similar to the Manual Training Course that was discontinued in 1908. It is true that the School Department tried to develop a relevant curriculum that would engage the interests of the Industrial Course students, but to claim the program was set up to train mindless, docile workers is false. (p. 6)

Finally, Violas claimed that as a result of the "enforced curriculum" a child of Fitchburg High School's industrial education program was "encouraged to believe that reality was limited to the factory and the machine that he was destined to tend" (p. 187). If Violas is correct then it would not be surprising to find that most of the young men who took part in the industrial education program in Fitchburg ended up in low-paying, dead-end jobs. Was this in fact the case?

Fitchburg, situated on a branch of the Nashua River, is located in north-central Massachusetts about eighty kilometers northwest of Boston. Incorporated as a city in 1872, Fitchburg enjoyed a national and international reputation for the manufacture of paper and pulp, cotton goods, woolen and worsted goods, and foundry and machine shop products.

Nation's First Cooperative Industrial Course

By the turn of the century, the Fitchburg School Committee and the city's school superintendent recognized the community's growing interest and need for industrial education. Introduced in 1908 and patterned after the program developed by Professor Herman Schneider at the University of Cincinnati, Fitchburg offered the nation's first high school cooperative industrial course. Known as the "Fitchburg Plan," it gained national and international recognition and was used as a model by many communities in setting up their own cooperative programs.

Between 1908 and 1928, 263 students were graduated from Fitchburg High School's Co-Operative Industrial Course. Using the alumni files and records of the high school, *The Fitchburg City Directories,* obituary material published in the *Fitchburg Sentinel,* and interviews with graduates and family members of graduates, Ringel (1980) collected occupational data on the graduates and their fathers. Of those students who completed the Course, it was possible to obtain intragenerational occupational data on 251 or 95.44 percent. Furthermore, he able to interview 71 of the 73 living graduates.

Fathers' and Sons' Occupations Compared

In order to determine whether there was a significant amount of intergenerational mobility, the occupations of the fathers, at the time they registered their sons at Fitchburg High School, were compared with the occupations of the graduates.[2] It was found that 133 of the 250 students—intergenerational data were missing for only 13 students—whose fathers' occupations were classified as blue collar ended up in occupations that were considered white collar. In other words, 53 percent of the sons of blue-collar workers ended up in white-collar occupations. Fifty, or 20 percent, remained at the same occupational level as the father. However, when one looks at occupational movement for all students, regardless of whether they moved from the blue-collar category to the white, it was found that 184 of the students, or 74 percent, moved to an occupational category higher than the father. Only in 6 percent of the cases was there downward mobility.

These data thus indicate that a substantial number of men, whose fathers were classified as "blue collar" when they registered their sons at Fitchburg High School, ended up in "white-collar" occupations. Thernstrom (1964) wrote, "the rise from an unskilled laboring position to virtually an nonmanual occupation represents significant upward mobility" (p. 217) and this definition of "mobility" can be applied here. Certainly the fact that more than half of the students who took part in the Co-Operative Industrial Course moved into white-collar occupations indicates that this group was definitely upwardly mobile.

Movement into High White-Collar Occupations

Ringel (1980) identified and contrasted the occupations of 251 of the 263 graduates with their fathers (pp. 286-311). One of his most significant findings was that 78, or 31.01 percent, of the graduates of the Industrial Course ended up in "High White-Collar" occupations (p. 224). Of this number, 65, or 25.89 percent, entered "Professional" occupations. Ninety of the graduates, or 35.86 percent, went into occupations that were classified as "Low White-Collar." Although significant in itself, when one combines the number of students in the Low and High White-Collar categories, it is seen that 168, or 66.93 percent, of the graduates entered "non-manual occupations" (p. 224).

As one might expect based on the kind of instruction given to the Industrial Course students, it is not surprising that 69, or 27.49 percent, of the graduates entered "Skilled Blue-Collar" occupations. Although not classified as "non-manual," the large number of students who entered the skilled trades is another indicator of the high caliber of student attracted to the Industrial Course and the quality of instruction received in high school. Although not actually crossing the "White-Blue-Collar" line, the fact that more than a quarter of the Course's students entered skilled occupations demonstrates that these men, many from humble backgrounds, were indeed upwardly mobile.

Only 14, or 5.58 percent, of the graduates of the Industrial Course entered "Semiskilled or Service" type work. With no graduates in the "Unskilled Laborer" category, this means that of the 251 occupations Ringel was able to identify for the graduates, 237, or 94.42 percent, found themselves in occupations at the "Skilled Blue-Collar" level or higher. Virtually *every* student who graduated from Fitchburg High School's Co-Operative Industrial Course was occupationally successful.

In 1928 the Co-Operative Industrial Course of Fitchburg High School was discontinued. For the most part, as has been pointed out, the students ended up in white-collar or skilled occupations. The data uncovered by Ringel's study incontrovertibly demonstrate that the young men who took part in the nation's first cooperative *industrial* course, were, as a group, upwardly mobile and vocationally and economically successful.

CONCLUSION

The revisionist educational historians have made wide-ranging, generalized assertions about industrial education. Contrary to their stated criticisms, American society has been open and fluid. It has always been difficult to strike the correct balance between the needs of the individual and the needs of society. Greene (1973) put it very well when she said,

A Response to the Criticisms of Job Training

Education, because it takes place at the intersection where the demands of social order and the demands for autonomy conflict, must proceed by means of the tension. (p. 9)

To paraphrase Professor Katz, the burden of proof no longer lies with those who argue that education is and has been equal. It lies, rather, with those who would criticize the system.

REFERENCES

Blau, P.M., & Duncan, O.D. *The American occupational structure.* New York: John Wiley & Sons, 1967.

Bowles, S., & Gintis, H. *Schooling in capitalist America: Educational reform and the contradictions of economic life.* New York: Basic Books, 1976.

Cohen, R.D. Urban schooling in twentieth-century America: A frame of reference. *Urban Education,* 1974, *8*(4), 423-437.

Cohen, S. The history of urban education in the United States: Historians of education and their discontents. In D.A. Reeder (Ed.), *Urban education in the nineteenth century.* New York: St. Martin's Press, 1978.

Cohen, S. The industrial education movement. *American Quarterly,* 1968, *20*(spring), 95-110.

Curti, M. *The social ideas of American educators.* n.p.: Charles Scribner's Sons, 1935: reprint ed., Totowa, N.J.: Littlefield, Adams & Co., 1974.

Featherman, D.L., & Hauser, R.M. *Opportunity and change.* New York: Academic Press, 1978.

Greene, M. Identities and contours: An approach to educational history. *Educational Researcher,* 1973, *2*(spring), 5-10.

Greenwalt, C.H. *The uncommon man.* New York: McGraw-Hill, 1959.

Greer, C. *The great school legend.* Basic Books, 1972; Viking Press, 1973.

Hays, S.P. *The response to industrialism, 1885-1914.* Chicago: University of Chicago Press, 1957.

Herschback, D. *Industrial education ideology, 1876-1917: A social and historical analysis.* Unpublished doctoral dissertation, University of Illinois at Urbana-Champaign, 1973.

Karier, C.J. (Ed.). *Shaping the American educational state: 1900 to the present.* New York: The Free Press, 1975.

Katz, M.B. *The irony of early school reform: Educational innovation in mid-nineteenth century Massachusetts.* Boston: Beacon Press, 1968.

Katz, M.B. Comment. *History of Education Quarterly,* 1969, *9*, 326-327.

Katz, M.B. *Class, bureaucracy, and schools: The illusion of educational change in America.* New York: Praeger Publishers, 1971.

Katz, M.B. Book Review: Roots of crisis. *Harvard Educational Review,* 1973, *43*(3), 435-442.

Kessner, T. *The golden door: Italian and Jewish immigrant mobility in New York City 1880-1915.* New York: Oxford University Press, 1977.

Lazerson, M. *Origins of the urban school: Public education in Massachusetts, 1870-1915.* Cambridge: Harvard University Press, 1971.

Lazerson, M., & Grubb, W.N. *American education and vocationalism: A documentary history, 1870-1970.* New York: Teachers College Press, 1974.

McBride, P.W. The co-op industrial experiment, 1900-1917. *History of Education Quarterly,* 1974, *14*(summer), 209-221.

McCann, M.R. The Fitchburg plan of co-operative industrial education. In *Bulletin* No. 50. U.S. Bureau of Education. Washington, D.C.: Government Printing Office, 1913.

National Education Association. *Report of the committee on the place of industries in public education.* n.p.: NEA, 1910.

Nelson, D. *Managers and workers: Origins of the new factory system in the United States, 1880-1920.* Madison: University of Wisconsin Press, 1975.

Perkinson, H.J. *The imperfect panacea: American faith in education, 1865-1965.* New York: Random House, 1968.

Ravitch, D. *The revisionists revised: A critique of the radical attack on the schools.* New York: Basic Books, 1978.

Ringel, P.J. *The introduction and development of manual training and industrial education in the public schools of Fitchburg, Massachusetts, 1893-1928.* Unpublished doctoral dissertation, Teachers College, Columbia University, 1980.

Spring, J. *Education and the rise of the corporate state.* Boston: Beacon Press, 1972.

Spring, J. Education as a form of social control. In C.J. Karier, P. Violas, & J. Spring (Eds.), *Roots of crisis: American education in the twentieth century.* Chicago: Rand McNally, 1973.

Susman, W.I. History and the American intellectual: Uses of a usable past. *American Quarterly,* 1964, *16*(summer), 243-263.

Thernstrom, S. *Poverty and progress: social mobility in a nineteenth century city.* Cambridge: Harvard University Press, 1964.

Thernstrom, S. *The other Bostonians: Poverty and progress in the American metropolis, 1880-1970.* Cambridge: Harvard University Press, 1973.

Tyack, D.B. *The one best system: A history of American urban education.* Harvard University Press, 1974.

Urban, W.J. Some historiographical problems in revisionist educational history: Review of roots of crisis. *American Educational Research Journal,* 1975, *12*(3), 337-350.

A Response to the Criticisms of Job Training

U.S. Congress. Senate. *Report of committee on industrial education of the American Federation of Labor, industrial education.* S. Doc. 936, 62d Cong., 2d sess., 1912.

Violas, P.C. *The training of the urban working class: A history of twentieth century American education.* Chicago: Rand McNally, 1978.

Reference Notes

1. Ringel, P.J. *Industrial education: A revised look at a revisionist's interpretation.* Manuscript submitted for publication, 1981.

Footnotes

1. Ringel (1980) interviewed 71 graduates of the Industrial Course. Among those interviewed were Mr. Robert Erickson, B.M.E., M.B.A., Executive Vice President (ret.) of Beckman Instruments, member of the National Committee for Co-Operative Education, and member of the Class of 1919; Dr. Edwin T. Holmes, Class of 1921; Professor Alfred Hobbs, (Professor Emeritus), Fitchburg State College, Class of 1920; and Mr. Edwin Nelson, B.S., M.A., Superintendent of Schools, (ret.), Brockton, Massachusetts, and member of the Class of 1917. Each of these men assured the author that Fitchburg's Industrial Course was rigorous and academically sound.

2. Using Thernstrom's five major categories of occupational rank, the occupations of both groups were identified and compared (1973, pp. 290-292).

A PERSPECTIVE ON VOCATIONAL EDUCATION'S CONTRIBUTION

Eli Ginzberg

FIRST IMPRESSIONS: THE EARLY 1950s

I first became aware of the tensions in the field of vocational education in the early 1950s when the National Manpower Council, whose Director of Research I was, published *A Policy for Scientific and Skilled Manpower* (1954), followed shortly thereafter by a volume of conference proceedings entitled *Improving the Work Skills of the Nation* (1955).

The subject of "skilled manpower" had been placed on the Council's agenda by Al Hayes, the president of the Machinists' Union, who persuaded his colleagues that the nation's economy depended not only on an adequate supply of professional and technical personnel (the Council's previous report) but also on an adequate supply of skilled workers and technicians.

As a result of the Council's effort I received numerous invitations to speak before assemblies of vocational educators, leaving me with the following strong impressions. The vocational education community contained a large number of dedicated persons, deeply committed to their task, suffering from feelings of isolation and inferiority because they were kept at arm's length from the mainline educational establishment. Further, they were largely isolated from the rapid changes under way in the economy and the occupational structure but were working hard to sustain one another and to protect their niche in the educational structure. One must remember that in the early 1950s the community college movement was in its infancy, which meant that vocational education was primarily tied to the secondary education system.

I must add a few more impressions: many vocational instructors appeared to me to have little acquaintance with or interest in such important groups as minorities or the urban poor and the curriculum was strongly sex-segregated, with young women concentrated in courses leading to clerical and sales jobs and to the acquisition of homemaking skills.

I came away from this early encounter with no deep convictions. It seemed to me that the United States had demonstrated during World War II that it had great flexibility to train the skilled manpower it needed for its industries; that it did not rely on the vocational education system to do much of the training; that classic apprenticeships in the U.S. contributed much less than in other advanced industrial countries to the total pool of skilled manpower and that the personnel shortages of skilled and technical personnel that Al Hayes had worried about were unlikely to occur. In short,

143

vocational education appeared to me to be a small, specialized sector in a highly differentiated secondary school system that was performing probably no better and perhaps no worse than the other main trends—the academic and the general.

SECOND IMPRESSIONS: MID-1950s TO LATE 1970s

During the intervening decades I had occasion both as Director of the Conservation of Human Resources Project at Columbia University and from 1962 to date as Chairman of the National Manpower Advisory Committee and later the National Commission for Employment Policy to add to my knowledge of vocational education.

In the late 1950s, as a result of several visits to Southern California, I was impressed to discover that the local aerospace industry was working very effectively with selected vocational high schools, assisting with curricula, staff and equipment. At that time and later, I also became acquainted with the impressive expansion of the community college system in California with its strong vocational offerings.

In 1962 when Congress debated the Manpower Development and Training Act (MDTA), the vocational education lobby played a determining role in securing its passage. And vocational education became a centerpiece of the new legislation, having the implicit responsibility for providing the "institutional training" that the federally funded trainees were to receive to hasten their reemployment. By the mid-1960s as the economy hit its stride it became clear that the groups who needed employability assistance were not regularly attached workers who had lost their jobs because of automation, but rather, members of marginal groups—minorities, the poorly educated, low income, inner-city groups. But these were the groups with which most vocational education systems had little concern or interest.

As succeeding administrations and Congresses became increasingly aware of the gap between the constituencies of vocational education and those eligible under MDTA and later under the Comprehensive Employment and Training Act (CETA), more and more of the federal funds were shifted to alternative organizations that could deliver training: the National Alliance of Businessmen, community-based organizations and eventually in 1973 to prime sponsors (local government entities). Vocational education lost out as a major factor in federal manpower programs but not without a fight.

The Most Recent Past

During the last decade and a half I have been impressed by the following important developments on the vocational education front. The rapid development of postsecondary training establishments from technical institutes to community and junior colleges facilitated the consolidation of resources into a smaller number of better staffed and equipped institutions which must have resulted in improved skill acquisition.

While it is never easy to modify any part of the educational system, offerings became more responsive to the changing economy, with substantial increases in health occupational areas and enlarged preparation for technical occupations and corresponding absolute or relative declines in training in agriculture and home economics. That is not to say that the vocational curriculum is well aligned with the new occupational structure but that it is less out of sync than it used to be.

I believe that slowly but surely many vocational education leaders became aware that they had not been responsive to the needs of the disadvantaged, particularly minority youth, and many of them took steps, some big steps and others small steps, to increase their offerings to those who were most in need of improving their employability.

As a long-time student of race (Ginzberg, Anderson, Bray & Smuts, 1956) and sex (Ginzberg, Berg, Brown, Herma, Yohalem & Gorelick, 1966; Ginzberg & Yohalem, 1973) in the labor market, I am concerned that instructors and counselors have misled many students by seeking to persuade them to forego training in occupational areas where discrimination exists in the job market. Most of them acted in good faith: why should a young black man or white woman study electricity when it was clear that the unions—or even non-union employers—would not hire them even if they became highly proficient? But laws and the labor market change and after the Civil Rights Act of 1964, these simplistic conclusions were no longer valid though many vocational education programs failed to adjust.

Evaluating Vocational Education

The large outpouring of federal funds in connection with the Great Society programs (Ginzberg & Solow, 1974) stimulated an interest in evaluations. Legislators and academicians alike wanted to know whether spending more money would lead to better outcomes and/or whether diverting resources in one direction rather than another made a significant difference. The last decade or so has seen a great many efforts to assess the value of vocational education relative to other educational and training programs. Beatrice Reubens (1974), a member of my staff, was the author of one of the earliest and best of these appraisals. She concluded from the data then available that there was no clear-cut gain over time in career progress and income for students who had pursued a vocational course of studies over others who followed less specialized curricula.

The bodies of data today are larger, the techniques of analyses more refined, but I do not believe that Dr. Reubens' findings have been upset. In fact, I consider the question moot because there have been no truly randomized trials in which individuals of equal competence, motivation and potential have been matched. Hence the results depend in no small measure on how one "corrects" for differences in the populations that are being compared, a correction that cannot be scientifically carried out.

A LOOK AHEAD

On the basis of about a half century of research into the world of work and almost as long a period as a consultant to the federal government, I have come to the following conclusions about vocational education. Let me stress that I have never studied vocational education in detail and know relatively little about its structure and its various methods of operating. What follows are the considered observations of an outsider whose research and policy concerns have been centered around the issues of employability and employment.

An Analytical Perspective

The following views are offered from an analytical perspective, as distinct from a policy perspective, which will be discussed later.

All education worth its salt must be concerned about what happens to the young people who pass through the system, most of whom will sooner or later have to earn their livelihood. Any educational system that fails to consider and deal in some sensible fashion with the linkages between school and work is not much of a system. Since I have recently set forth in some detail the distillations of my views on these linkages, I will do no more than draw attention to my monograph (1981).

But it does not follow that any educational system should find its beginning and its end in simply helping young people make the transition into the world of work. Education should have other goals, such as contributing to the development of trained intelligence and a value structure so that individuals can gain access to the spiritual and esthetic achievements of their society and other societies.

There is deep confusion, therefore, between vocational education and vocational training. The former must be much more comprehensive than the latter. In fact, much of vocational education must be coextensive with general education. To permit, much less to encourage, students to narrow their horizons while in high school so that they are underexposed to history, literature, science and the social disciplines in favor of "useful" subjects that will help them get jobs is a serious error that will cost them dearly. Important as jobs are, adults do more than work. They must be able to shape a total life and for that they need more than competences that will help them in the job market.

But there is the opposite danger that vocational education has failed to help many of the non-bookish respond effectively to their schooling experience. Regrettably, there are many slow readers, many who have trouble with mathematics as it is taught, many whose interest is not caught by the history texts. It has long seemed to me that vocational education's biggest challenge is to explore how these non-bookish students can be more interested in study by making their curriculum more relevant, practical, applied. To illustrate: how to teach arithmetic using card games; reading through practical instructions; science through simple laboratory procedures; social science through class projects.

I see a paradox in the fact that vocational education currently selects students who can master the three R's. But we know that the most disadvantaged students, when it comes to jobs and life, are those who have failed to master the three R's. It is the latter group that needs special attention and I believe, although I cannot prove it, that vocational education could make an important contribution to those most in need of help although it has failed to recognize the challenge, much less respond to it.

There is one last point. With 70 percent of all jobs in the U.S. economy in the service sector (Ginzberg & Vojta, 1981), the best preparation for the labor market is mastery of the three R's plus some acceptable level of socialization and maturity. Hence general education is the best of all training if the student learns how to deal effectively with numbers, words, concepts. Of course, there is much room for specialized occupational training on top of this base—but the base is what really counts.

A Policy Perspective

Now to a few concluding observations about policy.

Vocational education has shifted increasingly out of the high school into postsecondary institutions. I believe this is a necessary and desirable shift since it is too costly in terms of staff and equipment to run a large number of competent vocational education courses in small and medium-size communities. In large metropolitan centers good vocational schools at the secondary level are possible and do exist. Because of this shift, local and state authorities should be alert to the importance of opening postsecondary institutions to high school dropouts who give evidence that they have acquired the maturity and the competence to pursue one or another vocational offering.

In the present and prospective budgetary situation facing the federal government, it is unlikely that Congress will make any significant additional money available to vocational education, and the odds point to a reduction in recent levels of funding. It would probably be a waste of time and effort for the vocational education leadership to focus on Congress. Rather it should address state legislatures, which are the primary providers of funds.

If the leadership does a good job of moving aggressively to lower the sex and racial barriers that have for so long characterized vocational offerings and the composition of the student body, it may find itself with powerful new constituencies to help it—minorities and women. But to win their wholehearted support the leadership will have to do more than it has yet done (NCEP, 1981).

Congress is currently scheduled to address the reauthorization of the vocational education legislation and in 1982 CETA comes up for reauthorization. To the extent that the vocational education leadership can reestablish a better working relationship with the manpower community, and to the extent that both recognize the importance of raising the *quality* of the employability training for the large number of young people who are at risk (Freedman & Dutka, 1980), Congress may decide then, despite its fiscal conservatism, that more resources invested in hard-to-employ youth represents a sound national investment. The existence of the Private Industry Councils (PICS) may provide the umbrella for the much needed cooperation which, if

147

it is forthcoming, could prove highly beneficial to those most in need of help.

REFERENCES

Freedman, M., & Dutka, A. *Training information for policy guidance,* Washington, D.C.: U.S. Department of Labor, 1980.

Ginzberg, E., with the assistance of Anderson, J.K., Bray, D.W., & Smuts, R.W. *The Negro potential.* New York: Columbia University Press, 1956.

Ginzberg, E., Berg, E., Brown, A., Herma, J.L., Yohalem, A.M., & Gorelick, S. *Life styles of educated women.* New York: Columbia University Press, 1966.

Ginzberg, E., & Yohalem, A. (Eds.). *Corporate lib: women's challenge to management.* Baltimore, Johns Hopkins Press, 1973.

Ginzberg, E., & Solow, R.M., (Eds.). The great society: lessons for the future. *The Public Interest,* 1974, *34*(winter).

Ginzberg, E. *The school-work nexus: Transition of youth from school to work.* Bloomington, Ind.: Phi Delta Kappa Educational Foundation, 1981.

Ginzberg, E., & Vojta, G.J. The service sector of the U.S. economy. *Scientific American,* 1981, *244*(3), 48-55.

National Commission for Employment Policy. *Improving the earnings of disadvantaged women.* Washington, D.C.: Government Printing Office, 1981.

National Manpower Council. *A policy for scientific and professional manpower.* New York: Columbia University Press, 1954.

_____. *Improving the work skills of the nation.* New York: Columbia University Press, 1955.

Reubens, B. Vocational education for *all* in high school? In J. O'Toole (Ed.), *Work and the quality of life.* Papers for the Work in America Project of the Department of Health, Education and Welfare. Cambridge, Mass.: MIT Press, 1974.

THE EFFECTS OF JOB TRAINING

Morgan V. Lewis and Donna M. Mertens

In the early 1960s the federal government assumed a far more active role than it had previously played in the development of the human resources of the nation. This was carried out in many ways, including the passage of the Vocational Education Act of 1963, which led to major improvements and expansion in vocational education services. Together with these developments in vocational education, a nationwide system of manpower programs was created under the direction of the U.S. Department of Labor.

All this activity and expenditure of public funds has led to close scrutiny of programs that claim to prepare people for employment. Hundreds of attempts have been made to document, in a credible manner, just what the effects of these programs have been, resulting in an almost overwhelming number of reports.

APPROACH

In preparing this chapter, we did not attempt to review all of the individual reports on the effects of vocational education and other skill training programs. Instead we chose to synthesize a relatively small number of previous syntheses. By doing so, we were able to draw upon the thinking of a number of scholars who have examined the relevant literature. In turn, we were able to compare the conclusions reached by these separate reviewers and present a summation of what, in our judgment, can reasonably be inferred from the available evidence.

In choosing this approach, the selection of the syntheses to be included was, of course, crucial. In making these choices we were guided by a list of syntheses that had been developed as part of a comprehensive review of studies of the effects of vocational education (Mertens, McElwain, Garcia & Whitmore, 1980). We also asked nationally recognized scholars to recommend reviews to be included. The list of 13 previous syntheses that constitutes the source material for this chapter is thus selective, not exhaustive. It does present, however, a fairly representative sample that draws upon a total of 1,133 separate reports or papers concerning the effects of vocational education and other publicly supported, organized training programs. It seems unlikely that the inclusion of more reviews would significantly alter the conclusions presented here.

MDTA/CETA

In structuring the presentation of the evidence on effects, we adopted the traditional division of vocational education into secondary, postsecondary and adult. To our knowledge, however, there is no synthesis of studies on the effects of adult vocational education. There is instead a huge literature on the effects of what were earlier called manpower programs and what are now called employment and training programs. These are the programs that were conducted originally under the Manpower Development and Training Act (MDTA) and are now under the Comprehensive Employment and Training Act (CETA). Funded directly by the federal government, these programs are administered by state and local governments under contracts with the U.S. Department of Labor.

There is a tendency among many vocational educators, CETA trainers and even policy-makers to think in terms of vocational education versus CETA. Obviously, differences exist between the programs, primarily in the populations they serve. Vocational education is for all who need training and can benefit from it. CETA programs are targeted to the economically disadvantaged and provide training stipends and a variety of supportive services that vocational education usually does not offer. Nevertheless, the main component in CETA training programs (not public service employment or summer youth programs) is instruction in job skills. In fact, much of this training is conducted by vocational educators in public vocational facilities, either through direct subcontracts from prime sponsors or through individual purchase of services for CETA clients. Thus, even allowing for the differences in characteristics of the clients served, it seemed reasonable to include syntheses of research on MDTA and CETA training to provide some information on the effects of programs directed to adult, out-of-school populations.

One other crucial difference between vocational education and employment and training programs must be stressed. Vocational education had its origin in public education and is still a part of that system. MDTA and CETA began primarily as tools of economic policy, originally to correct skill imbalances in the labor force and later to move people out of poverty. These differences in origin have led to differing perceptions of goals and how the attainment of these goals should be measured. Evaluations of vocational education tend to go beyond employment outcomes and examine educational and personal effects. Evaluations of MDTA and CETA training focus primarily on employment and earnings. These differences are reflected in the kinds of conclusions that can be presented about secondary, postsecondary and MDTA/CETA programs.

Three Types of Effects

In the sections that follow, the conclusions on the effects of training at the secondary and postsecondary levels are organized into employment, educational and ancillary effects. *Employment* includes such outcomes as earnings, unemployment, relationship of jobs to training and satisfaction of both

employer and employee. *Educational* outcomes include continuing education, contributions of skill training to the acquisition of basic skills and satisfaction with the training itself. *Ancillary* effects refer to other results sometimes claimed for training programs, such as enhanced self-esteem or citizenship. The conclusions on the MDTA/CETA programs are limited to employment effects.

The conclusions on employment effects at all three levels are mainly
positive. Overall, training does seem to yield more positive employment
experience. The evidence on educational and ancillary effects is weaker.
There is a smaller body of research to draw upon and that which exists does
not provide strong support for the effects sometimes claimed for training.
These broad conclusions are discussed in more detail for secondary, postsecondary and MDTA/CETA programs.

SECONDARY EDUCATION

The nine review studies that addressed the effects of secondary-level vocational education were based on a total of 580 references—520 of which were
unduplicated titles. The majority of the review studies reported conclusions
about specific outcome variables in the three categories of employment,
education and ancillary effects.

Employment

The employment category is composed of a variety of outcome variables,
including unemployment experience, training-related placement, earnings,
employer satisfaction, employee satisfaction, occupational status and self-
employment. A discussion of the review studies' conclusions for each outcome variable follows.

    Unemployment. A summary of the seven studies' conclusions concerning
unemployment experiences are summarized in Table 1. Four of the studies
concluded that there were no or mixed differences in the unemployment experiences of vocational and nonvocational graduates (Carbine, 1974; Grasso
& Shea, 1979a; Mertens et al., 1980; National Commission on Employment
Policy, 1979). Three of the studies reported positive findings for select
groups of vocational graduates. Using the same data base, both Grasso and
Shea (1979a) and the Vocational Education Study (1980) concluded that
vocational females (especially those in a business and office program)
experienced less unemployment than general females. Based on a more recent national longitudinal survey (Borus, Crowley, Rumberger, Santos &
Shapero, 1980), the Vocational Education Study also concluded that male
vocational graduates would be less likely to be unemployed, especially if
they are black. Sparks (1977), using the measure "time needed to obtain first
job," concluded that vocational graduates have more favorable labor market
experiences.

Table 1
CONCLUSIONS CONCERNING UNEMPLOYMENT EXPERIENCES OF SECONDARY LEVEL GRADUATES

Study	Conclusion
Carbine, 1974	"There may be no net employment benefits attributable to the high school vocational curriculum" (p. 84).
Grasso & Shea, 1979a	"Findings relating to unemployment were mixed, in the sense that use of alternative measures yield conflicting evidence" (p. 183).
Grasso & Shea, 1979b	"We failed to find convincing evidence of an alleged labor market advantage of vocational education for young men. We did, however, find consistent labor market benefits of occupational training for young women" (p. 156).
Mertens et al., 1980	"The results suggest that a higher percentage of vocational graduates are employed upon graduation from high school—however, the unemployment rates for the two groups [vocational and nonvocational] are not significantly different" (p. 77).
National Commission for Employment Policy, 1979	"... statistical evidence from a variety of sources is accumulating that young men who have participated in vocational programs have no more success in the labor market than those who have not, after adjusting for other differences between the two groups" (p. 117).
Sparks, 1977	"Vocational job hunters generally require less time to secure their first jobs...." (p. 35).
Vocational Education Study, 1980	"After high school...the male vocational graduate is less likely to be unemployed, especially if he is black ...." (p. VII-4). "... the typical student in a commercial program is less likely to experience unemployment than the student in the general curriculum" (p. VII-5).

The Effects of Job Training

Training-related placement. Only three review studies presented conclusions concerning the percentage of vocational graduates who obtained jobs in areas related to their training. Based on 52 local, state and national studies, Mertens et al. (1980) concluded that the majority of secondary level vocational graduates (somewhere between 50 and 75 percent), find jobs that are related to the occupational area in which they were trained. This range of figures corresponds to those reported by Little (1970) and by the Vocational Education Study (1980) for business (and office) graduates.

Most of the data on training-related placement are based on students' self-reports. One study (Lewin-Epstein, 1979), which was cited in the Vocational Education Study, used an objective job classification measure and reported that 68 percent of business and office graduates, 41 percent of health graduates and 34 percent of agricultural graduates obtained training-related placement. Mertens et al. reported that business and health graduates had the highest rates of training-related placement overall.

The interpretation of these findings depends on the evaluation standards that are applied. Assuming the actual rate of placement in related occupations is somewhere between 50 and 75 percent, is this acceptable or not? Training-related placement rates of 100 percent or less than 50 percent would probably both be considered undesirable. In the former case, the argument could be made that the training is too effective in limiting the range of potential occupations and consequently unduly impedes individual choices. If less than 50 percent of the graduates are obtaining training-related placement, one might question whether the investment made to teach occupational skills was yielding a return through the use of these skills in the labor force. A trade-off between enhancing individual choice and realizing the best return on society's investment is involved in setting standards for evaluating this outcome measure.

Earnings. A summary of the seven review studies that addressed the outcome variable earnings is presented in Table 2. Carbine (1974) addressed differences within the vocational sample and concluded that males outearn females and only small differences exist between the races.

Little (1970) and Sparks (1977) concluded that vocational graduates outearn nonvocational graduates. Mertens et al. (1980) also concluded that vocational graduates tend to earn more initially but this advantage tends to disappear over time. In addition, differences by vocational program area were noted. Trade and industry graduates consistently earned the highest wages and the health and home economics graduates earned the lowest. This wage differential is undoubtably influenced by the sex of the preponderance of the persons in each occupational area.

Grasso and Shea (1979a and b) concluded that the relationship between earnings and curriculum for males was inconsistent or not statistically significant. For females, they concluded that vocational education provided a distinct earnings advantage. Based on more recent evidence (Borus et al., 1980), the Vocational Education Study (1980) concluded almost the opposite

153

of Grasso and Shea. They found inconsistent and small differences for females, and small, but usually positive differences for male vocational graduates.

Table 2
CONCLUSIONS CONCERNING
EARNINGS FOR SECONDARY LEVEL GRADUATES

Study	Conclusion
Carbine, 1974	Male vocational graduates outearn their female peers; small differences exist between vocational graduates of different races. (p. 82).
Grasso & Shea, 1979a	Earnings were unrelated to curriculum for males (although vocational graduates might experience slower rates of growth in wages). Female vocational (especially business) graduates outearned their peers. (p. 183)
Grasso & Shea, 1979b	Differences in earnings were inconsistent or not statistically significant for male vocational graduates. Female vocational (especially business) graduates outearned their peers. (pp. 156-157)
Little, 1970	Vocational graduates have an advantage in earnings (not always great) over their untrained cohorts. (p. 23)
Sparks, 1977	Most studies show vocational students to be slightly outearning other students shortly after graduation. (p. 35)
Mertens et al., 1980	Secondary level vocational education appears to confer an initial earnings advantage, but this advantage does not last more than a few years. Large differences exist among vocational program areas. (p. 78)
Vocational Education Study, 1980	Wage differences over time for males have been small, with average wages of vocational graduates generally slightly higher. The differences for females are also small, but the direction of the differences have been inconsistent. (p. VII-8)

Employer satisfaction. Only two of the review studies addressed the variable employer satisfaction (Mertens et al., 1980; Vocational Education Study, 1980). Both studies concluded that employers tend to be satisfied with the attitudes of vocational students toward work and their preparation in skills needed on the job. No national level studies were found which addressed this outcome.

Employee satisfaction. The conclusions of five studies that addressed employee satisfaction agree that vocational graduates express satisfaction with their jobs. For example, Grasso and Shea (1979b) concluded, "It is also true that, as of our latest follow-up data, vocational graduates were more likely than were their general curriculum counterparts to report enjoying their jobs" (p. 157). The Vocational Education Study (1980) concluded, "The vocational student is likely to express satisfaction with his or her job . . ." (p. VII-4). And Mertens et al. (1980) concluded that " . . . virtually all studies agree that former secondary level vocational students are satisfied with their jobs" (p. 78). Sparks (1977) and Little (1970) reached similar conclusions.

Self-employment. A possible effect of vocational education would be that graduates are prepared to start their own business. Only the Vocational Education Study (1980) addressed the variable of self-employment, and it stated, "Within the first four years after high school, the secondary school vocational graduate is no more likely than the general curriculum graduate to be self-employed, with the possible exception of the graduate of an agricultural program . . ." (p. VII-4).

Occupational status. Two studies examined the types of jobs that vocational graduates obtained in terms of their occupational status. Based on the Class of 1972 data, the Vocational Education Study (1980) concluded that " . . . a greater percentage of male graduates of secondary vocational education programs than of the general curriculum were employed in semi-skilled (operative) or skilled (crafts) occupations, while a greater percentage of male graduates of general than vocational programs were employed as unskilled workers (laborers or unskilled service workers)" (p. VII-8). They also concluded that a much larger percentage of female vocational graduates than general graduates was found to be in clerical jobs.

This contrasts with the conclusion of Grasso and Shea (1979a), which was primarily based on the National Longitudinal Survey data. They reported that the occupational distributions for each curriculum overlap one another to a great extent. Among males, 67 percent of vocational graduates and 59 percent of general graduates held crafts and operatives jobs. Among females, 74 percent of former business and office graduates worked in clerical and secretarial positions, but so did 52 percent of their general program peers.

Education

The education category is composed of a variety of outcome variables including continuing education, satisfaction with training, drop-out, basic skill attainment and occupational awareness. A discussion of the review studies' conclusions for each outcome variable follows.

Continuing education. A wide array of alternatives exist for persons who want to continue their education beyond the secondary level, ranging from four-year colleges to technical institutes to employer-sponsored training. Most of the studies agreed that a larger percentage of nonvocational than vocational graduates attain more formal school or post-school institutional training (that is, from business colleges, technical institutes and four-year colleges) (Carbine, 1974; Grasso & Shea 1979a and b; Mertens et al., 1980). The Vocational Education Study (1980), however, reported no difference between vocational and general graduates.

The studies also agreed that between 30 and 50 percent of vocational graduates did continue their education (Little, 1970; Carbine, 1974; Mertens et al., 1980) and that vocational graduates were likely to take advantage of such educational alternatives as company-sponsored training (Grasso & Shea, 1979a).

Satisfaction with training. The research literature consistently reports that vocational graduates are satisfied with their training. For example, Sparks (1977) concluded that "... the great majority of vocational graduates rate their prior vocational instruction highly" (p. 35). Mertens et al. (1980) reported, "The percentage of satisfied graduates was generally between 80 and 90 percent, supporting the hypothesis that vocational graduates perceive their training as being satisfactory" (p. 80).

Grasso and Shea (1979b) concluded, "Despite the absence of a clear economic advantage to male high school graduates from a vocational program, they were less likely than were their peers from a general program 'to feel hurt' by a lack of additional education. This statement, however, does not apply to young black men" (p. 157).

School dropout. Six of the syntheses found that vocational education seemed to prevent school dropouts for specific types of vocational students. Carbine (1974) concluded, "Dropout rates in college preparatory programs are higher than for vocational and general, which are about equal" (p. 88). Grasso and Shea (1979a and b) and the Vocational Education Study (1980) found that the female business and office student is less apt to drop out of high school before graduation than a student in the general curriculum. Mertens et al. (1980) concluded that insufficient information was available to answer the question "Does vocational education serve to retain students in school who might otherwise have dropped out?" They did, however, find evidence to suggest that programs that include some outside work experience provide additional motivation to stay in school.

Grasso and Shea (1979a and b) reported mixed results for male vocational students. They found that cross-sectional data suggested that vocational education had a positive effect on staying in school. However, longitudinal data suggested that male vocational education students were not more likely to finish high school than general students. These apparently contradictory results can be accounted for by the movement of students between ninth and twelfth grades, resulting in a net increase in vocational enrollments from one year to the next. This net flow toward vocational studies, among those who stay in school, contributes to a positive association between enrollment in a vocational program and grades in school. The shift imparts a positive bias to any cross-sectional regression results linking most recent curriculum to highest year of school completed.

The National Commission for Employment Policy (1979) acknowledged that vocational education appears to have increased the percentage of people completing high school. However, the Commission warned, "While promoting the completion of high school might reduce youth unemployment, it will have to do so by actually improving their competencies as contrasted with simply providing more of them with a credential" (p. 116).

Basic skills. Argument exists as to whether or not basic skill attainment should be considered an "effect" of vocational education. As Corman (1980) noted, "It could be that vocational education students function poorly in basic skills at the time they enter vocational programs in secondary school, if not long before" (p. 24). Both Mertens et al. (1980) and Corman (1980) concluded that insufficient evidence is available to determine the effects of vocational education on basic skill attainment, although Corman did conclude " . . . that vocational education students in secondary school perform below average in reading comprehension, vocabulary, and mathematics" (p. 24).

The Vocational Education Study (1980) concluded that the " . . . typical vocational student reads, writes, and computes with about the same level of proficiency as a student in the general curriculum . . ." (p. VII-4). This study also found that the typical student in a business and office program has similar reading proficiency and better writing skills than the average student in general or other vocational programs, although the business and office student is less proficient in computational skills.

Grasso and Shea (1979a) found that the evidence on the net effects of vocational education in the area of basic skills is unclear. They hypothesized that there might be both " . . . (1) positive effects, such that vocational students are motivated to greater academic achievement because they perceive the real-world applicability of academic subjects, and (2) negative effects resulting from less time being spent in school subjects that foster the development of basic skills" (p. 182).

Occupational awareness. Grasso and Shea (1979a and b) and the Vocational Education Study (1980) both concluded that male vocational graduates know less than their peers about a variety of occupations. The reverse is true among the young women. This lack of awareness raises the question of the thoroughness of vocational guidance and the ability of students to choose their curriculum on an informed basis.

Ancillary Effects

The ancillary effects category is composed of a variety of outcome variables, including aspirations, attitudes, feelings of success and citizenship.

Aspirations. Overall, curriculum assignment was found to be congruent with occupational and educational aspirations. Mertens et al. (1980) concluded that the majority of vocational education students aspire to skilled occupations that do not require a college degree, although approximately one-third of the vocational students did plan to attend college. Grasso and Shea (1979a) found that enrollment in a vocational program had a depressing effect on aspirations for college, although they did find, "The vast majority of NLS respondents out of school expressed a desire to obtain additional education or training, and this did not vary by high school curriculum" (p. 182).

Concerning occupational aspirations, they further concluded, "The occupational goals of high school students follow seemingly a logical pattern: male vocational graduates are especially likely to desire to work in the crafts, female business and office students in clerical and secretarial jobs, etc." (p. 181).

Attitudes. Generally, the attitudes of vocational graduates appear to be positive toward the value of their courses and course content (Grasso & Shea, 1979a and b; Mertens et al. 1980). This is interesting in light of Grasso and Shea's finding that vocational education students do not like high school as much as other students. The fact that they like their vocational programs might explain why some students find their way into such programs.

Feelings of success. Mertens et al. (1980) reviewed a number of studies that examined how vocational students felt about themselves. They concluded that no significant differences existed for feelings of success between vocational and nonvocational students, although the overall picture of the vocational graduates' personal and social characteristics appears to be positive.

Citizenship. Low rates of voting behavior were reported by both Carbine (1974) and Mertens et al. (1980). Although vocational graduates did report that their program had helped them become better citizens, this was not reflected in their activity at the voting booth.

POSTSECONDARY EDUCATION

The five review studies that addressed the effects of vocational education at the postsecondary level were based on a total of 418 references—379 of which were unduplicated titles. These numbers tend to over-represent the amount of research that exists concerning the effects of postsecondary vocational education. The number of references counted for each review study included many studies that addressed secondary-level effects. Much less research is available concerning the effects of postsecondary than secondary vocational education. Because less research is available, the results are discussed at a more general level than was true for secondary-level effects, although the three broad categories of employment, education and ancillary effects are discussed.

Employment

The employment category includes the following variables: unemployment experiences, training-related placement, earnings, employer satisfaction and employee satisfaction.

Unemployment. The reviews that presented summary statements on the effects of postsecondary programs on unemployment are presented in Table 3. Mertens et al. (1980) and the Vocational Education Study (1980) both reported that graduates of business and office, trade and industry, and technical programs had lower rates of unemployment than did general curriculum graduates.

Table 3
CONCLUSIONS CONCERNING
UNEMPLOYMENT EXPERIENCES
FOR POSTSECONDARY GRADUATES

Study	Conclusion
Carbine, 1974	Junior college vocational graduates experienced significantly higher employment than either postsecondary or secondary vocational graduates. (p. 93)
Mertens et al., 1980	Postsecondary vocational graduates tend to have lower rates of unemployment than individuals with no postsecondary training or those who were enrolled in a nonvocational postsecondary program. (p. 82)
Vocational Education Study, 1980	Community college graduates in office, trade and industry and technical programs experienced significantly less unemployment than general curriculum graduates (based on one study with a small sample). (p. VII-7)

Carbine (1974) compared the employment experiences of junior college, postsecondary vocational-technical and secondary vocational graduates. He concluded that junior college vocational graduates experienced a significantly better employment rate than graduates of the other two programs.

Training-related placement. Little (1970), Mertens et al. (1980) and the Vocational Education Study (1980) all concluded that a majority of the postsecondary graduates find employment in the occupational areas in which they trained. The results were slightly more positive for the postsecondary than the secondary-level vocational graduate.

Earnings. Two of the reviews that examined the effects of postsecondary training on earnings disagreed on their conclusions (Table 4). Grasso and Shea (1979a) concluded that postsecondary training produced benefits. Mertens et al. (1980) judged the evidence to be insufficient to draw comparison between vocational and nonvocational postsecondary programs, but did report notable differences in earnings across vocational areas. Technical programs were consistently associated with the highest earnings, and home economics were associated with the lowest. Males outearned females in every program area.

Table 4
CONCLUSIONS CONCERNING
EARNINGS OF POSTSECONDARY GRADUATES

Study	Conclusion
Carbine, 1974	Junior college vocational graduates experienced significantly higher wages than postsecondary vocational-technical or secondary vocational graduates. (p. 93)
Grasso & Shea, 1979a	Postsecondary training appears to produce benefits in wages and earnings for high school graduates in either sex. (p. 183)
Mertens et al., 1980	Insufficient information is available to draw conclusions on the impact of postsecondary vocational education (as compared to nonvocational education) on earnings, although earnings differences are apparent among vocational program areas. (p. 82)

Employer satisfaction. Mertens et al. (1980) and the Vocational Education Study (1980) both reported that employers are satisfied with graduates of vocational programs. In addition, Mertens et al. reported that in some cases employers are more satisfied with vocational graduates than other entry-level employees.

Employee satisfaction. Mertens et al. (1980) and the Vocational Education Study (1980) both reported that postsecondary vocational education graduates expressed satisfaction with their jobs.

The Effects of Job Training

Education

Very little research is available concerning the educational effects of postsecondary vocational education. No studies were found that addressed the basic skills and occupational awareness variables at this level. A discussion of the review studies' conclusions for the outcome variables of continuing education, dropout rates and satisfaction with training follows.

Continuing education. Mertens et al. (1980) reported that a very low percentage of community and junior college graduates go on to four-year institutions (between 10 and 20 percent). Carbine (1974) concluded that junior college graduates were more likely to go on to a four-year college than postsecondary vocational-technical graduates.

Dropouts. Mertens et al. (1980) reported that dropout rates differ considerably from study to study (ranging from 25 to 66 percent), although a large percentage of community college dropouts indicated that they planned to return at a later date.

Satisfaction with training. Similar to the secondary level studies, postsecondary level research also indicated that a majority of the graduates report satisfaction with their training (Mertens et al. 1980).

Ancillary Effects

Mertens et al. (1980) were the only authors to address ancillary effects at the postsecondary level. They reported that insufficient information was available to draw conclusions in the areas of aspirations, attitudes and feelings of success at the postsecondary level. Postsecondary vocational graduates exhibited the same low rate of voting behavior found at the secondary level, although the evidence did suggest that vocational graduates belonged to or were officers in civic clubs more often than nongraduates.

ADULT PROGRAMS (MDTA/CETA)

In the introductory section of this chapter we noted that MDTA/CETA programs were developed primarily as a tool of economic policy, originally to deal with structural unemployment and later to assist the poor to improve their economic condition. This emphasis has been reflected in the criteria by which these programs have been evaluated. The emphasis has been almost totally on the extent to which participation decreased unemployment and increased earnings. A frequent concern has also been whether the increase in earnings experienced by participants exceeded the costs of their training. The conclusions presented in Table 5 indicate that in the overall judgments of the five sources cited, the effects of these programs have been positive. These conclusions are based on 224 separate sources, 29 of which were cited more than once in the five syntheses quoted.

Borus (1980) and the National Council (1977) made estimates of the increases in earnings associated with institutional (classroom) training. The National Council range was a $400 to $800 increase in the year following training, and Borus reported a more modest $300 to $400 increase. These

Table 5
CONCLUSION CONCERNING OVERALL EFFECTIVENESS OF MDTA/CETA TRAINING PROGRAMS

Study	Conclusion
Borus (1980)	"What we do know, based on gains in participants' earnings as the major criterion of success, is [that] classroom, on-the-job and work experience training programs appear to justify their costs." (p. 39)
Mangum and Walsh (1973)	"MDTA has been worth the cost and effort. The weight of evidence supports its effectiveness as a device to increase the employment and earnings of its enrollees." (p. 14)
National Commission for Employment Policy (1979)	"Training appears to have a significant positive impact on the subsequent labor market experience of youth." (p. 162)
National Council on Employment Policy (1977)	"The overwhelming body of evidence, then, supports the conclusion that employment and training efforts have had a positive impact on participants earnings." (pp. 681-683)
Stromsdorfer (1980)	"Skill training appears to be effective, but its effects decay rather rapidly over time. Some estimates suggest the decay rate may be as high as 15 percent per year." (p. 108)

may seem like relatively minor gains, but most of the data on which they are based were collected in the 1960s, mainly from low-income participants. If it is assumed that the earnings advantage found in the first year after training will continue for some time into the future, the benefit-cost ratios for most of the programs studied were greater than one. The return to society as a result of providing this training will probably exceed the cost of the training.

CONCLUSIONS
What does this synthesis of syntheses allow us to conclude about the effects of the two main types of publicly supported training for civilian jobs? The

following matrix attempts to reflect our overall judgments arranged by the major framework for this chapter.

Effects Variables

Level	Employment	Education	Ancillary
Secondary	+ to ?	+ to ?	?
Postsecondary	+	?	Ins.
Adult (MDTA/CETA)	+	Ins.	Ins.

+ = in general, the evidence is positive
? = evidence is conflicting, either positive or no significant difference
Ins = insufficient evidence to make a judgment.

In making these global judgments we have obviously had to ignore the many qualifications that should be included. To those who wish to explore the sources of uncertainty in more detail, we recommend they consult the original syntheses, particularly Mertens et al. (1980), pp. 85-86 and the National Council (1977), pp. 690-693.

Two points stand out in this matrix. The first is that there are no negative entries. The accumulated evidence on the effects of training is either positive or indicates no significant difference. Very few studies have found training to be associated with detrimental outcomes, such as less earnings or more unemployment. The other major point is that the question marks and indicators of insufficient evidence outnumber the plus signs. Questions still are more numerous than answers, but this will probably always be the case.

In evaluation research it is unlikely that any one study or even a large body of studies will be conducted that can answer every possible methodological criticism. Evaluators must strive to assemble the most credible evidence possible. Policy-makers must evaluate this evidence together with other sources of information and make the best decisions they can. The National Council on Employment Policy (1977) expressed this same idea when it stated that

> policies must rest on informed judgments rather than unequivocal findings. Evaluations can be improved but even the best studies will leave many questions unanswered. If it must be proven beyond a reasonable doubt that efforts work, there is no such proof. (p. 679)

Overall, the evidence presented here points to positive effects from training, especially for the employment variables. More and better evaluations are needed, but the best evidence indicates that training programs yield their intended results. It seems unlikely that more evaluations are likely to change this general conclusion.

REFERENCES

Borus, M.E. Assessing the impact of training programs. In E. Ginzberg (Ed.) *Employing the unemployed.* New York: Basic Books, 1980.

Borus, M., Crowley, J.E., Rumberger, R., Santos, R., & Shapero, D. *Pathways to the future: A longitudinal study of young Americans. Preliminary report: Youth and the labor market—1979.* Columbus: Ohio: The Ohio State University, Center for Human Resource Research, 1980.

Carbine, M.E. Evaluations of vocational education. In A. Lecht. *Evaluating vocational education—Policies and plans for the 1970's.* New York: Praeger Publishers, 1974.

Corman, L. *Basic skills proficiencies of secondary vocational education students. Vocational Education Study Publication No. 4.* Washington, D.C.: U.S. Department of Education, 1980.

Grasso, J.T., & Shea, J.R. Effect of vocational education programs: Research findings and issues. In *The planning papers for the Vocational Education Study. Vocational Education Study Publication No. 1.* Washington, D.C.: National Institute of Education, 1979a.

Grasso, J.T., & Shea, J.R. *Vocational education and training: Impact on youth.* Berkeley, Calif. The Carnegie Council on Policy Studies in Higher Education, 1979b.

Lewin-Epstein, N. Vocational education. In J. Coleman et. al. *High School and beyond: Policy issues and research design.* Chicago: National Opinion Research Center, 1979.

Little, J.K. *Review and synthesis of research on placement and follow-up of vocational education students.* Columbus, Ohio: The National Center for Vocational and Technical Education, Ohio State University, 1970.

Mangum, G.L., & Walsh, J. *A decade of manpower development and training.* Salt Lake City, Utah: Olympus Publishing, 1973.

Mertens, D.M., McElwain, D., Garcia, G., & Whitmore, M. *The effects of participating in vocational education: Summary of studies reported since 1968.* Columbus, Ohio: The National Center for Research in Vocational Education, 1980.

National Commission for Employment Policy. *Expanding employment opportunities for disadvantaged youth.* Washington, D.C.: Author, 1979.

National Council on Employment Policy, The impact of employment and training programs. In M. Guttentag & S. Saar (Eds.) *Evaluation studies review annual, Volume 2.* Beverly Hills, Calif.: Sage Publications, 1977.

Sparks, D. *A synthesis of research findings which describe selected benefits and outcomes for participants in vocational education.* Washington, D.C.: Bureau of Occupational and Adult Education, 1977.

Stromsdorfer, E.W. The effectiveness of youth programs. In B.E. Anderson and I.V. Sawhill (Eds.) *Youth employment and public policy.* Englewood Cliffs, N.J.: Prentice-Hall, 1980.

The Vocational Education Study: *The interim report. Vocational Education Study Publication No. 3.* Washington, D.C.: The National Institute of Education, 1980.

SECTION V

THE CONTINUING CHALLENGE TO MEET INDIVIDUAL AND SPECIAL NEEDS

For the past two decades, the list of special groups and needs that federal legislation has asked vocational education to address has grown considerably. Beginning in 1963 with targeted funds for handicapped and disadvantaged individuals, the list was much enlarged in 1976 when targeted funds were set aside to address the needs of women, limited English-speaking persons, incarcerated persons and displaced homemakers.

This section takes a broad view of the track record of vocational education in meeting special needs of people. Edwin Herr reviews research and concludes that "there seems little doubt that job training serves the needs of certain groups of people ... disadvantaged persons and women have gained on both educational and economic indicators from job training." Herr also provides some observations that will help continue the impact that vocational education can have on special groups.

From another perspective, Kermeta "Kay" Clayton points to the lack of women in policy-making, management and conceptual leadership roles and identifies changes that must occur if vocational education is to have its male-female leadership ratio in tune with contemporary times.

Robert E. Nelson and James A. Leach call attention to yet another special group which is becoming a growing priority for vocational education—the entrepreneur. These authors offer a good argument for entrepreneurship training as an integral part of vocational education for the future.

DOES JOB TRAINING SERVE THE NEEDS OF PEOPLE?

Edwin L. Herr

INTRODUCTION

As some observers have suggested, "In its broadest sense vocational education is that part of education which makes an individual more employable in one group of occupations than another. It may be differentiated from general education which is of almost equal value regardless of the occupation to be "pursued" (Evans & Herr, 1978, p. 3). If one assumes that occupations differ in the work activities, content and settings by which they are manifested, implicit in such a definition is the provision of job training as an important aspect of vocational education.

The problem that one immediately confronts in considering such an implication is the nature of the job training that should be provided by vocational education. Anderson and Sawhill (1980) have captured the essence of the issue.

> No strategy for addressing youth labor market difficulties can ignore the importance of employability development. The key question is what type of employability development (and what combinations of program services) will be most effective? (p. 149)

Within such a context, several specific questions arise. Should job training be occupation-task specific or should it include tasks that are useful across several occupations? Should job training, as defined by the technical skills of work performance, be the primary objective of vocational education? Should trainability be the major goal of vocational education? These are important and debatable questions. There are advocates of each of the positions these questions reflect. Indeed, there is a substantial body of argument which contends that providing job readiness, trainability, industrial discipline and the motivation to learn basic academic skills are each more important objectives of vocational education than providing specific job training, particularly if the latter is construed in very narrow terms.

In support of the position just described, current critics of vocational education target job training as a waste of taxpayers' money, unrealistic or inappropriate in the face of how persons actually enter primary labor markets and advance in them, unnecessary because of the degree to which on-the-job training is provided by employers, and often obsolete because of

169

the dynamics of the shifts in the occupational structure and the constant lag of educational responses (Stern, 1977; Thurow, 1977; Wilms, 1980).

SOME POSITIVE PERSPECTIVES

While each of these criticisms of vocational education, and specifically job training, has its own limited validity, the argument here will focus on the view that, collectively, such criticisms tend to oversimplify the complex matter of whether and how job training serves the needs of people. This chapter will attempt to focus on the positive aspects of job training, as well as on recommendations about the future of such training in vocational education. In doing so, three types of questions will guide the discussion:

- First, are there advocates of job training or does research exist that supports it? And if so, under what conditions?
- Second, what types of job training are at issue? Is all job training the same?
- Third, what future role can be conceived for job training in vocational training and under what circumstances?

Advocates and Research

While it is quite true that research findings and government rhetoric can be cited that do not support the utility of job training, an opposite case can also be made. There are advocates of job training and there is research that supports it. However, like the body of findings that argues against job training, many of the research studies are methodologically flawed (Stern, 1977). In other cases, job training is not viewed independently of a larger program of which it is a part, thereby reducing the ability to speak of its specific treatment effects. Further, the findings about job training are often not disaggregated by subpopulations served, thus creating an all-or-none mentality about whether such processes should be supported.

Among the most recent and positive support for job training are the reports published by the Vice President's Task Force on Youth Employment (1980a), which reviewed the research on the effects of training and educational programs on youth employment through a series of analytic papers. The Task Force reports that the papers "share some basic messages," which include:

1. Employment, training and education programs can work and probably are working better than the gainsayers claim. Increased education *does* pay off in the labor market. Job Corps is cost effective as a comprehensive development program for those most in need. Employment programs produce useful social products and increased work is correlated with higher future earnings. There is diversity in performance but there are consistent elements in the consistent programs.

2. No strategy works for everyone, and perhaps the biggest short-coming is not in the institutions and what they offer but in not being able to steer individuals to the appropriate institutions and offerings in a reasonable fashion.

3. Many of the shortcomings of the programs are straightforward but ignored in seeking "panaceas." For instance, employment and training programs suffer extraordinarily from instability but we continue to fund them year-to-year. Alternative educa-tion approaches clearly make sense for a minority of youth but the resources and flexiblity are not provided. We give in to the pressure to spread limited resources broadly and then decry the lack of measurable impacts . . . . Supportive services and longer duration treatment are needed for youth with the most severe problems, but we tend to judge these efforts by the same standards applied to other programs . . .

4. The basic problem is not in identifying what works, but in replicating the positive approaches. We continue to experi-ment looking for answers when in fact there are many success stories and the issue should be how we can increase their incidence. (pp. 6-7).

In a separate summary report, The Vice President's Task Force on Youth Employment (1980b) reported the following:

Employers told the Task Force that even though they don't al-ways expect vocational schools to keep up with the latest tech-nological changes, they prefer to hire the graduates of these schools. Why is this?

Again we are faced with a paradox, but this time there is a key. Vocational schools are good at doing many of those things which the Task Force has identified as being central to running ef-fective programs. They link learning with doing and they spell out their goals in ways which both students and parents can ac-cept and understand.

Vocational schools incorporate the learning of reading and writing into their training in actual job skills, so that the participants can see the connection between the ability to read and doing good work (p. 22).

The same report indicated that for federal employment and training programs to be effective, they need to be made simpler and more flexible. The Task Force also found that while youth need job and career information, they must also receive "support and assistance from community networks during the increasingly difficult transition from school to work" (p. 10).

Increase in Earnings

Mangum and Walsh (1978) have reported on the research on classroom or institutional employment-related training programs with respect to four components: (1) orientation: (2) pre-vocational training; (3) skills training and (4) remedial education. Pertinent to institutional training for out-of-school youth and adults, they cite evidence which suggests that the average institutional enrollee in programs under the Manpower Development and Training Administration (MDTA), which used the public schools to provide skill training, had experienced increased earnings of about $1,250 a year because of enrollment in the program. They indicate that a similar increase in earnings has been experienced by Job Corps enrollees. They further contend that underlying the annual earnings gains just reported.

> it is significant that disadvantaged workers appeared to profit more than those not so disadvantaged, that completers profited more than non-completers, and that longer training was more effective than shorter training ... Given the charge that employment and training programs more often recycle disadvantaged workers through a secondary labor market rather than providing breakthroughs into the primary market, it is also significant that post-training jobs were far more likely than pre-training jobs to provide the fringe benefits and job securities of the latter markets (p. 90).

Mangum and Walsh also report on their analyses of classroom training for in-school youth. Citing Project Baseline data for 1971-74 (Lee and Fitzgerald, 1975), they indicate that of those available for placement following school completion, vocational education has a remarkable placement record. In addition, they indicate that unemployment rates are also low when it is remembered that almost the entire graduating group is between 17 and 20 years of age. Measured a few months after graduation, the unemployment rates of vocational graduates are persistently 9 to 10 percent, about the same as rates for 20 to 24-year-olds and below the 12 to 15 percent rates experienced by 18 and 19-year-olds in the years 1971-1974, which represented the data bases (p. 93).

Mangum and Walsh suggest that, in general, available studies support the usefulness of the additional investment necessary for vocational education. They cite the analyses of the National Longitudinal Survey data by Adams, Mangum, Lenninger and Stevenson (1978), which found no appreciable differences in income for those emerging from various education tracks, but did identify a substantial income differential in favor of the vocational students two years later. Earnings differentials ranged from $1,500 per year for all whites to more than $2,300 for black women. They further contend that

172

other studies have measured earnings differentials in favor of vocational graduates, with a return on investment in vocational education of 10 to 20 percent. Quoting the work of Lecht (1974) they report that "income differentials between Blacks and whites were less for persons from vocational education than for other curricula, suggesting that Blacks gained relatively more from vocational education than did Blacks enrolled in other education tracks" (p. 94).

Three-Year Follow-Up Findings

A different but related type of support for job training can be found in follow-up studies of graduates in particular states. A good example is the research of Allen (1975) who conducted a three-year follow-up study of 364 vocational graduates from the state of California. He found that 75 percent of the respondents were working and 72 percent had jobs related to their high school vocational training. Seventy percent said the high school vocational training was helpful in their present jobs and 88 percent would recommend vocational training to other students. Fifty percent had enrolled in advanced training, and 49 percent had had additional training on the job. When respondents were asked about what changes they would recommend in the program, 71 percent of the respondents recommended more applied practice; 66 percent, more job-related information, and 67 percent, better help in job placement.

The National Commission for Employment Policy (1979) in its Fifth Annual Report to the President and the Congress has comprehensively reviewed much of the evidence related to youth employment. At various points the report draws specific conclusions about vocational education and about job training. It concludes that vocational education can improve youth employability either because it imparts salable skills to participants or because it encourages them to obtain more schooling. In general the latter is interpreted to mean remaining in school until high school graduation. The report further concludes that vocational education has been more successful for women than for men, in both of these areas (p. 129).

Citing essentially the same data as does Mangum and Walsh about MDTA institutional skills training, the National Commission for Employment Policy concludes similarly that the studies of classroom training show that it has had a significant positive impact on the earnings of enrollees. Earnings gains were particularly significant for females, slightly less so for males. A further conclusion in the report of the commission is that "training appears to have a significant, positive impact on the subsequent labor market experiences of youth. However, this benefit may be obtained more in those programs that provide quality instruction and equipment, offer the needed supportive services, and assist the trainee in finding a job after he/she leaves the program" (p. 162).

173

Characteristics of Job Training

Frequently, the matter of job training is treated as though it is confined to the technical skills of work activity and that it is monolithic, always the same for all occupations. This is obviously untrue, but when job training is acknowledged as potentially different for different occupations and different circumstances, it enormously complicates finding easy answers.

Freedman (1980) has contended that "training encompasses maturation in general, socialization to work and the workplace, basic education, and, finally, occupationally-related skills. In real life, among real people, these aspects are interdependent; successful work experience depends on their co-existence" (p. 1). She then goes on to discuss skill training by contending that "the patterns of entry and skill acquisition are complex, and they vary considerably by occupation." In general she divides skill acquisition into two categories: pre-employment training and on-the-job training. She asserts that

> about one-quarter of all jobs have well-established pre-employment training requirements where there is a clear transition from school or training program to work. These jobs are, in turn, divided between, on the one hand, professional occupations requiring two or more years of preparation in colleges, graduate or professional schools and, on the other hand, a mix of technical, clerical, and service occupations that require from three months to two years of pre-employment training. Among the latter, the most familiar are nonprofessional health specialties and, the single most numerous category, office clericals. (p. 1)

With respect to on-the-job training, she contends that over 60 percent of all jobs do not routinely require pre-employment training. Among these are occupations, like the better jobs in the insurance industry, where recruiting takes place among liberal arts college graduates who then learn the necessary job-related skills after they are hired. At the other end are low-skill clerical, sales, blue-collar and service occupations that are learned entirely on the job in less than three months. This latter group accounts for about 37 percent of all jobs in the United States (p. 2).

Freedman also asserts that there are a large number of skilled and semi-skilled jobs that she calls *mixed* because the dynamics of the particular locality may either require pre-employment training or that the job be learned on the job. Included are jobs that range in complexity from air traffic controller to auto mechanic. She asserts that, "the most general statement one can make is that, given a local labor market, employers will hire the most experienced people available, and only then will they seek out partially trained or altogether untrained entry workers" (p. 2).

Stable Worker Skills

What further complicates the perspectives advanced by Freedman is the nature of the hiring practices of firms in the primary labor market, presum-

174

ably the most attractive employment sector because of the opportunities for career ladders, good pay, promotion, security, training and other fringe benefits. Osterman's (1980) research suggests that the key issue to such firms is who will become a stable worker. This concern is often more important to the firm than prior skills or relevant experience. Being a stable worker is an abbreviation of sorts for saying that what is desired is a reliable and mature worker and "one who is able to learn future jobs, not necessarily the job they are being hired for, since that job is simply the first rung on the bottom of the internal ladder" (p. 26). These ingredients also underlie the consistent use of 'attitude' as an important criterion in hiring.

Osterman further argues that because of internal labor markets, which promote people already within a firm to skilled and better-paying jobs, as well as the frequent requirement for on-the-job training of firm-specific technology, the advantage of previous experience and job training is diminished. However, Osterman suggests in what almost verges on contradiction that "firms do not generally consider previous skills a disadvantage; on balance it probably helps" (p. 27).

More relevant to our general concern is Osterman's observation that even though many firms are heavily engaged in training, they do not want to train people in industry-specific skills; blueprint reading or typewriting would be such examples. Thus they try "to shift costs of this training to the school system and to other firms by giving preference to applicants with some previous work experience and by supporting vocational programs in the public schools" (p. 28). What they are concerned about providing themselves is firm-specific training, which does not stimulate worker mobility except within that firm.

Advantages of Industry-Specific Skills

What is not fully elaborated in these views of skill training is the diversity within firms. Larger firms are more likely to be able to afford the losses of productivity that occur when master or veteran workmen are assigned to train new workers. Small firms and geographically isolated firms frequently cannot afford this type of luxury. They must find workers whose skills allow them to be trained quickly and whose attitudes and other work behavior will cause them to be stable. Thus industry-specific skills, those which Freedman identifies as pre-employment skills, are likely to have a more generalizable attraction than on-the-job training skills that are firm-specific. On the one hand, industry-specific skills that can be taught in a classroom on a pre-employment basis are likely to increase the labor pool from which large and small firms can choose their work force. On the other hand, such skills provide workers with a freedom of choice which training in firm-specific technology does not.

Thurow (1977) speaks to these points by arguing that employers are "interested in obtaining employees who occasion low on-the-job training costs rather than completely trained workers. Although on-the-job training may be informal, it is still costly in that production slackens while the training occurs" (p. 40). He further argues that vocational education should focus on establishing a complementary relationship with on-the-job training and on placing trainees in those internal labor markets that offer training and promotion opportunities.

Thurow also identifies some advantages associated with job training within vocational education. One is that it is a cheap place for employers to determine whether workers do or do not have good habits. In this sense, student attendance records are excellent indicators of such work habits and provide a way by which employers can hire workers who are potentially reliable in their attendance.

A second advantage is that in those job skills that are industry-specific, vocational education can provide for economies of scale, which firms cannot. This advantage is obviously increased as firms get smaller and employ fewer workers of particular types. A third advantage according to Thurow is that the best way to teach motivation, industrial discipline, general literacy and trainability may be in the transmission of very specific cognitive job skills. The cognitive job skills may never be used, but they can serve as the vehicle around which those other skills are taught. "Without learning job skills, students may not sit still long enough to learn the skills that have the long run pay-off" (p. 42).

PERSPECTIVES ON THE FUTURE OF JOB TRAINING

There seems little doubt that job training serves the needs of certain groups of people. As research findings cited here have suggested, disadvantaged persons and women have gained on both educational and economic indicators from job training. It is also likely that many young people have remained to graduate from high school as a function of the job skills they were acquiring and the motivation these engendered to improve their literacy, work habits, occupational information and general motivation.

In somewhat less direct terms, job skills training, especially that focused on industry-specific rather than firm-specific skills, creates a labor pool from which firms in both the primary and secondary sectors can secure workers. The job training provided by vocational education responds to economies of scale which firms, especially small firms, cannot. Thus, job skill training can be viewed, to some degree, as a public subsidy to industry, by which a trainable work force is provided to reduce on-the-job training costs. Beyond these perspectives is the reality that there are specific occupations in which classroom and lab training are the most efficient methods of skill development.

It can also be argued that job training in industry-specific skills gives workers a mobility and a freedom of choice which on-the-job training in firm-specific technology does not. In an era where cost/benefits tend to be the ultimate accountability criteria, increasing individual options or freedoms can be undervalued factors in models which are primarily economic, even though such individual outcomes are of fundamental importance to larger social principles.

176

Conditions of Effectiveness

Although this chapter has focused on the positive things that can be said about job training, it is well to acknowledge the conditions in which it tends to be most effective. The National Commission for Employment Policy (1979) suggests that vocational education and job training would be improved where:

(1) there is emphasis on combining classroom learning with a work-related component;
(2) there is concentration on those occupations which are best learned in the classroom setting;
(3) there is an effort to link training to known labor market opportunities;
(4) there is emphasis on a sustained, integrated approach to youth employability combining the provision of basic skills, job skills, job-seeking skills and placement (p. 117).

If there is an overarching perspective about job skill training, it is that it cannot be seen in isolation from other parts of a program leading to employability. Job training must be seen as part of a developmental process by which participants gain labor market information, an orientation to the adult behavioral norms and expectations that characterize the work place, a commitment to future trainability, the work habits by which personal productivity can be maximized and the tools of job search and interview by which access to the work force can be enhanced. There is no right way or right program for every individual but with flexibility in the time and intensity of training, as well as the provision of support services tailored to individual needs, job training does, can and will meet the needs of people.

REFERENCES

Adams, A.V., Mangum, G., Seninger, S.F., & Stevenson, W. *The lingering crisis of youth unemployment.* Kalamazoo, Michigan: The W.E. Upjohn Institute of Employment Research, 1978.

Allen, D. *A three-year follow-up study.* Los Angeles: Division of Vocational Education, University of California, 1975.

Anderson, B. E., & Sawhill, I. V. (Eds.). *Youth employment and public policy.* Englewood Cliffs, New Jersey: Prentice-Hall, Inc., 1980.

Evans, R.N., & Herr, E.L. *Foundations of vocational education* (2nd Ed.), Columbus, Ohio: Charles E. Merrill Publishing Co., 1978.

Freedman, M. Training and motivation. Chapter 11 in *A review of youth employment problems, programs & policies,* Volume 3. Washington, D.C.: The Vice President's Task Force on Youth Employment, January, 1980.

Lecht, L.A. *Evaluating vocational education—policies and plans for the 1970's.* New York: Praeger Publishers, 1974.

Lee, A.M., & Fitzgerald, D. *Learning and living across the nation.* Volume IV. Flagstaff, Arizona: Project Baseline, University of Northern Arizona, 1975.

Mangum, G., & Walsh, J. *Employment and training program for youth: What works best for whom?* A Report to the Office of Youth Programs, Employment and Training Administration, U.S. Department of Labor. Washington, D.C.: National Council on Employment Policy, May 1978.

National Commission for Employment Policy. *Expanding employment policies for disadvantaged youth.* Report No. 9. Washington, D.C.: Author, December 1979.

Osterman, P. *Getting started, the youth labor market.* Cambridge, Massachusetts: The Militi Press, 1980.

Stern, Barry. *Toward a federal policy on education and work.* Washington, D.C.: Government Printing Office, 1977.

The Vice President's Task Force on Youth Employment. *A review of youth employment problems, programs & policies.* Volume 3. Washington, D.C.: Author, January 1980a.

_____. *A summary report.* Washington, D.C.: The White House, February 1, 1980b.

Thurow, Lester C. Technological unemployment and occupational education. In T. Powers (Ed.) *Education for Careers, Policy Issues in a Time of Change.* University Park, Pa: The Pennsylvania State University Press, 1977.

Wilms, Wellford W. *Vocational education and social mobility: A study of public and proprietary school dropouts and graduates.* Washington, D.C.: The National Institute of Education, 1980.

INCREASING OPPORTUNITIES FOR ENTREPRENEURS

Robert E. Nelson and James A. Leach

INTRODUCTION

The Small Business Administration estimates that 80 percent of the 50,000 new businesses started each year will eventually fail. Despite these overwhelming odds, entrepreneurs continue to organize, manage and assume the risks of small business ownership and management. With the exception of agriculture and a few experimental programs, vocational education has not made any systematic effort to prepare youths and adults for self-employment. Entrepreneurs are rarely taught the basic knowledge, attitudes and skills necessary for operating a business successfully. Instead, these skills are learned primarily by self-employed individuals through trial-and-error methods in the day-to-day operations of a business. It might be assumed that a relationship exists between this method of learning essential management skills and the high rate of small business failures.

Owners of small business firms may be called entrepreneurs because they have chosen to assume risks, identify business opportunities, gather resources, initiate action and establish organizations to meet some demand or market opportunity. A distinguishing mark of entrepreneurs is that they tend to be independent and self-sufficient, and they have some resistance to working with government or any other agency to meet common goals. Many entrepreneurs want to be left alone to operate their businesses in a very individualistic manner, and this factor presents one of the major barriers to providing help to the small business sector. However, statistics concerning small business presented at the White House Conference on Small Business (1980) highlight the need for attention to this sector of the economy.

- Of over 14 million enterprises in the United States (including farms, franchises and professional firms), two million are corporations, one million are partnerships and approximately 11 million are sole proprietorships.
- Of the 14 million enterprises, 99.2 percent employ fewer than 100 persons.
- Eighty percent of all small businesses fail within the first five years.
- Nine out of 10 small businesses fail because of poor management. Specific reasons include lack of planning, inadequate controls, poor accounting methods, inability to read and understand financial statements, and inability to locate expert advice when needed.
- Minorities form 17 percent of the total population, but own only 4.3 per-

cent of all businesses and generate only .7 percent of all business receipts.

- Women make up 48 percent of the work force, but own only 4.6 percent of all businesses and generate only .3 percent of all business receipts.

Despite their high failure rates, small firms are of vital importance to the American economy. Small business in the United States accounts for 43 percent of the Gross National Product (Quimby, 1980, p. 23) and generates 60 percent of all jobs (Birch, 1979, p. 29). In slower growing areas and in rural areas, small firms may be the only significant providers of jobs. Most economic development programs to stimulae new job opportunities have been aimed at a relatively few large corporations. However, it is the thousands of anonymous smaller firms that employ fewer than 20 employees that are the job providers in the older sections of our cities, as well as offering the major share of new jobs in expanding areas.

During the 1980s and beyond, the United States will face enormous challenges regarding employment and productivity. One way to create new jobs and increase overall productivity in the economy is to promote the health and survival of existing small businesses and to develop an environment that will foster the growth and vitality of new firms.

INCREASING ENTREPRENEURIAL OPPORTUNITIES

Increasing entrepreneurial opportunities depends, in a large part, upon the births and expansion of small firms. Entrepreneurs have the ability to spark new ideas and new products that create businesses, which in turn create the need for new jobs. David Birch (1979) recently conducted a study based on Dunn and Bradstreet's files of 5.6 million businesses. From the results of this study, it appears that entrepreneurs in smaller firms are aggressively seeking out new opportunities, while the larger ones are primarily maintaining their current status. Quimby (1980, p. 23) states that it is well known that productivity is increased through small innovative firms. This segment of the economy is creating employment and increased productivity by utilizing the results of research and development efforts. In addition, innovation, new products and new processes developed by creative small business people spur productivity in established larger businesses.

High Failure Rates

Over 50 percent of all new businesses fail during their first two years of existence. This serious problem is compounded by estimates which indicate that over half of the money used to start new small businesses is generated through private sources such as personal family savings and borrowing from friends or relatives. The failure of a small business is a financial tragedy, but it is also a family tragedy, and the psychological problems of the people involved may be as great or greater than their financial losses.

During the past 10 years, the literature has highlighted the importance of the small business sector in achieving economic goals. It is now time to focus attention on how specific problems relating to the small business sector can be solved. Solving these problems will allow small businesses to be more successful, to grow and expand, resulting in the creation of new job opportunities at the local level.

Small business experts or consultants are especially helpful in solving specific business problems. However, their numbers are limited and those who are available may be considered a first generation because they have received no specific training for dealing with the problems of small businesses. Few educational programs, extension services or support organizations exist to prepare people as small business consultants.

A Comparison with Agricultural Assistance

In developing new types of assistance for the small business sector, the educational programs and assistance given to farmers through the U.S. Department of Agriculture (USDA) and its network of cooperative extension services might provide a model for duplication. Although the principles and problems in business are in many ways unrelated to agriculture, the basic concepts remain the same.

A sharp contrast exists between the abilities of the U.S. Small Business Administration (SBA) and the USDA to provide services to the two respective economic sectors. For every 20 farms in the United States, there is one USDA employee; for every 2,200 firms there is one SBA employee. The total SBA staff of 4,500 is inadequate to satisfy the demands of approximately 11 million small businesses.

A major priority for the growth and expansion of the small business sector is the development of integrated policies. In January, 1980, the White House Conference on Small Business identified issues and made proposals concerning small business policies for the 1980s and beyond. Twelve policy issues addressed at the conference highlight the potential for increasing opportunities for entrepreneurs: (1) capital formation and retention, (2) federal procurement, (3) economic policy development in government programs, (4) women in business, (5) government regulations and paperwork, (6) inflation, (7) international trade, (8) minority business development, (9) innovation and technology, (10) energy, (11) veterans in business and (12) education, training, and assistance. Additional proof that the federal government is interested in the small business sector is reflected in a recent survey that indicated more senators applied for membership on the Senate Select Committee on Small Business than any other Senate committee.

Contributions of Small Businesses

During the White House conference, it was noted that small businesses:
1. Strengthen the ability of local communities to withstand national economic turmoil.
2. Provide more than half of the major innovations and technological breakthroughs in business and industry that have contributed greatly toward raising the standards of American life.

3. Because of their greater flexibility and ability to relate more directly to workers, small businesses find it easier to motivate their employees to achieve increased productivity.
4. Provide the means by which deprived groups such as women, minorities and the poor are brought into the economic mainstream.
5. Greatly enrich the lives of local citizens because of the diversity of their products and services and their emphasis upon courteous, individualized service to their customers.

The Issue Paper on Education, Training and Assistance, which was discussed at the conference, indicated that:

> There is an urgent priority in the current national "crisis of confidence" to encourage the expansion and vitality of small enterprises as a long-term factor in the American economy. It seems apparent that there is a need for reestablishing a strong base for small businesses and a reintroduction of the small business option to the American public. In other words, there is a need for a systematic nationally-directed program of education for entrepreneurship. (The White House Conference, 1980, p. 377)

To increase entrepreneurship opportunities, continuing education and training in the form of management assistance and updating specific technical skills should be provided. There is also a need for increased general public awareness of the problems and potentials of owning and operating a small business.

The Need for a National Program

In recognizing the need for a systemic, national program of education to encourage entrepreneurship, the White House Commission on Small Business specifically recommended that:

(1) A National Policy should be established for the support of entrepreneurial education and training, continuing education and management assistance, provided by the public and private sector, as an opportunity for every American who wishes to own his or her small business and should receive recognition as a priority from the highest levels of government.

(2) Congress should enact legislation that would provide tax credits or other tax incentives for: a) expenses incurred to educate small business owners and operators regarding the management of business, and b) expenses incurred to conduct continuing education and training and to provide on-the-job entrepreneurship experience. (1980, p. 91)

Responding to these training needs, Congress passed the Small Business Development Act of 1980, which includes a provision that authorizes $20 million in federal matching grants for Small Business Development Centers

(SBDCs) to provide technical and management assistance to small entrepreneurs. These centers would be operated through state institutions.

IMPLICATIONS FOR VOCATIONAL EDUCATION

Vocational education has had a proud history of preparing people with the skills they need for employment. Since the early 1970s, vocational education has focused on broader non-skill programs and has played a leadership role in developing and implementing career education at all levels. Recent indications are that vocational educators are becoming more involved in assisting students in attitude development. Occupational survival skills such as problem-solving, human relations, decision-making and effective communication are examples of concepts that might be included in career preparation programs (Nelson, 1979).

Because vocational education is open to new ideas concerning the preparation of people for work, preparation for self-employment is receiving attention as a career option for inclusion within vocational education programs. The National Advisory Council on Vocational Education stated in a recent Issue Paper on Self-Employment (1979) that entrepreneurship activity is a by-product of the vocational education experience which should be more strongly developed. In addition, the council indicated that vocational education should provide encouragement and training to aspiring entrepreneurs to assist them in establishing and expanding their own businesses.

A Role in the Demand Side

Vocational education has always been a primary factor in the supply side of the economic equation of supply and demand of skilled workers. However, there is no reason to believe that vocational education cannot also be involved on the demand side. Demand for trained workers comes with the initiation of new businesses and the expansion of existing businesses. When people become self-employed, they must hire workers who will also need training. It is the preparation of people with self-employment skills that will enable vocational education to approach the educational process from a totally different perspective.

The evidence suggests that vocational education has a role in training potential entrepreneurs. Of the approximately 15 million students enrolled in secondary and postsecondary vocational programs (National Advisory Council on Vocational Education, 1979) a sizable portion prefer and/or become self-employed. Wenzel (1979) reported that a survey conducted in Middlesex County, New Jersey, indicated that of those persons graduating from vocational programs 25 years ago, nearly 9 percent eventually owned their own businesses.

Many Desire Entrepreneurial Setting

The American desire for independence was revealed in a study published in 1979 by The Survey Research Center at the University of Michigan. For five successive years (1974-1979), the center interviewed two million graduating high school seniors to determine what type of work setting they preferred. The results indicated that they strongly prefer an entrepreneurial setting: working for themselves, with a small group of partners or in a small enterprise, rather than in a large organization (SBA, 1980, p. 1).

Nelson (1980) estimated that of those students currently enrolled in vocational education programs, three or four students in a typical vocational education class will eventually own their own businesses and that many more students may have the potential and desire to become self-employed.

Four Levels of Training Identified

Baker (1980) presented four tiers of relationships between the entrepreneur and the educational system. The first tier focuses on teaching people who have some interest in becoming entrepreneurs. The second provides vocational education an opportunity to offer management training to people who have already chosen to be entrepreneurs and are in business. The third tier consists of training workers for small business firms. The final tier involves the training of people such as government small business administrators, bank managers and consultants to work together to increase the vitality of the small business environment in the local community.

Another way to make distinctions among the various groups in need of education and training is to identify target groups. The first target group might be labeled *future entrepreneurs,* or those young people in school who are considering small business ownership as a career option. A second group could be called *potential entrepreneurs,* comprised of those persons in the labor force who are ready to initiate action to become self-employed. The third target group, *existing entrepreneurs,* are those persons who currently operate small businesses and are in need of assistance. A final group could be identified as *growth-oriented entrepreneurs.* These people have viable businesses which they are interested in expanding.

The primary objective of designing programs for these four groups is to increase their chances of success as small business owners. This education should begin at the elementary and secondary education levels and be continued at the adult level. People need to know the problems and prospects for self-employment, how to initiate action to become self-employed, the types of skills necessary to operate a business and the strategies and opportunities which can help businesses expand.

Developing New Approaches

Vocational education must define and develop new methods to link training to the small business sector. These methods need to be designed to meet the specific needs of potential and existing self-employed individuals. The following assumptions, which resulted from a survey conducted concerning entrepreneurial training efforts for the Illinois Advisory Council on Adult, Vocational, and Technical Education (University Consultants, Inc., 1980), might be helpful when initiating new approaches:

- Within the business and education communities, opinions vary sharply on the value of entrepreneurial training.
- There has been a great deal of concern expressed about the availability of entrepreneurial training, especially for minority group members and, more recently, women.
- There are different types of entrepreneurial training, with the differences related to the nature and length, sources and purposes of the training.
- Foundation support for entrepreneurial training does not exist on a significant scale.
- Those training opportunities that do exist are very popular, which suggests that if more were offered, more people would participate.
- A good deal of entrepreneurial training is being provided directly by the academic community, much of it in cooperation with the Management Assistance Division of the SBA.
- Entrepreneurial training for prospective farmers is *not* available to the same extent as it is for other small business aspirants.
- Entrepreneurial training opportunities are not equally accessible throughout the state to all who might be interested.
- Most of the available training activity is concerned more with the sustenance and expansion of existing businesses, rather than with the preparation of new entrepreneurs.
- There seems to be a direct correlation between certain personality characteristics, which may not easily be developed through training and entrepreneurial success.
- In general, free forms of technical assistance are poorly publicized and regarded by most of the entrepreneurs who utilize them as being less useful than the instruction and orientation services for which they pay a fee.
- The effects of entrepreneurial training are not carefully evaluated.

These assumptions, coupled with the new enthusiasm to meet the challenges that entrepreneurship education offers, may provide the basis for a new dimension in vocational education. Vocational education can have a significant impact on increasing the opportunities for entrepreneurship in the United States through education and training efforts designed to prepare people for self-employment and to assist those individuals already self-employed to operate viable and growing enterprises.

RECOMMENDATIONS FOR VOCATIONAL EDUCATION

The following recommendations are designed to initiate an expanded vocational education effort to emphasize the importance of the small business sector and to provide needed education and training.

Provide leadership for a national emphasis to include small business development and growth in the revitalization of the American economy. By utilizing the voice and existing structure of the vocational education network throughout the nation, including the national and state advisory councils, a general public awareness of the problems and potential of the small business sector can be created. Vocational education should strive to encourage work-force policies that include and emphasize incentives for self-employment.

Emphasize education and training for self-employment at all levels of education. The concept of owning and operating a small business should be introduced in career education programs at the elementary level and explored further at the secondary level. Opportunities for education and training for self-employment should be made available to all students through vocational education programs at the secondary and postsecondary level.

Community colleges should be encouraged to expand their efforts to provide education and training in small business management. How educational programs can be modified to better prepare people for self-employment needs to be determined. Special efforts should be undertaken to prepare women and minorities for self-employment.

The universities need to place emphasis in their teacher education programs on the training of vocational educators to work with small business owners and managers and to become knowledgeable and competent in teaching skills necessary for teaching successful self-employment. The universities can also help to train needed small business consultants and conduct research to learn more about entrepreneurs and how to nourish entrepreneurial characteristics.

Define new approaches to link vocational education and training efforts to the small business sector. In order to provide education and training to meet the specific needs of self-employed individuals, new methods and concepts of delivering instruction will need to be explored. Small business owners and managers are extremely busy people who generally will not take time to travel to traditional classroom settings for theoretical instruction. No-nonsense practical approaches with flexible scheduling and instruction tailored to meet specific needs must be devised.

Staffing of instructional programs must utilize successful small business entrepreneurs. Methods to capitalize on the practical business experience of these individuals and on the pedagogic strengths of educators must be developed. Serious consideration must also be given to developing ways to work with other agencies, institutions and organizations (e.g., SBA, SBDCs, economic development corporations, CETA), which are attempting to provide training and assistance to small businesses.

CONCLUSION

Vocational education must define new approaches to link education and work. An economy maintains its vitality through change and it is entrepreneurs who are willing to make changes by taking risks and being innovative. It is primarily small businesses that initiate change and it is the large businesses that tend to perfect and refine those changes.

Some critics of vocational education have accused vocational educators of conspiring with business and industry to "condition" the work force, to produce employees who come to work on time, do what they are told, be complacent and respect authority. It is time to look at ways that vocational educators can prepare more entrepreneurial workers, to focus national attention on education for entrepreneurship, and to re-study education and work-force programs in terms of this concept.

Strategies must be developed to create new employment opportunities. Public policies should be reviewed to find out how government may be discouraging the formation of small businesses. The concept of work-force policies needs to be enlarged to include and emphasize suitable incentives for self-employment. Business needs to be encouraged to redefine employment in more entrepreneurial terms, and there is a need to modify educational programs to prepare people better for entrepreneurially defined work. Although entrepreneurial skills are quite different from technical skills, vocational educators may be in the best position to show the relevance of entrepreneurial skills to the development of technically skilled workers who want to be creative in their employment or become self-employed in the future.

The real training needs of persons who operate small businesses are not being met adequately. Vocational education can provide more and better training for potential entrepreneurs and for those who are already self-employed.

In order for this new emphasis to have a substantial impact, however, vocational education will have to re-shape some of its traditional concepts. New methods of providing training in this area need to be developed and methods need to be devised to work cooperatively with other agencies and institutions to present a united effort to rekindle the vitality and spirit of the small business sector.

REFERENCES

Baker, D.E. Reaction paper to: Increasing the productivity of the small business sector. In J.A. Leach (Ed.), *Productivity in the workforce: A search for perspectives.* Urbana, Ill.: Office of Vocational Education Research, Department of Vocational and Technical Education, University of Illinois, December, 1980.

Birch, D.L. *The job generation process.* Cambridge, Mass.: M.I.T. Program on Neighborhood and Regional Change, 1979.

National Advisory Council on Vocational Education. *Preparation for self-employment: A new dimension in vocational education.* Washington, D.C.: Government Printing Office, January 1979.

Nelson, R.E. *Perceptions concerning occupational survival skills.* Urbana, Ill.: Department of Vocational and Technical Education, University of Illinois, 1979. (Monograph) (ERIC Document Reproduction Service No. ED 181 250)

_____. *The role of state and local vocational education in job creation.* Paper presented at the American Vocational Association Convention in New Orleans, Louisiana, December 1980.

Quimby, J.W. The Small Business Administration and education. In S. Sniegoski (Ed.), *The role of education in the re-industrialization of the United States.* Washington, D.C.: Office of Occupational Planning, Bureau of Occupational and Adult Education, U.S. Department of Education, March 30, 1980.

University Consultants, Inc. *Education for entrepreneurship and entrepreneurial development activities in Illinois.* Cambridge, Mass.: Author, 1980.

U.S. Small Business Administration, Office of Chief Counsel for Advocacy. Small business and economic growth in the 1980's. *Current Topics.* Washington, D.C.: Government Printing Office, September 1980.

Wenzel, W. Comments at the job creation conference. Somerset, New Jersey, November 1979.

White House Commission on Small Business. *America's small business economy: Agenda for action.* Washington, D.C.: Government Printing Office, April 1980.

White House Conference on Small Business. *Issue paper on education, training and assistance.* Washington, D.C.: Government Printing Office, January 1980.

WOMEN IN VOCATIONAL EDUCATION ADMINISTRATION: WHY SO FEW?

Kermeta "Kay" Clayton

Vocational educators were charged with the task of eliminating sex discrimination and sex role stereotyping in the Education Amendments of 1976 (P.L. 94-482). This challenge has been met with increased efforts to assure equal access of males and females to all vocational education programs. Another area that is receiving considerable attention is that of the leadership within vocational education. With few exceptions, men have traditionally predominated the top decision-making positions in the field, both at the local and state levels. King (1974) reports one universal rule: the higher the position, the fewer the women.

Although slight progress was made during the late 1970s, women continue to be underrepresented in administrative positions in vocational education (Bowers & Hummel, 1979). In order to focus attention on areas of possible reform during the 1980s, this chapter will address several factors that appear to contribute to the uneven distribution of men and women in vocational education administration. Factors to be addressed include: (1) academic preparation and credentials; (2) professional aspirations; (3) professional perseverance; (4) geographic mobility; (5) the recruitment and selection process and (6) role models in the profession.

ACADEMIC PREPARATION

One of the most common explanations for the shortage of women in administration is that most women lack the appropriate academic preparation to qualify for these positions (VanMeir, 1975). Cohen (1971) and Howard (1975) report that men are simply more likely than women to seek advanced training and certification in educational administration. Schmuck (1975) reports that when women do return to the college or university for graduate training, it is not likely that they will enter programs leading to an administrative credential. Of the 7,230 degrees earned in 1969 in the areas of supervision, administration and finance, 22.2 percent were conferred to women and 77.8 percent to men (Koontz, 1969). A 1975 study by Cirincione-Coles reports that approximately 92 percent of all students in educational administration or related programs were males. These figures suggest a lower percentage of women trained in administration than men, but they also reveal greater numbers of women with credentials than are being utilized for administrative posts (Recruitment, Leadership and Training Institute, 1974).

PROFESSIONAL ASPIRATIONS

A second explanation for the shortage of women in administration is that proportionally fewer women than men aspire to administrative positions. It would then appear that few women desire to leave teaching for administration. Schmuck reported in 1975 that most of the superintendents surveyed could not recall even one women applying for an administrative position within the last 10 years. In the few instances where a female applicant could be recalled, the event was remembered "whimsically and was not viewed as a serious application" (Schmuck, 1975, p. 70). Krchniak (Note 1) also reports that even when they have the appropriate credentials, women apply for administrative jobs less often than men. In 1977, Funderburk conducted a nationwide study of participants in the vocational education leadership training program funded under the Education Professions Development Act (EPDA). It was found that following the program 19.6 percent of the women went into administration as compared to 44.4 percent of the men.

Because of the socialization process that results in what Horner (1969) calls a "motive to avoid success," women do not see themselves in leadership roles typically assigned to men. Because women *seem* to be less motivated to attain these positions, they may require more support and encouragement to become administrators. Numbers of women applicants alone, however, should not be used as evidence of a lack of interest in administrative positions. Perceived low advancement possibilities prevent many women from striving to achieve, and the social conditioning of women may deter them from making an aggressive attempt to enter areas where they feel themselves to be unwanted.

PROFESSIONAL PERSEVERANCE

A third explanation for the underrepresentation of women in administration is that women typically show less professional perserverance than men (Schmuck, 1975). One criterion often used in the selection of administrators is the length of service to the school system. A study done by the National Education Association (Note 2) indicates that 45.2 percent of men teachers surveyed had taught in only one school system in contrast to 30.9 percent of the women teachers. Since preference is usually given to teachers with tenure when filling administrative posts, men have somewhat of an advantage (Taylor, 1966).

Related to this "lack of perseverance" is the fact that women interrupt their careers to bear and rear children, although the length of these interruptions has decreased considerably in recent years. The NEA report reveals that at least one extended absence from teaching is taken by two-thirds of the married women teachers. Over the past 15 years, however, there has been a trend for women to continue their educational careers while bearing and rearing children (Schmuck, 1975). It has been argued that because of the interrupted career patterns of female teachers, male teachers get promoted because they have more experience (Howard, 1975). However, studies by Hoyle and Randall (cited in Mickish, 1971) and Gross and Trask (1976) report that men advance *faster* and with *less experience* than women. Gross and Trask (1976) found that female administrators tended to be older than male administrators and that these women had three times as much teaching experience as the men.

GEOGRAPHIC MOBILITY

A fourth reason for the disparity in the percentages of men and women in educational administration is lack of geographic mobility of women in general. On the average, women are more constrained than men in taking advantage of strategic career opportunities when these opportunities require geographic moves (Marwell, Rosenfeld, & Spilerman, 1979). Funderburk (1977) found that of the EPDA awardees studied, 19.4 percent of the men and 27.9 percent of the women felt limited in their career advancement by a lack of geographic mobility. Findings from a study by Centra (cited in Marwell et. al., 1979) reveal that 49 percent of the married female Ph.D.s and Ed.D.s studied viewed their spouses' jobs as a major deterrent to considering positions in other geographic areas. Only 4 percent of the married male Ph.D.s and Ed.D.s held this view. These findings seem to support the idea that change of locale is more closely associated with a status improvement for men than it is for women (Marwell et. al., 1979).

Marital and family status seem to be factors that affect geographic mobility and, hence, the percentage of women in administration. Gross and Trask (1976) and Krchniak (Note 1) found that most female administrators are single. Of those who are married, few report having young children. Gross and Trask (1976) suggest that women who do pursue positions in educational administration often forego marriage and childbearing, or they wait to assume these positions after the childbearing years or after children are older.

RECRUITMENT AND SELECTION

A fifth explanation for the sexual imbalance in educational administration is the recruitment and selection process itself. Epstein (1970) describes a "protege," or sponsorship, system that male professionals use to bring other men into the upper echelons of the profession. It is known that the informal training grounds for administration are settings such as the golf course and the locker room. Women are intentionally or unintentionally excluded from the informal socialization process in which the aspiring administrator learns "crucial trade secrets" (Epstein, 1970).

Because there are no valid criteria for predicting administrative performance, administrators who do the selecting and hiring often use informal processes to recruit persons for administrative positions. Women are at a disadvantage in terms of these informal contacts which may help to insure career advancement. It is also true that posting notices of job openings is often just a formality and that people are recruited by word-of-mouth.

Oftentimes, hiring decisions are made even before jobs are announced and active recruiting of women cannot occur under these circumstances.

In addition, screening committees or personnel directors are usually men and, as the "gatekeepers" to the profession, they generally recruit other men. Related to the recruitment and selection process is the fact that women administrators are often viewed as a "threat" to men in the profession. As Schmuck (1975) states:

> to share responsibility with women will be to share prestige with women. In our society, women as second class citizens detract—rather than add—to the prestige of the occupational position. Men in education cannot validate their self-worth when women share the responsibilities and prestige of their occupational position (p. 105).

In most cases, a committee or personnel director genuinely wishes to select the best person for the job, yet many do not believe that women have the capabilities to carry out administrative responsibilities. Even women tend to see themselves as less competent than men (Schmuck, 1975). A number of studies indicate that there is no reason to believe that men are more effective than women as elementary and secondary administrators (Bach, 1976; Grobman & Hines, 1956; Gross & Trask, 1965; Hemphill, Griffiths, & Frederiksen, 1962; Morsink, 1970; Norman, 1970). People who hold the notion that men are better suited to educational administration will not choose a women for a position unless she stands "head and shoulders" above her male colleagues in ability. Hence, one comes to understand why the few women who have made it to the "top" are usually outstanding.

ROLE MODELS

The sixth reason for the lack of equal representation of women in educational administration is inextricably related to the five previously cited explanations. Because (1) women fail to prepare themselves academically for administrative roles; (2) have lower career aspirations; (3) show less professional perserverance; (4) lack geographic mobility and (5) are discriminated against in the recruitment and selection process, there is (6) a lack of female role models in the administrative levels of vocational education. Because there are so many male role models, men do not often think about suggesting a woman for an administrative post. Likewise, few women consider the idea of becoming administrators because they do not see other women at these levels. "An important aspect of occupational socialization is the availability of role models—those 'ego-ideals' who provide an example of who to be like and what to strive for" (Schmuck, 1975, p. 111). It appears that both men and women are greatly influenced by the prevalence of male role models and the lack of female role models in educational administration.

CONCLUSION

It becomes apparent upon investigation that there is not one simple answer to the question of why women are underrepresented in vocational administration. Rather, there are several complex, interrelated explanations. The outlook for women in administration will improve only when actions and attitudes change. Changes must occur in the systems and procedures that discriminate against women. Additionally, women themselves must become more positive about their own abilities and the abilities of other women. They must become willing to (1) develop their potential; (2) assume administrative responsibility and (3) encourage other women to do the same. While discriminatory practices, marital/family constraints and stereotypes are not readily nor easily changed, the greatest responsibility for change in the 1980s lies with those having the vested interest—women themselves.

REFERENCES

Bach, L. Of women, school administration, and discipline. *Phi Delta Kappan,* 1976, 463-466.

Bowers, E., & Hummel, J. *Factors related to underrepresentation of women in vocational education administration: a literature review.* Columbus, Ohio: The Ohio State University, The National Center for Research in Vocational Education, 1979. (ERIC Document Reproduction Service No. ED 182 462).

Cirincione-Coles, K. The administrator: male or female? *Journal of Teacher Education,* 1975, *26*(4), 326-329.

Cohen, A.C. Women and higher education: recommendations for change. *Phi Delta Kappan,* 1971, *53,* 164-167.

Epstein, C.F. Encountering the male establishment: sex-status limits of women's careers in the professions. *American Journal of Sociology,* 1970, *75,* 965-982.

Funderburk, K.C. *A comparative study of career advancement of female and male participants in the vocational education leadership development program under the Education Professions Development Act.* Unpublished doctoral dissertation, Texas Woman's University, 1977.

Grobman, H., & Hines, U.A. What makes a good principal? *The Bulletin of the National Association of Secondary School Principals,* 1956, *40,* 5-16.

Gross, N., & Trask, A.E. *Men and women as elementary school principals.* Cambridge, Mass.: Harvard University, Graduate School of Education, 1965.

_____. *The sex factor and the management of schools.* New York: Wiley, 1976.

Hemphill, J.K., Griffiths, D.E., & Frederiksen, N. *Administrative performance and personality.* New York: Bureau of Publications, Teachers College, Columbia University, 1962.

Horner, M.S. Women's will to fail. *Psychology Today,* 1969, *6*(3), 36-62.

Howard, S. *Why aren't women administering our schools?* Arlington, Va.: National Council of Administrative Women in Education, 1975.

King, E.C. The status of women educators in community colleges. *American Vocational Journal,* 1974, *49*(8), 38-39.

Koontz, E.D. *1969 handbook of women workers.* Washington, D.C.: U.S. Government Printing Office, 1969.

Marwell, G., Rosenfeld, R., & Spilerman, S. Geographic constraints on women's careers in academia. *Science,* 1979, *205,* 1225-1231.

Mickish, G. Can women function as successfully as men in the role of elementary principal? *Research Report in Educational Administration.* Boulder, Col.: Bureau of Educational Research, University of Colorado, 1971, *4*(2).

Morsink, H.M. Leader behavior of men and women principals. *The Bulletin of the National Association of Secondary School Principals,* 1970, *54,* 80-87.

Norman, B. A study of women in leadership positions in North Carolina. *The Delta Kappa Gamma Bulletin,* 1970, *36,* 10-14.

Recruitment, Leadership and Training Institute. *Women in administrative positions in public education.* Philadelphia: Temple University, Recruitment, Leadership and Training Institute, 1974.

Schmuck, P.A. *Sex differentiation in public school administration.* Arlington, Va.: National Council of Administrative Women in Education, 1975.

Taylor, H.A. Women in administration. In M.C. Nolte (Ed.), *An introduction to school administration.* New York: The MacMillan Co., 1966.

U.S. Congress. Education amendments of 1976. Public Law 94-482, 94th Congress, October 12, 1976.

VanMeir, E.J. Sexual discrimination in school administration. *The Journal of the National Association for Women Deans, Administrators, and Counselors,* 1975, *38*(4), 163-167.

Reference Notes

1. Krchniak, S.P. *Variables associated with low incidence of women in school administration: towards empirical understanding.* Paper presented at the annual meeting of the American Education Research Association, Toronto, March 1978.

2. National Education Association. *Twenty-sixth biennial salary and staff survey of public school professional personnel, 1972-1973* (Research Report 1973-R5). Washington, D.C.: National Education Association, 1973.

SECTION VI

STRENGTHENING CURRICULUM AND INSTRUCTION

This section of the yearbook was included to address recurring themes that have begun to influence the design and scope of instruction for vocational education. All three authors take positions on the level and quality of instruction in vocational education.

John Skinkle views competency-based instruction as a future necessity for vocational education. He indicates how this approach offers more flexibility for meeting the needs of diverse groups who will enroll in vocational programs.

Dolores M. Robinson discusses the needs for employability skills training as a vital and integral part of any vocational program. She views this kind of training as essential for youth as well as for adults, a complement to skills training per se.

Beatrice Reubens provides a perspective of vocational education in America in comparison to European models. She warns against underestimating the potential of the secondary school to prepare persons for employment, stressing that vocational training must meet the needs of youths as well as adults. Systems must be designed and maintained to assist all ages who can benefit from vocational education.

THE PROMISE AND LIMITATIONS OF COMPETENCY-BASED INSTRUCTION

John D. Skinkle

During the 1980s and on into the future, the field of vocational education will continue to expand beyond the traditional secondary vocational programs. With the expectation of an increasingly older population, a continuing growth of high technology within society and the concomitant interest in and need for occupational education by those persons seeking upgrading and retraining, vocational educators can expect a formidable public demand for their programs. The challenge for the vocational education leadership will be to develop instructional systems that can meet the needs of students—as individuals or collectively as a society.

With the advances in technology, training institutions will be required to prepare workers with sophisticated skills and competencies. Persons leaving vocational programs will be expected to be capable of mastering job responsibilities. Therefore, professionals involved with occupational education activities will be charged with the obligation of providing relevant learning experiences. But there must also be a reasonable assurance that those persons who complete specific learning exercises can perform as expected within the work setting.

Many individuals will prefer to engage in short-term occupational development, for example, training that is characteristic of upgrading, retraining or training under such programs as the Comprehensive Employment and Training Act. In such cases, it will be desirable to have a curriculum capable of serving a unique clientele, either groups or individuals, who desire training that is several weeks long, as opposed to semester- or year-long secondary programs and the postsecondary or associate degree programs.

As a consequence, vocational educators should recognize the necessity for developing instructional programs, learning materials and progress reporting systems that embody the concepts of competency-based vocational education, mastery learning and individualized instruction (Knaak, 1977). The purpose of this chapter will be to present a rationale for using such a curricular approach to better serve participants in vocational training programs. Attention will be focused on a discussion of competency-based occupational programs in terms of a definition, program components, justification and the operation of such programs. Caveats to be considered when implementing competency-based programs also will be presented.

A DEFINITION

Competency-based occupational training programs are primarily concerned with the specific activities (competencies) that a person performs in a given occupational role. These competencies are identified and expressed in terms of what a person should be able to do when employed in a particular job. The word "do" is the key dimension of competency-based education, at least the skill training aspect of it.

This type of vocational program is unique because the student engages in training that (1) focuses on developing skill that can be *observed* and *measured* and (2) is evaluated to determine whether or not he or she is developing the competencies necessary to be employable and perform at an acceptable level of productivity. In essence, competency-based vocational education is that training which is concerned with the development of skills that individuals are expected to perform at a given level of proficiency within a specific occupational role.

BASIC COMPONENTS

A competency-based vocational education program is initiated by first developing an occupational description of the generic work role for which training is to be provided. To accomplish this task properly, it will be desirable to use several resources: the *Dictionary of Occupational Titles,* journals, task listings and other resources available from various curriculum centers. In addition, advisory committees are very important to competency-based vocational programs because they have the capacity to provide insightful, up-to-date, detailed information for program development and improvement.

With a functioning advisory committee, the previously mentioned resources, the commitment of the instructional staff and the necessary support of administrative leadership, it will be possible to develop a comprehensive, realistic description of a particular occupation within a reasonable time frame.

The second major component of this curricular framework is concerned with identifying the specific competencies to be developed through the training activities. This is achieved by listing those aspects of job performance that are both observable and measurable. Competencies are expressed in terms of specific activities that a person performs in an occupation. They indicate what a person is able to accomplish. A competency is a skill (or group of skills) which must be mastered at minimal levels of performance prior to employment in an entry-level position within the world of work.

It should be noted that after developing the initial competency list for a training program, it is desirable to update the list periodically, perhaps yearly. It is also important to continue the active involvement of the advisory committee with the program. If this group meets four times a year, one of the meetings could be devoted to reviewing the competency list to determine if there are new technological changes that need to be incorporated into the curriculum. Once the list has been finalized, at least for a period of time, related competencies should be grouped together. This categorization of competencies will afford the specific program curriculum structure and organization in terms of the sequence of instruction, the relative difficulty of the competencies to be developed and the interdependence of competencies (such as the need to be proficient at one competency in order to learn another).

Program Blocking

The third major dimension of competency-based vocational education involves program blocking. This is essentially a visual representation of the occupational training to be provided. In order to understand the concept of blocking, it might be helpful to think of competencies as "units of instruction." Blocking begins by identifying competencies which students need to develop first. Generally, easier competencies are developed initially, with more difficult ones being developed later. When coupled with various modes of individualizd instruction, the student is actually given the opportunity to achieve his or her maximum potential.

After blocking a program of instruction for a given occupation, a list of tasks to be performed must be developed for each competency. This task list specifies the entry-level skills that individuals should be able to perform once they have accepted employment within an occupational setting. Tasks are the general work activities that students must be able to perform in order to fully develop a particular competency—the actual learning experiences of the student. For instance, if an individual is enrolled in a welding program and one of the competencies to be developed is "prepare the torch for welding," then securing the necessary equipment, setting the proper level and mixture of gases and adjusting the flame are tasks associated with that particular competency.

General and Specific Objectives

At this point, the occupational description has been completed and the occupational competencies have been listed. The program has been blocked and task lists have been generated. During the latter phase, it was essential to determine what the student needed "to do" and "to know" with respect to performing these tasks. Subsequently, attention is focused on the general and specific objectives of instruction. General objectives refer to the competencies being developed whereas specific objectives relate directly to the tasks the student engages in during the learning experiences. As expected, the conditions, level of performance and standard of acceptability must be established for each program competency.

Once these objectives have been identified, decisions regarding the technique(s) and extent of student evaluation must be determined. It is essential to decide how to assess whether or not students have achieved a particular level of occupational competence. Too often, vocational educators proceed immediately with the development of instructional materials without directing sufficient attention to the intent, scope or process of evaluation, which is the ultimate measure of student achievement. Instructional staff members working with competency-based vocational systems must know at the outset what criterion standards of performance they are going to measure students against. For instance, it is possible to tell whether a postsecondary student enrolled in a masonry program will have achieved a satisfactory level of performance with respect to a particular competency. Mastery may be shown if he or she is able to lay a minimum number of bricks on a line within a given time period using specific types of equipment. Once the level and conditions of performance have been established, the evaluation mode and process can be formalized by the use of performance checklists, multiple-choice test items or other forms of measurement. Also, once the standards of acceptable performance for each competency have been determined, parameters are defined specific to the method of individualized instruction and the resource materials to be used.

Developing Materials

Finally, the instructional staff along with program coordinators (supervisors) can begin developing learning materials. The materials developed for each competency (unit of instruction) are usually referred to as modules, packets or packs. The development of these modules proceeds through several steps, and therefore, demands a substantial commitment by those associated with a particular program.

It is absolutely essential that the teaching staff be actively involved in preparing instructional materials for the competency-based system. If materials developed elsewhere are to be incorporated within the program content, instructors must devote time to evaluating the documents, resources and student achievement measures to ensure that the materials have been adapted to their unique competency-based program. It is only through the active participation of the instructional staff in developing the curriculum that a *commitment* to and subsequent *utilization* of materials can be expected.

In addition, the support of the administrative and supervisory staff is critical because of the instructor time and effort required for the development of quality materials. The administration will need to establish a "reward" system to encourage the active participation of the supervisory and instructional staff members who are preparing and actually implementing this type of curriculum.

Inservice Training

Furthermore, in order for competency-based vocational education to succeed, it will be imperative to provide an inservice training program to train staff for: writing curriculum, teaching competencies and following the overall concepts of competency-based education. Generally, this is no small task. Because most instructors have participated in a traditional educational process all their lives, competency-based education is often viewed as a curricular approach which, at best, must be tolerated but not necessarily adopted for use without proven results. Therefore, instructors must be: (1) provided with a basic understanding of competency-based education; (2) given reasons for its adoption along with examples of proven success; (3) motivated to develop the professional skills required to write and teach competencies; (4) given an opportunity to personally experience competency-based education in action and (5) provided with the time, resources, guidance and support needed to write curriculum and teach using the competency-based approach.

When preparing instructional modules, introductory materials are presented to define the respective competency to be developed. Next, include materials that inform the student of the purpose for developing a specific competency—he or she will learn why it is important to acquire a particular occupational skill. The general performance objectives are then outlined. The students are told what they will be able to do once the learning experience has been successfully completed. Specific performance objectives are then noted in terms of the activities students will engage in and the resources (learning guides, equipment, etc.) they will be using.

It should also be noted that a quality resource center is critical to the implementation of a competency-based, individualized system. Without the many necessary resources—films, manuals, handbooks, slide-tape presentations and other materials—and without access to these resources, the system is doomed to failure.

JUSTIFICATION

Having previously provided a brief explanation of competency-based vocational education and identified some of the basic program components, it is desirable to consider why such programs should be linked to individualized instruction.

In the traditional curriculum, the time allocated to developing a particular type of skill or academic knowledge base is generally fixed; so is the content. In addition, if one method of instruction is being used for a class of 30 individuals, there is the apparent assumption that everyone learns in the same way—that a fixed learning style exists. As a consequence, the educator directs as though the students are a homogeneous group.

This approach to public education is contrary to results of research in educational psychology, but it is characteristic of the state-of-the-art in classroom instruction. The implications of accepting this condition as unchangeable are significant. If everything in the curriculum is fixed (time, content and instructional technique), then the skill attainment levels of the students are going to be variable. Some students are going to perform better than others. True, some students will still perform better than others in competency-based programs, but in the latter case, students will achieve a higher level of knowledge and skill relative to the specific competencies that they are capable of developing.

When the entire competency-based vocational education system is individualized, the amount of time the student needs to spend on a given competency is variable. The content within a given area of instruction is also variable because various businesses and industries desire students—their employees—to cover certain content while others may desire something else. This is not meant to imply that business and industry would, or should, strictly control vocational training. It means that part-time students can be served by the system very effectively by focusing their learning experiences on certain aspects of the training program. *The student still has the option of completing the entire program if he or she desires.*

Variable Learning Styles

This same system serves the variable learning styles of individual students. It is reasonable under varying circumstances to use printed materials, audiovisual materials, peer group teaching, and/or one-to-one interaction between the learner and instructor when developing various competencies. For example, it seems that the potential of the competency-based system is best characterized by the following situation. A young, moderately retarded student was working on a lathe developing a certain skill and competency required of a machinist. At the same time, on the other side of the shop, another student (a college graduate) was developing a different competency on a numerical control machine. Through the flexibility of the competency-based instructional system, which had been individualized to the needs of each student, teachers are able to function as managers of the learning environment. They can be responsive both to students who have the potential of the moderately retarded youth *and* the graduate of a prestigious higher education institution. Certainly, it was never expected that the retarded student would develop all of the competencies which the other student might, even with an unlimited amount of time. But the potential was there for the retarded student to achieve the highest possible level of skill development of which he or she was capable.

Toward Articulation

Another justification for advocating the development of competency-based education programs concerns articulation. Most educators would probably prefer, and hope, to achieve effective articulation of their education programs. In fact, competency-based programs help this goal to be realized. How might this be possible? Considering the example noted above, it is evident that people may enter a program at varying levels of competency and continue until they have achieved their potential or until they desire to leave the program to begin working. Under such conditions, it is possible to accept high school students regardless of their ability level—before or after graduation. These students can be helped to develop competencies in a specific occupational area, which will not only prepare them for the world of work, but also afford them the opportunity for further training at a college or university or through an associate degree program. It can also serve as the means to illustrate the need for developing certain basic educational skills in the areas of reading, mathematics and writing, which are generally important to successful participation in an occupation. With the proper emphasis on evaluation, it is also possible for individuals who already have certain competencies to continue their training without having to repeat learning experiences. The student simply "tests out" of a particular competency and moves on to another.

How does the competency-based vocational education system mesh with the entire curricular effort? Individuals in the system may be secondary, postsecondary or adult students. They may be handicapped, disadvantaged or they may be neither. No one, however, is refused admission to a program of occupational preparation.

How is this possible? Fortunately, competency-based systems do not place levels of expectation on students. They simply present students with a description of what they must do and know to develop certain competencies. The services, resources and people to be involved in the learning are also identified. Eventually, it is expected that students will be able to perform competencies at such a level that they can become economically self-sufficient.

IMPLEMENTING THE CURRICULUM: A SCENARIO

Once students have been enrolled in a vocational training institution, they participate in a pre-assessment diagnosis. Basically, this process involves considerable testing. All individuals participating in occupational training programs should be tested in order to determine how their characteristics, interests and abilities coincide with those required of individuals employed in occupations for which the vocational program provides preparatory training. At this point, it is extremely important that the necessary vocational guidance be provided. Competency-based vocational education programs rely on effective guidance because it is critical to identify the learning experiences and the services that are needed by students to ensure the development of their full potential.

The next stage is program assessment. The individual student is required to meet with the instructional staff to determine whether or not he or she realizes what skills and competencies are needed to work within the particular occupation, and what his or her future work environment is going to be like. This helps students decide if they are willing to make the necessary commitment to the given occupational training. The individual is also asked to carefully examine the entire competency list and note which—if not all—competencies he or she wishes to develop.

Students May Leave and Re-Enter

At times, students may wish to develop only a portion of the competencies associated with a program because they have only a limited amount of time to spend in vocational training. Possibly, they simply do not have the financial resources to continue for an extended period of time. In a competency-based program, the student identifies needed competencies, develops them effectively and subsequently secures employment with an expectation of considerable success. Does this mean that students are "out" of the system once they have left school? Quite the contrary. In a competency-based program, students may return at any time and continue their training by developing additional competencies on a full-time or part-time basis. They may also leave and re-enter the system as many times as they feel necessary.

Finally, the student will participate, at different times, in evaluations to determine how well he or she can perform certain competencies. At these points, one of several things will happen. First of all, during an evaluation, the instructional staff will diagnose how well the student can handle an occupation-related activity. The instructor may then decide that it is necessary for the student to continue his or her training on that competency, or the student may move on to the development of a new competency. On the other hand, at the end of a particular evaluation phase, it may be time for the individual to seek employment. If not, the student may decide to continue with advanced training in another institution. In either case, the student—and others—are reasonably assured of the extent of a student's capabilities because they have been observed and measured. In addition, there is substantial information that students and others can use to plan and make decisions about their continuing occupational growth and development.

CONCLUSION

When vocational education leadership seriously considers the development and implementation of competency-based vocational programs, it is essential that persons responsible for the effort be aware of the problems associated with this curricular approach as well as the benefits. For instance, competency-based programs are not a panacea; they will not solve all instructional problems. In fact, if this approach does help to solve some problems, others will arise.

Attention will have to be directed to the time needed for developing (and/or conducting an in-depth review of) instructional materials according to a consistent format, professional development of staff (including preparation needed to individualize instruction), careful monitoring of program operations, recording students' progress using a well-developed information system and open-entry/open-exit policies.

In the end, what is important are policy changes, a formalized student accounting system, considerable planning activities, a "reward" system designed to encourage a commitment and participation of the professional staff and the involvement of active vocational advisory committees. These will be the benchmarks of success in implementing competency-based vocational education programs.

REFERENCES

Hennepin Technical Centers. *A delivery system for competency-based vocational education.* Unpublished manuscript, circa 1977. (Available from Hennepin Technical Centers, 1820 N. Xenium Lane, Minneapolis, Minn. 55441).

Knaak, W.C. *Competency-based vocational education: A review* (Information Series No. 115). Columbus, Ohio: ERIC Clearinghouse on Career Education, 1977.

EMPLOYABILITY SKILLS TRAINING: A WEAPON AGAINST YOUTH UNEMPLOYMENT

Dolores M. Robinson

"If a young person cannot get a job in the formative years of life, there is a feeling of despair, discouragement, a loss of self-esteem, and a lashing out against the authorities who are responsible." Former President Jimmy Carter, speaking in 1977, saw the dire social and economic consequences of youth unemployment. His administration and previous ones tried to face and solve the problem of youth unemployment. Yet solutions were—and are—elusive and expensive. Because there is no single cause of youth unemployment, there is no single answer to the problem. What is needed is a broad mixture of strategies aimed at different aspects of the situation.

One element that has been targeted in the battle is the school-to-work transition. Studies have shown that youth unemployment is highly attributable to difficulties students experience in leaving school and going to work (Stern, 1979, p. 267). Too many students leave school unable to meet the demands of finding, getting and keeping a job. Yet if youth unemployment is to be alleviated, strategies must be designed to provide students with these skills. One good possibility seems to be through adding an employability skills component to existing job training programs.

BACKGROUND OF THE PROBLEM

The dilemma of youth unemployment in this country is not new. It is a problem that has developed and worsened over the past three decades; and it has resisted the efforts of federal, state and local legislation to alleviate or reduce it.

Although teenage unemployment rates have always been higher than those of adults, teenage unemployment has escalated to record levels in recent years. The U.S. Department of Labor reported (July, 1980) that the jobless rate for adult males was 6.5 percent while unemployment among teenagers rose to 19 percent—a rate approximately three times as great as that reported among the 25-to-64-age group.

Frightening as these statistics sound, the figures may actually understate the scope of the problem. Many believe that the Bureau of Labor Statistics' methods of collecting unemployment data are inexact, since the bureau bases its conclusions on queries directed to just a small sample of households across the nation. Most importantly, many researchers feel that official estimates as currently measured are inaccurate, especially in cities, since the figures do not include the scores of young people who become discouraged and quit looking for work (Mister, 1979). Richard Ruggles (1978) agrees that, when the "discouraged" worker is counted, statistics often indicate such workers actually outnumber their employed counterparts in many areas of the country.

Discouraged Workers

Who are these discouraged workers? They may be classified as persons who are technically not in the labor force, but who do want to work. They are not looking for work, only because they think they cannot get jobs. Kerry Helmeke and others (1977) postulated that such persons are not looking for work because (1) work is not available in occupations related to their training; (2) they have looked for jobs but are unable to find work; (3) they lack the necessary education, training, skills or experience and/or (4) employers think they are too young or too old for the position sought.

Sar Levitan (1976) agrees that unemployment statistics do not reflect reality. He opposes the current categories that consider only those persons working or not working, or how many hours they work. He urges adding another dimension to "look at the number of persons who are unable to attain an adequate standard of living through work." This technique would count not only employment and unemployment, but would take into consideration earnings and time worked. According to Levitan, current employment statistics do not differentiate between adequate and substandard employment. These additional figures would reveal family incomes and provide information on those persons who work, but at marginal jobs with low salaries. It is clear that current unemployment statistics reveal neither the breadth nor the depth of the problem. Only with accurate data can the full scope of the problem be revealed and suitable policies devised to resolve it.

THE IMPACT OF UNEMPLOYMENT

The fact that so many of this country's youth are unemployed is detrimental both to those individuals and to society. Kalacheck (1969) says that "labor force participation by persons in their teens and early twenties is of significance for two reasons. First, it contributes to the output of the society and provides current employment and income to persons desirous of both. Second, it presumably results in a significant acclimatization" (p. 66). In emphasizing the significance of labor force participation, Kalacheck also noted that there are carryover effects of early labor market experiences that we are still not able to completely understand.

The implication is that the chronic employment problems young people experience during the period of transition from school to work can be expected to have long-run consequences on their labor market experience. There is increasing evidence that the problems of unemployment are not temporary for some youths. Youths who have repeated periods of unemployment are also unemployed for longer periods of time as adults.

Adams and Mangum (1978), in their assessment of youth unemployment problems, point to the relationship of early labor market success and future employability. They also suggest that those who have unfavorable early labor market experiences are less likely than others to have favorable subsequent experiences. These authors conclude that youths who have steady work will have higher future earnings than those who are chronically unemployed. The Vice-President's Task Force on Youth Employment (1980) agreed that those with early labor market experience have more stable and remunerative employment as adults. The Task Force report goes further, asserting that the vibrant economy this country needs will depend on an increase in employment of young people.

REASONS FOR YOUTH UNEMPLOYMENT

Because unemployment is highest among those who start looking for work immediately after high school, it is important to examine the difficulties associated with the school-to-work transition.

A number of explanations have been advanced for the difficulties experienced by youths who are making the transition from education to work. Sinclair (1977, p. 9) suggests that the inability of young people to make the initial entry into the job market is a lack of employment experience, a deficit of job-specific skills, inadequate preparation for career development and unsatisfactory attitudes toward work. Other reasons associated with the difficulty in transition from school to work are: (1) the lack of basic skills (Ginzberg, 1980); (2) frictional unemployment (Bobrow, 1976; Kalacheck, 1969) and (3) inadequate labor market information (Parnes, 1975).

Lack of Basic Skills

Inability to read, write and perform basic mathematics is a significant problem for unemployed youths. Former Vice President Walter Mondale's Task Force on Youth Unemployment (1980) asserts that the underlying reason for many young people not finding a job is that they lack the basic educational skills crucial to training and employment.

Ginzberg (1980) shares the same view, saying that the basic skills of reading and mathematics are critically important for all U.S. citizens, particularly in a society whose economy is tilting ever more toward service.

Further emphasis on the need to improve basic educational competencies of youth appears in the executive summary of the National Commission for Employment Policy (1979). According to this commission, "without basic literacy skills, youths are unable to take advantage of further education or training and will be permanently consigned to the bottom of the economic and social ladder" (p. 4).

Frictional Unemployment

Bobrow (1976), in summarizing studies that have examined the reasons for youth employment problems (Folk, 1968; Barton, 1972), found that high youth unemployment is attributable to frictional unemployment. She pointed out that, unlike members of the adult unemployment group who have acquired an interest in job stability, the teenage group consists largely of new entrants to the labor force and re-entrants, who come back into the job market after a period of nonparticipation.

Adams and Mangum (1980, p. 41) share Bobrow's viewpoint that the rates are similar for teenagers aged 14 to 19 and adults over 20 once the new entrants and re-entrants are eliminated from unemployment figures. In explaining the process of high turnover and frequent job search, these authors pointed out that "the teenage group can be expected to spend more time in the job search effort associated with job turnover, interruptions in employment and initial labor market entry" (p. 42).

Such findings are in line with Kalacheck's (1969) study. His analysis of unemployment rates from June, 1964, through June, 1966, indicated that high teenage unemployment was a direct result of the search for a job after a period of non-labor force participation. When the "job-search group" was eliminated from the unemployment figures, teenage unemployment was 3.1 percent, while the overall rate was 2.6 percent. Based on these findings, it would appear that the gap between adult and teenage unemployment rates was minimal for those who had had long periods of regular employment.

In the same vein, Freeman (1976) analyzed youth unemployment and concluded that 16-to 19-year-olds had an unemployment rate of 5.1 percent, while the overall rate for all workers was 3.2 percent.

Yet even if the high rate of youth unemployment is a function of frictional unemployment, the severity of the situation cannot be discounted as hundreds of youth cannot get started on a career or even gain an understanding of what work is about. Unemployment for these individuals also represents a serious economic hardship for those who not only support themselves but help to support their families.

Lack of Relevant Labor Market Information.

There is also evidence to indicate that youths need better labor information. Parnes (1975) identified four kinds of labor market information needed by youths: "a) general labor market information, or information about career alternatives; b) specific labor market information, or information about alternative employers; c) information on effective ways to search and apply for a job; and d) information on employers' behavioral expectation of employees" (p. 33).

In addition to these factors, a lack of skills in nonvocational but job-related areas is crucial. Stern (1979, p. 267) observes that very little effort is put into seeing what can be done about individuals moving directly from high school to work. He suggests that there is little evidence to indicate that schools have been successful in providing training in skills such as choosing an occupation, filling out an application form, getting along with people on the job and practicing good work habits. Instead, "Students as a rule do not know much about the world of work. They lack information about employment prospects and about the educational and experience requirements for jobs." Stern further notes that "most students lack the ability to 'sell themselves' to a prospective employer, even when the student has mastered skills that could land a suitable job."

Poor Interpersonal Skills

In summarizing the findings of several studies, Evans (1978) reported that 78.2 percent of the Youth Opportunity Center counselors surveyed reported that personality problems hampered the adjustment of youths in the work world. "More specifically, 72 percent mentioned job-seeking and/or on-the-job behavior as a major problem" (p. 317). Feldman (1967) suggested that the maladjustment of secondary students in the world of work may be related more to poor interpersonal skills than to inadequate technical skills.

A survey administered to more than 75 percent of the high school seniors in the state of Wisconsin asked students their perceptions of the usefulness of various available resources in making plans for the following year. Most reported that they received little help from high school counselors and teachers. Less than 5 percent of those responding reported receiving help or information from the state employment service. At the same time, nearly half of all respondents reported needing help with career-related counseling and job placement.

In a similar survey in the Florida public school system, 75 percent of high school students reported that they received little job-related counseling; they needed help in making plans for the future and they wanted more work-related courses. Students were also asked if they needed more career-related counseling. Three-quarters of those responding said that career information and career counseling programs in the school needed to be improved and expanded. Only 22 percent reported that they needed no additional help.

Given the seriousness of the problem and the nature of its underlying causes, an effective policy must be devised to improve the labor market prospects of youth.

WHAT CAN BE DONE

Employability skills training may be used as one strategy to provide those skills which will not only enable youth to increase their chances of getting a job, holding a job and achieving promotion, but it will also place them in a better position to compete for jobs with adults. The lack of knowledge of the world of work, how to look for work and how to conduct oneself in a job interview make the first labor market entry difficult for some youth. For others, the problem of entering and re-entering the labor market several times during the teenage years is an additional cause of concern.

To what extent can schools contribute to the solution of the problem? Many believe that the public schools in our society should be responsible for preparing youth with both occupational and employability skills. Thus, schools should be held responsible for placing greater emphasis on labor market-related curricula and programs, especially for those youths who will not go on to higher education (Anderson & Sawhill, 1977).

Further, these authors indicate that greater efforts should also be made to teach younger people how "to identify and pursue available job opportunities" (p. 152). They reason that this job-related training should be supplemented by appropriate labor market information so that youths develop not only marketable skills but also the knowledge and abilities to engage in effective job searches.

According to Bottoms (1980), "Money needs to be targeted through vocational education for employability and job skills for in-school and out-of-school youth" (p. 8). Outside of school, the approach must be remedial and is most often associated with school dropouts who plan to enter the labor market but lack sufficient orientation to the world of work. The preventive approach, on the other hand, is typically an in-school strategy designed to develop employability skills for students who plan to enter the labor force directly from high school. Through both preventive and remedial efforts, students need to be taught those skills that will enable them to compete in the job market, to make good impressions on employers and to help them "get their feet in the door."

EMPLOYABILITY SKILLS CONCEPTS

There are three major employability skills concepts that may comprise an appropriate course of action in assisting youth who look for jobs but cannot find work and for youth who find jobs but cannot maintain them.

The first concept in the employability skills approach is making students aware of the relationships between finding a job and conducting an active, well-planned job search.

Many of the students who plan to enter the labor market directly from high school are enrolled in cooperative education classes and are, therefore, working part-time while enrolled in school. Given the role of cooperative coordinators in providing assistance to youth in finding their first job, some students are lulled into a sense of false security. Even currently employed students who are participating in cooperative education programs need to have real knowledge of the difficulties associated with job hunting.

Skills for Job Searching

Employability skills training is one strategy that can be used to provide the knowledge that job hunting takes time and that, therefore, one must set time aside for the job search. In addition, the student must learn that job searches must be planned and acquire skills in planning them (*Your Job Search,* 1978). How does one find a job? How does one find leads about job openings? Finding a job isn't easy—it is a time-consuming and challenging task. But employability skills training can help to reduce the time a young person spends in the effort through explicating job-hunting activities and strategies. Since there are many ways of finding out about jobs—from friends and relatives, want ads, employment agencies, former employers and many more, employability skills training teaches the concept that not one, but all possibilities should be explored.

Adams and Mangum (1978) observed that the average number of job-search methods used by teenagers is lower than the number of other job seekers. Data from this study reveal that the average number of job-search methods used for this group is 1.58, compared to 6.3 methods for other groups. Teenagers, aged 16 to 19, are more likely to apply directly to employers and less likely to apply to a public employment agency than other job seekers.

According to Billhartz (1980) job hunting may be broken down into four parts: (1) know what you want; (2) know yourself; (3) go after it and (4) go after it again and again. The employability skills training concept includes these parts but adds the idea that the more action one takes each day, the sooner one finds a job. Students need to be given some ideas while they are still in school on ways to find job openings through employment agencies, both public and private, and when to use or not to use each kind.

The second concept basic to the employability skills training approach is to show that applying for a job can be easier and more successful if one is prepared for it.

"Everyone who wants a job must fill out an application." Billhartz, writing in 1978, sees the application as a basic necessity for all prospective employees when they go job hunting, even though they may be applying for positions other than initial labor market entry.

Included in the basic concept in applying for a job, employability skills training provides practice in general principles of (1) completeness and correctness and (2) interviewing for a job.

Completeness and Correctness

Applications are the principal means by which employers get information about a job applicant; therefore, information given on these forms must be complete and correct. A concept that should be taught is that "if the student skips or doesn't answer questions completely on the application form, there is a good chance the employer will skip over the student." Citing problems concerning youth unemployment, one employer described how an incomplete or partially filled out application form not only slows down the hiring process but may prevent a youth from getting a job that provides a positive work setting as well as needed income and an alternative to street life. A personal fact sheet that contains information about the applicant, including the home address, education, work experience and references should be carried along when the applicant applies for a job. It saves time for both the employer and applicant, and information will be accurate. Although there are many kinds of application forms, the general principles of neatness, completeness and correctness apply to all.

Interview Behavior

For this activity, the main point that should be emphasized is that the impression given by the applicant at the interview is important. Students need to practice the behaviors that will be used in the interview, but these behaviors should be performed correctly. Although interview behaviors may vary from job to job, it seems appropriate to take a look at the behaviors that are acceptable by most employers. (1) Interviewers are usually interested in an applicant who exhibits an interest in doing the best possible job for the company, so it is the applicant's responsibility to get as much information about the company as possible before going to the interview. (2) Interviewers want prospective employees to wear clothes that are acceptable to the employer's standards. (3) Interviewers are interested in applicants who exhibit positive attitudes and show signs of maturity.

If an applicant wants a job, he or she must make every effort to be chosen over other applicants. Chances are that the one who exhibits the best behavior will be chosen for the job even though his or her skills may not be the best. If the first interview, however, is not successful, the applicant should not become discouraged as the interview experiences may help the student do better in the next one.

The third concept of employability skills training is that work habits are as important as technical job skills in keeping a job. Employees are more often fired for their poor work habits than for their poor job skills.

Technical Skills Are Not Enough

Evans and Herr (1978) add the perspective that "technical skills alone are insufficient for work adjustment and satisfaction." Youths also need the employability skills, the attitudes and the values that most adult workers bring to the job. Through the employability skills project students can be made aware that employers want workers who have good work habits, dress appropriately, avoid waste, arrive at work on time, perform their duties conscientiously and follow instructions.

Emotional maturity is also evaluated by some employers as an indication of potential for success. A survey designed to determine why 4,000 people were fired (Frost, 1976) indicated that nearly 70 percent of those fired lost their jobs because of their inability to get along with others. Job-related instruction needs to stress that even though a person gets a job, there is no guarantee that he or she will keep the job without constant effort and cooperation. Employability skill training stresses that job skills, of course, are necessary to be a good worker. But it also stresses that employers feel that good work habits, a good attitude and the ability to get along with others provide solid indications of a potentially successful worker.

CONCLUSION

The evidence indicates that while in recent years the proportion of teenage unemployment has been increasing, for most teenagers, unemployment can be attributed to the job search effort associated with initial labor market entry. To what extent can schools contribute to the solution of this problem? Authors Stern (1979), Sinclair (1978) and Evans (1978) reveal the urgent need to improve young people's preparation for working life while they are still in school. This need can be addressed in many ways. One such strategy would be to identify and develop programs that would get the public schools more involved in employment by providing employability and job skills within the school system.

The school should be held accountable for this role, particularly for those youth who will enter the job market before or upon completion of high school. Therefore, the appropriate place for teaching job-related skills is in the school before youth go out into the job market. Employability skills training does not provide an instant cure, but it does seem to be an effective way for improving the labor market experience of youth.

REFERENCES

Adams, A., & Mangum, G.L. *The lingering crisis of youth unemployment.* Kalamazoo, Mich.: W.E. Upjohn Institute for Employment Resarch, June 1978.

Anderson, B., & Sawhill, I.V. *Youth employment and public policy options.* Englewood Cliffs, N.J.: Prentice Hall Publishing Co., 1977.

Barton, P.E. Youth transition to work: The problem and federal policy setting. In National Commission for Manpower Policy, *From school to work: Improving the transition.* Washington, D.C.: Government Printing Office, 1976.

Billhartz, C. *The complete book of job hunting, finding, changing.* Akron, Ohio: Rainbow Collection, 1980.

Bobrow, S.B. *Reasonable expectation: Limits on the promise of community councils.* Washington, D.C.: National Institute of Education (HEW), November 1976.

Bottoms, G. We are challenged. *VocEd,* March 1980.

Carter, J. *Youth unemployment initiatives: background report.* Washington, D.C.: The White House, January 1980.

Evans, R.N., & Herr, E.L. *Foundations of vocational education,* 2nd ed. Columbus, Ohio: Charles E. Merrill Publishing Co., 1978.

Feldman, M. We must prepare students for work, not jobs. *The Chronicle of Higher Education,* September 5, 1978, p. 56.

State of Florida, Department of Education, Division of Vocational Education. *Your Job Search: Instructor's Guide.* Tallahassee, Fla.: Author, January 1978.

Folk, H. The problem of youth unemployment. In *The transition from school to work,* a report based on the Princeton Manpower Symposium, 1968.

Freeman, R.B. *The declining economic value of higher education and the American social system.* New York: Aspen Institute Program on Education for A Changing Society, 1976a.

Frost, K. Why 4,000 people were fired. *Administrative Management,* February 1974.

Ginzberg, E. Education, jobs, and all that. *New York University Education Quarterly,* Winter, 1980.

Helmeke, K., et al. *Groups with historically high incidence of unemployment.* Washington, D.C.: Employment Standard Administration, Department of Labor, July 1977.

Kalacheck, E. *The youth labor market, institute of labor and industrial relations.* Washington, D.C.: The University of Michigan-Wayne State University and the National Manpower Policy Task Force, 1969.

Levitan, S. *The unemployment number is the message.* Columbus, Ohio; The National Center for Research in Vocational Education, The Ohio State University, December 1977.

Mister, M. How not to change the counting of the unemployed. *Journal for Employment and Training Professionals,* 1979, *1*(3), 315-328.

Mondale, W. *Youth unemployment initiatives: Background report.* Washington, D.C.: The White House, January 1980.

National Commission for Employment Policy. *Expanding employment opportunities for disadvantaged youth,* Fifth annual report. Washington, D.C.: Author, December 1979.

Parnes, H.S. "Long-Run Labor Market Experience," in S.L. Wolfbein (Ed.), *Labor market information for youths,* Philadelphia, Pa.: Temple University School of Business Administration, 1975.

Ruggles, R. *Employment and unemployment statistics as indexes of economic activity and capacity utilization.* Unpublished paper, New Haven, Conn.: Yale University, September 1978.

Sinclair, M. Public policy to improve the employability of young people. *Educational Planning,* 1977, *4*(28), 94-105.

Sterns, B.E. A federal policy on education and work. *Journal for Employment and Training Professionals,* 1979, *1*(3).

U.S. Department of Labor, Bureau of Labor Statistics. *Monthly Labor Review,* 1980 (July), *103*(7), 5.

AN INTERNATIONAL PERSPECTIVE ON SECONDARY SCHOOL VOCATIONAL EDUCATION

Beatrice Reubens

During the past several years, I have traveled outside the United States a great deal, visiting a dozen or more countries and studying the latest developments in apprenticeship, vocational education, the transition from school to work and youth unemployment. As I review what I have learned abroad, several common trends stand out.

First, with the exception of Austria, Switzerland, Germany and Japan, whose situation the U.S. cannot expect to replicate for many reasons, the industrialized market economy countries have been faced with high youth unemployment since the mid-1970s. This followed an earlier period of little unemployment. Taking a gloomy view of the medium-term economic future as well, most of these countries show more concern than we do about the adverse effects of unemployment on young people at the beginning of their working lives.

Second, throughout the world governments are placing a great emphasis on steering young people into vocational education and vocational training. They are discouraging types of academic education that have no specific vocational content. Vocational education has a better image abroad than it has here, especially at the high school level. This is not to suggest that middle-class parents in other countries select vocational education for their children or that vocational education has equal social standing. But vocational education is regarded as a necessary and useful part of the educational system.

INTERNATIONAL TRENDS

If one looks at the trends in initial vocational training around the world, it is clear that the share going to school-based training, which is a fair description of vocational education in the United States, is increasing. It is increasing at the expense of industry-based training, of which apprenticeship is a leading example. The main reason is that as occupations become increasingly technical and theoretical, the classroom is judged to be the superior location for learning to take place.

Studies in these countries show that those who complete vocational education fare better on most labor market indicators than those who complete an equal number or even more years of academic education. Recent American studies, especially for boys, have been negative on that issue. A 1979 report by the Carnegie Council entitled *Giving Youth a Better*

Chance suggests a dismantling of American high school vocational education. All of the European countries, as well as Canada, Australia, New Zealand and Japan, would find that a shocking recommendation.

I disagree with the Carnegie Council recommendation to phase out high school vocational education for several reasons. I find that the alternatives suggested by the Carnegie Council are not adequate or likely to become so, either quantitatively or qualitatively. Apprenticeship, for example, was cited as one alternative. But in the United States apprenticeship is a small program, concentrated in the construction trades, on males and on age groups that deliberately slight teenagers. In fact, young adults are not even the majority in most U.S. apprenticeship programs. Neither were the other alternatives offered by the Carnegie Council satisfactory.

Another reason to hold back on the destruction of high school vocational education is that some parts of it actually may be productive in terms of labor market outcomes. Most of the recent studies have necessarily evaluated all who were registered as vocational students, without regard to the subjects studied or the proportion of total hours devoted to vocational subjects. Additional studies are under way to correct this data problem. Until all the results are in, we should continue to try to improve high school vocational education.

Third, within vocational education the trend in many countries is toward the inclusion of a compulsory period of practical work experience in a firm as a prerequisite for completion of the course. Naturally, this development is heavily dependent on the cooperation and understanding of the business and labor communities. In France, which previously provided only classroom learning, the national decision to incorporate a practical element is being introduced gradually after discussions between government, the employers' associations and the representatives of teachers. Because of a shortage of employer work places, it may cover only a portion of vocational students. In Scandinavia it is easier to obtain industrial cooperation, but there still are problems, including competition for employers' work places among a number of different youth programs.

On-the-Job Training

American vocational education, especially at the high school level, must come to grips with the issue of on-the-job training for a large proportion of vocational students. Cooperative education already provides the model to be followed. There should be an expansion of the subjects to which it applies and of the number of students who are placed in firms for part of a course. All evidence suggests that pedagogical and career outcomes are improved. Moreover, this may be the main route to survival for high school vocational education.

Fourth, there is a growing interest in making greater use of employers' premises for educational purposes in many countries. Specifically, there are drives to increase the number in apprenticeship. In spite of a drop in total employment after 1974, many nations were able to increase the number of apprentices who are usually 15-to-16-years-old. I believe that an enlarged apprenticeship system with a lower age requirement for entrance is very desirable in the United States. But I am not sure that it can be realized, even with government subsidies to employers, such as other countries are offering. Still, vocational education and apprenticeship are the two main systems of initial skill training and their administrative and research integration should be a high priority in the United States. Such integration exists in most countries.

Fifth, there is a convergence of training methods under vocational education and apprenticeship in most countries. Not only do apprentices spend an increased amount of time in schools and training centers, but in many nations the newest pattern is to have one or more years of full-time vocational education conclude with a shorter apprenticeship than was customary. In these countries full-time vocational students usually spend time in a firm. It is becoming increasingly difficult to distinguish apprenticeship from other forms of on-the-job experience. The congruence of vocational education and apprenticeship is increasing. None of these trends are yet apparent in the United States.

More Attention for Those Unprepared for Work

Sixth on the list of general trends is the increased attention given in all countries to the residual group of youth who leave school poorly prepared for working life. The schools receive most of the blame, being charged either with not serving the group's needs at all or serving them poorly, as in the United States. It appears that the proportion of the age group which leaves school poorly prepared is somewhat higher in the United States than in some other countries. Many new programs, designed for young people who do not fit into the traditional programs, have been developed abroad, both inside and outside of the schools. But there has been less effort than in the United States to open vocational education to the academically unprepared. Special preparatory courses are offered, but on the whole, vocational education maintains its admission standards. A few countries have attempted to revise apprenticeship admission standards and training regulations to permit young people with low academic achievement to enter. But in many cases it is expected that they will do no more than reach semi-skilled status. American vocational education should not regard remedial or supplementary programs as a threat. Nor should it try to serve every last youth, even while fulfilling its mission to aid the disadvantaged.

Last, there is a marked tendency to group occupations into a few basic categories for training purposes. The purpose is to give young people a wider choice, to provide greater occupational mobility and to streamline training courses. There is a similarity to the occupational cluster approach in this country.

Great Diversity

This review of trends abroad is somewhat misleading in that these other countries appear to be uniform and in full agreement. In fact there is great diversity, although these countries are all quite different from the United States.

Switzerland offers a case study of low adult and youth unemployment and a comparatively easy transition from school to work for the majority of young people, including the children of foreign workers. There is a sense in Switzerland that one has returned to the nineteenth century and that it works! The family is strong and influential and young people are obedient. Schools are traditional, maintain strict discipline and give a great deal of homework. Families from other European countries commented to me on the difference between the education their children were receiving in Switzerland and what they would have had at home—all in favor of the Swiss way. Even the tiny fraction that has organized rebelliously in the largest cities makes the conformity of the vast majority all the more striking.

To be fair, one of the reasons for low unemployment is the Swiss willingness to let the large body of foreign workers bear a disproportionate share of joblessness. As the work contracts of the foreigners come to an end, the surplus laborers are simply forced to return home. This exportation of unemployment is not, however, the major reason for the relatively smooth transition from school to work. A substantial share of the credit belongs to the extensive apprenticeship system which Switzerland, along with Germany and Austria, strongly supports.

Expanding Apprenticeships

Germany has avoided substantial unemployment by persuading employers to expand the number of apprenticeship plans. This policy brings youth directly into the private sector and places no financial burden on government. Even when the training is not for jobs we would regard as highly skilled, apprenticeship offers young people security, continuity and status. It also gives an assurance to other employers that basic work habits have been instilled. Youth jobs that might be viewed as dead-end are thus transformed into socially acceptable positions, although the job tasks and earnings are not impressive in themselves.

To take the other side of the coin, I found evidence in Switzerland that higher skill levels may be achieved than we produce. The director of a precision machinery factory, who was very familiar with the United States and did business with some of our major corporations, said that it would be advantageous for sales to locate a factory in the United States. However, he was hesitant to do so in 1979 because he could not find American workers trained in the Swiss manner. He did not like work attitudes in this country and was fearful that he would not be able to maintain the standards of operations on which the company's worldwide trade and reputation depend. (A Japanese report in 1981 took much the same position).

220

Perhaps Switzerland ought to specialize in high precision manufacturers, and we should not try to compete in this area. But may we not be missing some important aspects of training that would create more jobs for Americans? Work attitudes are a different sort of issue. Countries like Switzerland, Germany and Austria have begun to worry about changing attitudes among youth, including less respect for traditional work values, such as many other countries are already experiencing. Their time may be limited to enjoy an obedient work force. Another possible disadvantage is, that as a consequence of a widespread apprenticeship system, relatively few Swiss go on to higher education. Most of the emphasis is on developing very good technical schooling through the secondary level. Obviously, there is a trade-off here. The Swiss may ultimately suffer in occupations requiring more advanced education.

BEYOND APPRENTICESHIP

Turning from the apprenticeship countries to another group where apprenticeship is of less consequence, one sees different developments. Denmark, for example, has recently instituted a new system that parallels apprenticeship or replaces it, according to the desires of the employers and trade unions in each industrial sector. In essence, the employers' organizations and trade unions make the decisions about vocational education, replacing the dominant rule of educators. Educators, however, still play a prominent role.

The new system offers a year of basic vocational education in school, focused on clusters of occupations. In the second year the student specializes in a particular occupation. In the third year the pupil has to find an employer who will provide a year of practical experience under a contract that pays the pupil at the same rate as a third-year apprentice. In this period of practical experience, the employer is bound by the curricula developed jointly by management and unions.

Representatives of employers and unions are proud of the political achievement represented by the new system. As long as full-time vocational education was controlled by educators, both employers and unions felt that no matter how much they tried to participate, their opinions were never fully considered. There was always a lag in adjusting the curricula to the newest technological demands of industry. The only way to prevent this would be for the people who knew best what was going on in industry to have the most influence over the curricula.

In Denmark, trade unions and management associations cooperate fairly easily. They each maintain large education and training departments staffed by well-trained people, most of whom have been teachers at one time. They decided that permitting the employer to control the apprenticeship system made training too narrow, while letting the schools have complete control over vocational education made the training too remote. So they are striving for a new model.

OTHER APPROACHES

What is being done for youth not accepted by apprenticeship or by vocational education? There are several different approaches. One of the most common is to offer employers subsidies to take young people on for a given period of time. France has done this on a very large scale. The British use an approach called work experience, which again involves the firm. In order to get the agreement of the trade unions, who were afraid that such a program might take jobs away from ordinary workers, an arrangement was made in Britain that the youth would come only to learn about how the business was organized. They would not do any actual production work, though admittedly, this is not easy to control. This type of program has led to the permanent placement of many young people who otherwise would not have had access to these firms. Once private employers can be induced through subsidies to take a chance on a doubtful youth, many find that a person who would have been rejected by the personnel office can make a good employee. Under such programs, the rate of permanent placements has been quite high. But rising unemployment in Britain has greatly reduced the rate.

We may think that we are the only country whose young people have insufficient math or do not know how to read or write properly. This complaint, however, is heard all over the English-speaking world, as well as in some other nations. It is said that the current crop is not as proficient as earlier generations. This is a somewhat irrelevant conclusion, because we are not talking about the same group of young people as in the past. Moreover, our tests and comparative measurements are not really that reliable. But the main reason to discount comparisons of generations is that today much higher knowledge and performance standards are needed in some jobs. Therefore, it is sufficient to indicate a problem if many young people cannot perform well enough to hold a job—especially a good job.

No Specific Answer for Skills Deficiencies

This basic skills deficiency is a common problem for which I have not seen any remarkable programs for coping. Most of what is offered is remedial work, some provided by employers who cannot get apprentices of suitable standards, usually in mathematics. Since an employer's remedial program takes up valuable training time, there is great pressure to keep youngsters in school until they achieve a certain level of proficiency.

Highly educated students face their share of problems as well. Most countries I visited complain that the jobs considered appropriate for university graduates are not increasing as fast as the number of graduates. Students hedge their bets by getting vocational education in combination with an academic or higher education. In Germany some who complete the upper-secondary level school (at about 19 or 20 years) often take desirable apprenticeships in the white-collar and administrative fields. After completing the apprenticeships, they decide whether to try for a job or go to a university.

LOOKING TO THE FUTURE

Fears about the future employment situation—not just for youth, but for everybody—are widespread abroad. They arise in part because labor-intensive industries have been losing jobs to less developed nations. Some nations, which do not recognize that this is happening to other countries also, tend to blame factors in their internal situations. However, this economic phenomenon affects every developed country. It appears impossible to stem that tide because the forces behind it are the capital and business interests in the developed nations themselves. These interests are transferring their capital to underdeveloped countries, setting up operations overseas to increase production and profits, employing workers of the underdeveloped nations and thus causing specific unemployment in their own lands.

Some analysts believe that the developed nations should concentrate on the things they can still do best. This policy would mean hardship for many individuals who would be displaced and might not be easily retrained. But such displacement is not likely to be stopped by legislation nor by programs that attempt to train youth for the jobs that are moving out of the country. Problems are not created by youth who lack training, but rather by the relatively lower costs of labor in the less-developed nations and the possibility of training their workers for these jobs.

A new threat to employment in Europe, which we are beginning to hear something about in the United States, is seen in the microprocessor, or the silicon chip. Since European firms have only recently automated banking and insurance and in the process experienced substantial displacement of labor, the threat of the potential displacement because of the microprocessor has gained a wide audience. Furthermore, these nations have not had the rise in employment that we have had since 1975. Specifically, Europe may be worse off than the United States for some years to come in terms of total new jobs. Private services in those countries have simply not developed at the same rate as ours.

For vocational education, this is an important point. There is no doubt that the service sector is the growth sector in terms of jobs. In the past 20 years the proportion of the work force in service industries in the United States has grown markedly. Vocational educators need to look at the state of training for service occupations to determine where new job opportunities exist for high school boys as well as for girls for whom the vocational courses in high school already perform reasonably well, according to latest evaluation reports.

SECTION VII

NEW ISSUES AND NEW DIRECTIONS FOR THE 1980s

This last section of the yearbook includes viewpoints on how vocational education can respond to the immediate challenges of the 1980s. Leonard A. Lecht identifies and elaborates on the policy options available to vocational education in light of major developments expected in the economic climate of the 1980s.

Following an in-depth project of the American Vocational Association on the role of vocational education in economic development, Krishan K. Paul and Ellen A. Carlos provide valuable insight on this specialized function of vocational education and report on what some of the states are doing to facilitate economic development.

Rupert N. Evans addresses the relationship between vocational education and the reindustrialization of the nation needed in the next decade. From upgrading equipment and facilities to ideas for keeping current with changing technologies, Evans provides an overview of one of the strongest challenges facing vocational education today.

In the final chapter in this yearbook, Clyde Maurice points to the necessity of the role that vocational education can play in coordinating alternative systems of job training. According to Maurice, coordination "can no longer be considered a superficial exercise. Rather, it must be viewed as an essential instrument for survival and a major challenge to the vocational education enterprise."

THE ROLE OF VOCATIONAL EDUCATION IN ECONOMIC DEVELOPMENT

Krishan K. Paul and Ellen A. Carlos

Until recently, states and communities generally believed that for economic development to occur they only had to offer substantial tax and financial advantages to industries interested in locating in their areas. For a while, it worked. However, industry requires more than just tax benefits to make its location and relocation decisions. Demands from industries and competition from other states and communities have resulted in the offering of additional services and incentives to attract new and expanding industries. Important among these is free customized training. Vocational education, as the leading institutional training system in the country, has been called upon to play an important role in the economic development of many states and communities. This emerging role is the subject of this chapter.

ECONOMIC DEVELOPMENT DEFINED

Economic development is defined as a planned sequence of programs and activities designed to improve the "quality of life" in a region or a community. It is the process of expanding the productive capacity and improving the overall welfare of the citizens of an area or a region (Bruno & Wright, 1980; Winnie, 1977; Ledebur, 1977). Economic growth, which usually means an increase in employment opportunities and earnings, is a necessary and important condition for economic development. However, most economists agree that economic development, in addition to economic growth, also means improvements in health, security and a host of other tangible and intangible qualities that make a community a better place to live and work. Economic development and economic growth are used together with the belief that if economic growth takes place, economic development is bound to follow.

Analytically, economic growth is easier to measure than economic development. Increases in the number of jobs, wage rates, family income or per capita income are all rather precise measures of economic growth. Economic development, on the other hand, is determined by the improved "quality of life," "job security," "productive capacity" or "good and satisfying job opportunities," all good and worthwhile objectives, but very hard to measure. This is another reason why communities and organizations plan and work for economic growth although the ultimate goal remains economic development.

227

Factors of Growth

Given the demand for output (products and services) of an industry, two groups of factors are important for economic growth (Vaughn, 1979). The first group is comprised of all economic inputs in terms of costs and availability, which include, *inter alia*

- Land and other natural resources
- Raw materials
- Skilled labor
- Energy
- Finance
- Transportation
- Management
- Taxes and fees
- External economies such as those of scale and agglomeration.

These factors determine not only the level of production of goods and services, but also the cost thereof, which itself is an important factor of economic growth. Communities and states that offer the optimum opportunities to industries for production of goods and services at a cost *lower* than all other communities and states tend to grow the most and the fastest, other things being equal.

The second group of factors for economic growth consists of local characteristics, or what is generally called the *infrastructure*. Local characteristics include municipal services and amenities such as schools, recreational facilities, police and fire protection, and availability of cultural opportunities. Local and state leadership, especially their commitment to facilitate industry and business growth, is another important component of the infrastructure.

Both groups of factors are equally important for economic growth of a community or a state. However, within each group, the prevailing economic conditions and the nature of industry determine the contribution of each factor to economic growth. Often, environmental and political considerations will limit the optimum use of a factor. For example, a chemical plant may be the optimum use of a given piece of land, although it may not be feasible because of environmental considerations. Similarly, sociopolitical considerations constrain the optimum use of other factors listed in the two groups. Thus, although they are all important factors for economic growth, their importance, relative to each other, changes for different communities and different industries.

ROLE OF VOCATIONAL EDUCATION

Whatever the relative importance of labor as compared with other factors of economic growth, increased labor utilization is very important for communities and states. Increased labor utilization by industry means more job opportunities within the community, which of course, is a primary objective of economic growth. It is the reason most communities and states seek new businesses and industries and at the same time help existing industries to grow. For industries, on the other hand, opportunities to increase the utilization of their labor, relative to other economic factors, generally means increased profitability. And that is the reason they prefer to locate plants where opportunities to increase profitability are readily available.

Education and *skill* are two important attributes that affect the potential use of labor. Schooling, training and experience are the most accepted methods to improve the educational and skill levels of the work force. With the estimated 18,000 secondary and postsecondary institutions providing vocational training to more than 17 million youths and adults, vocational education represents the best potential for the community to train its work force.

Vocational education's role in helping communities to create new jobs, however, is relatively new. The traditional role of vocational education since the passage of the Smith-Hughes Act in 1917 has been to train youths to create a supply of skilled job seekers from which business and industry draw according to their needs. The demand side has been viewed only as a source of information to plan vocational education programs. Thus, the role of vocational education has been reactive as far as the expressed or projected needs of business and industry.

A significant change in the role of vocational education for economic growth occurred in the early 1960s, resulting from the post-war rise in agricultural production. Declining prices of farm products with a concomitant decrease in the agricultural employment further widened the existing income gap between the rich industrial North and the poor and predominantly agricultural South. During the late 1950s some of the Southern states, in order to increase their industrial base, started offering tax rebates and other financial incentives to industries in the North to move to the South. For a while, many industries did move from Northern industrial cities to Southern rural areas. However, by and large, the industries that took advantage of the generous offer were highly labor-intensive industries that also benefitted from the abundantly available cheap labor. A number of textile and apparel industries moved from New York, New Jersey and Pennsylvania to the Carolinas, Georgia and Alabama. It was, perhaps, during this period that the legend of the "Sunbelt" as a potential rival for industrial growth was born.

The Advent of Custom Training

However, soon after the first wave of industrial migrants, Southern states realized that unless they could match the skill level of the work force in the North, attraction of technology-based industries was not possible. Some of them decided to offer special vocational training programs specially tailored to client needs as an added incentive to new industries. The innovative "custom training" programs started in North Carolina and soon spread to most Southern states, and later to many Northern and Western states as well. A recent survey (Bottoms, p. 57) indicated that in 1979 all states offered some type of training assistance to new industries, although only 14 had organized statewide programs with track records of five or more years. In most of the state programs, vocational education plays an important part.

Involvement in special or customized training affords vocational educators a direct stake in the economic growth of their communities and states. By helping the communities, they play a proactive role in job creation and economic development. Vocational educators who have been involved in the economic development efforts of their communities for any length of time find that the investment of their time and resources pays handsome dividends. Not only does this involvement add another dimension to vocational education, but it also helps youth and adults obtain better job opportunities.

Advantages of Economic Development to Vocational Education

The following is a summary of the most important advantages that accrue to vocational education by its involvement in economic development efforts:

1. Given the mission of vocational education to train youth and adults for gainful employment in existing or expected job opportunities, a logical extension of the mission is to help increase the number and quality of job opportunities for vocational students. The latter is especially true in areas where job opportunities are limited due to economic or social reasons.
2. Increasing the total number of jobs helps the placement function of the vocational institutions.
3. Participation in economic development makes vocational institutions more responsive to labor market demands.
4. Since the introduction of new industries in a community generally brings in new technology, participation affords vocational education an opportunity to keep current with the changing technology at the work place.
5. Involvement in economic development is a politically sound effort. It helps to create a constituency for vocational educators among the business community and the economic development agencies, which generally fare well in state and local legislatures.
6. Participation in economic development helps the on-going vocational education programs since the capacity to deliver services for industry can also be used to support existing in-school programs.
7. Coordination and cooperation with other state and local agencies increases with participation, thus building better relations within state and local government and within communities.
8. Participation in economic development efforts creates a better image for vocational education and boosts its prestige in the community.

Types of Participation

The type and level of vocational education's participation vary considerably from state to state and from community to community. Although the basic purpose is the same (that of providing special training services to a new or an expanding industry), every state and community has evolved its own way to deliver the services. Following are two examples of training programs that may be considered typical of vocational education's involvement at a state and a community level. These examples, as well as those quoted later, are based on studies conducted as a part of its Economic Development Project, sponsored by the U.S. Department of Education.)

State Program

The Division of Special Schools for Industry Training in Oklahoma is perhaps one of the best examples in the country of a statewide training service provided by vocational education. The Department of Vocational and Technical Education plays an important role by preparing and offering special training programs that are specific to industry needs and are flexible enough to be tailored to an individual company.

The Department of Vocational and Technical Education (Vo-Tech) maintains a close liaison with the development activities by maintaining two industrial coordinators in the Department of Economic Development. This affords Vo-Tech the opportunity to establish contacts with industries at an early stage of their contemplation to expand their business in Oklahoma. By explaining and demonstrating the range and extent of training services available to industries, the industrial coordinators reinforce the economic development efforts initiated by the Department of Economic Development, state and local chambers of commerce, and other professionals who recruit industries to locate in Oklahoma.

Over the years, Oklahoma has acquired a reputation for delivering training services to industries efficiently and on time. The training service provided by the Special Schools Division is coordinated by a team of professionals who perform the following tasks:

Employer training needs assessment. Assessment includes determining how many persons need to be trained for what kind of jobs, what the training schedule should be, and what resources—equipment, curriculum materials, instructors—are needed to deliver the training.

Training program development. The jobs for which training is required are analyzed to determine the training objectives. Tasks analysis, curriculum development and production of instructional materials are important parts of program development.

Delivery of training. Most of the machines and equipment are acquired from the state equipment pool, and the facilities for training are located at a site convenient to the employer. Recruiting (for pre-employment training), screening applicants and instructor training are some of the activities prior to the delivery of the training program. Monitoring the progress of trainees during the program and evaluation of skill training at the end are some of the subsequent activities.

Post-completion follow-up. The Special Schools Division is required to keep close liaison with the client industry at least six months after delivery of the program. Any problem areas are identified and solutions are found to solve the problems.

Services provided by the Special Schools Division to the industries that decide to expand their operations in Oklahoma are essentially similar to those offered to new industries, except that the expansion programs are often run either at the nearby area vocational school or on the company premises, and sometimes a combination of the two.

Since 1968, Vo-Tech has trained approximately 37,000 persons, out of which 28,000 persons were placed in *new* jobs in new and expanding industries. During that time, the Department serviced 270 industries that located new plants or that expanded their production facilities in Oklahoma.

Local Program: Portland, Oregon

One of the most successful partnerships among a prime sponsor under the Comprehensive Employment and Training Act (CETA), a community college and a foreign manufacturer was born in 1977 in Portland, Oregon. After much negotiating, a memorandum of understanding was drawn up among the Portland Community College (PCC), the City of Portland and Wacker Siltronic. The memo stipulated that Wacker would agree to sign a sole source training agreement with the city and it, in turn, would agree to contract with the community college's vocational education training program.

In the resulting contract, the city agreed to provide the funds for the overall program. The city was to conduct the task analyses needed to identify the skills, knowledge and abilities required of the trainees, as well as to recruit, screen, and assign trainees to the PCC program. The city also assumed the responsibility for covering the program's costs for supplies and materials. The specialized training equipment, crystal slicers, growing equipment and polishing machines were to be provided by Wacker Siltronic.

The contract included a detailed training schedule and was designed to accommodate three waves of trainees and three phases of training. The first phase covered such topics as basic metric measures and the history of silicon wafers. Phase II covered the job training itself in a laboratory setting which enabled the trainees to develop hands-on experience with the actual tools and equipment provided by Wacker. Phase III of the training was then carried out at the new plant itself.

A facility located at the site of an abandoned shopping center in southeast Portland was acquired and remodeled to accommodate the simulated production line. The training equipment was installed by Wacker engineers assigned by the parent company in Germany.

The staff of the training program consisted of a project manager, a curriculum developer, nine instructors who were qualified engineers, nine assistant instructors, two maintenance technicians and one maintenance helper. A unique feature of this program was the agreement between Wacker and PCC that the instructors would ultimately be hired as managers of the trainees for whom they were responsible. Initially, 12 instructors were recruited and immediately assigned to six weeks of observation and curriculum planning in Burghausen, Germany.

Key to Success: Interagency Cooperation

As an example of effective interagency cooperation, the Portland case stands out. First, the leadership and initiative shown by the mayor of Portland was essential. Second, the responsiveness of Portland Community College and its staff to the mayor's requests helped to reassure the Wacker Siltronic management that the City of Portland would deliver on its promise. The ability of the curriculum planning and development staff to work with Wacker engineers in Germany, the willingness of the Wacker management to consider CETA eligible trainees and the responsiveness of the CETA staff to the understandable concerns of Wacker Siltronic for meeting high standards of employee selection—all of these factors coalesced to insure a successful experience. Had the top management of the Wacker plant not been willing to devote both time and energy to working with the city officials throughout the span of the project, the serious problems that erupted along the way could not have been handled as well as they were.

Among some of the questions raised, for example, were who should take responsibility for the supply of materials, who should install the training equipment, and who should pay for the time of the Wacker staff involved in the curriculum development? While each represented a potential barrier at the time of its occurrence, the cooperative and committed stance taken by the key parties helped to insure that such problems were resolved in a timely manner.

Initially, out of a thousand or so CETA eligible trainees screened, 734 were referred for training. They came from all walks of life and included displaced homemakers, minorities and ex-offenders. Of these, 480 were actually able to complete all three phases of the training program and 450 were eventually hired by Wacker Siltronic.

All things considered, the return on the initial investment of approximately $3.5 million of federal, state and local monies was probably substantial. Not only were several hundred new jobs added to Portland's economy, but the opportunities opened up for suppliers, builders and other service companies were impressive as well. For those trainees who were able to move from the ranks of the unemployed to positions with a growing company, the opportunity meant considerably more than just another job.

Job Preservation

As competition for new industries grows among states and communities, those at the receiving end of industrial recruitment efforts find it necessary to hold on to what they have. The concept of job preservation grew in the North, initially to counter the enticements and incentives offered to industries to move to the South. Now, when even Southern industries are being targeted for moves to neighboring states or abroad, job preservation efforts are finding acceptance among most states. Essentially, job preservation involves helping the businesses and industries to analyze and solve their problems so that they may remain competitive and not be tempted to move elsewhere. Since quality labor is one of the most important factors in industries remaining competitive in the marketplace, vocational education can play an important role in job preservation efforts.

Job preservation involves providing financial incentives and special services to existing industry even when they do not expand or create new jobs. A recurring need of existing industries is a good supply of skilled labor, a need met primarily through vocational education institutions, community colleges and other instructional training programs. In most states, vocational education schools try to match their training programs with the current and projected needs of the industries and businesses in their respective areas by inviting employers to be represented on state, local and program advisory committees, by conducting needs surveys and by holding occasional meetings with employer groups.

However, the vocational education system is large and sometimes fails to meet the ad hoc and specific needs of individual employers, especially if the employers are from small industries. Yet, small and medium industries are the ones that need help the most. They often do not have the resources to train their own work force, as do many large industries, and must rely on the local labor pool for recruitment. If that fails, they are forced to curtail production, go out of business or move elsewhere where a larger labor pool is available.

Assisting Small Industries Through An Area School

Some states have initiated programs to serve and assist industries that suffer from a scarcity of skilled workers. The Industry Training Program at the Upper Valley Joint Vocational School in Piqua, Ohio, though simple in design, is quite innovative in its approach to provide training service to small businesses and industries in the area. For a small annual membership fee ($600.00 at this time), companies benefit both from the school's ongoing programs as well as from special training programs designed for their individual needs.

Among the services offered to employers through their participation in the Industry Training Program are the following: vocational counseling with fully certified counselors; career assessment and exploration center; vocational evaluation and testing center; on-site task analysis, curriculum development and planning; vocational instruction for skilled and semi-skilled areas; in-service instruction for management and skilled areas; instruction to upgrade personnel; on-site video taping to facilitate training; apprenticeship training; and technical learning resource material support. The school also runs workshops to develop management skills and other areas of professional development for the benefit of member companies. The services are well received by the 17 participating industries in the Upper Valley region and already have proved useful to employees who can upgrade their skills or learn new ones.

The Business and Industry Liaison Program at Mid State Technical Institute in central Wisconsin and the Small Business Encouragement and Rescue Program at the Westchester Community College in New York are two other examples specially aimed at helping small existing businesses and industries cope with competition from their big brothers. These programs assist small entrepreneurs by increasing their management skills and other required job skills.

A NEW ROLE

The role of vocational education in community economic growth, whether in recruiting new industries, assisting industries to expand or helping small industries to be competitive, is relatively new. It has evolved during the last two decades and has yet to be universally accepted either by the state and local leadership or by vocational educators themselves. However, the economic decline of communities, rising unemployment and mounting competitive pressure from countries such as Japan and West Germany are forcing this country to revitalize our industries and to make our businesses more competitive in the domestic and the world marketplace. Collaborative efforts among state and local development agencies, vocational education and communities have demonstrated that community economic growth can be achieved.

A study of 17 state and local economic development programs is being conducted by the American Vocational Association under a contract with the U.S. Department of Education, Office of Occupational and Adult Education. Following are some of the characteristics common to all 17 programs.

Strong and dedicated leadership is essential to develop effective linkages between vocational education and industry. Not only is it essential to select effective coordinators and other staff, but it is also critical that state leadership make a commitment to developing the linkages. All successful programs enjoy strong support from state and local leaders in vocational education and government.

Flexibility is another essential characteristic of all successful programs. In order to deliver training service to industry, it is not always possible to tailor employer needs to the existing school program structures. The school must be willing to make changes. Without flexibility, it is well nigh impossible to maintain an effective training service.

Mutual respect and trust is important to any relationship. But, it is even more important to linkages between education and industry. Only when industry is convinced that the educational system is willing and capable of delivering training programs suited to their (industry) needs, will they go the extra mile to help the schools with their facilities, equipment and personnel. In some cases, companies even underwrite a part of the cost through direct support or tuition reimbursements. In almost all cases, company personnel are made available to work on school or advisory committees.

Another important factor in a successful linkage is the absence of any strings attached to the training programs. In most programs, even when the program is developed specifically for an employer, the latter is under no obligation to hire all graduates or to pay any predetermined minimum wage. Instead, the program is made as flexible as possible so that it proves a resource rather than a binding contract.

In the ultimate analysis, however, the extent to which vocational education is involved in economic development is largely up to vocational educators themselves. In states, and even in some communities, where public vocational education willingly collaborated and worked closely with the private sector and other agencies, it proved to be a valuable partner. In other states, where vocational education opted to remain uninvolved, it was bypassed, and other agencies and institutions took over the job of customized training. Those states that did take a chance and developed vocational education customized programs are now in the forefront of the movement, which portends to sweep the nation in the 1980s. After all, training *will* occur. Whether vocational education is a part of it is up to us to decide.

REFERENCES

Bottoms, G. *The vocational education enterprise in 1980.* Arlington, Va.: American Vocational Association, 1979. (Position paper)

Bruno, L., & Wright, L.M., Jr. *Rival job creation: A study of CETA linkage with economic development.* Washington, D.C.: U.S. Department of Labor, Employment and Training Administration, 1980.

Ledebur, L.C. Regional economic development and human resource requirements. In P.V. Braden (Ed.), *Human resources and regional economic development.* Washington, D.C.: U.S. Department of Commerce, Economic Development Administration, 1977.

Vaughan, R.J. *State taxation and economic development.* Washington, D.C.: The Council of State Planning Agencies, 1979.

Winnie, R.E. Outcome measures of state economic development programs. In P.V. Braden (Ed.), *Human resources and regional economic development.* Washington, D.C.: U.S. Department of Commerce, Economic Development Administration, 1977.

VOCATIONAL EDUCATION AND REINDUSTRIALIZATION

Rupert N. Evans

WHAT IS VOCATIONAL EDUCATION?

Ever since the beginning of World War I, Congress has spent tax dollars to encourage the states to provide education that helps youth and adults to qualify for new or better jobs. The states pass this subsidy on to secondary and postsecondary schools that offer approved training programs. The emphasis is on the development of the skills, knowledge and attitudes that are needed in productive work that normally requires less than a baccalaureate degree for entry. The only professionals trained under this program are vocational educators, though many vocational graduates eventually go to four-year colleges and become professionals.

No one is required to participate. But almost all high schools and community colleges, in every state and territory, have elected to provide vocational education. In fact, local and state governments have chosen to spend more than $10 of their own tax funds on vocational education for every federal dollar they receive. Obviously, local school officials feel it is good for their communities.

A Matter of Choice

Similarly, the trainees decide whether or not they want vocational education. If they are full-time workers or have left school and are unemployed, they can choose to spend their free hours in many ways other than in vocational classes. In addition to giving up their free time, vocational students at the postsecondary level must pay tuition fees and, unlike the trainees in government training programs, they receive no stipend. If they are full-time high school students, they have a choice of three curricula: vocational, college preparatory or general. The latter "does not necessarily prepare you either for college or for work, but consists of courses required for graduation plus subjects that you like" (Flanagan et. al., 1964, p. 5). It is generally considered to be the least demanding of the three and is the curriculum choice of the majority of students who later drop out of school (Combs & Cooley, 1967). Obviously, both the full-time and part-time trainees who have chosen to participate in vocational education feel that it is good for them.

Similarly, adults support it. When asked about the high school subjects they had taken and which they "found to be most useful in later life," commercial subjects and shop are listed in the top five (along with English,

237

mathematics and extracurricular activities). Those who did not participate wish they had. Typing and other secretarial skills, mathematics and shop are listed as the three subjects which would be of "special help...now" (Gallup, 1978).

Vocational education grew slowly but steadily throughout its first 50 years (though it had a brief, major expansion during World War II when school shops ran 24 hours a day training workers for war production). In the 1960s, it began to expand rapidly to accommodate the post-war baby boom and in the 1970s it expanded again because a higher proportion of youth and adults chose it instead of other educational activities.

Today, according to the National Association of State Directors of Vocational Education (1980) the principle roles of Vocational Education are:

1. Preparing individuals for work, for entry jobs, upgrading, retraining, and cross training.
2. Providing orientation to work.
3. Ensuring equity for individuals and population groups in pre-paration for work (p. 3).

Vocational Education Serves 17 Million Yearly

More than half a million instructors provide vocational education to 12 million youth and 5 million adults each year. About a third of these students receive "occupational" training and two-thirds get work orientation, consumer and homemaking instruction and other "non-occupational" instruction (NIE, 1980, p. VI-4). More than 5,000 high schools and more than 2,000 community colleges and technical institutes each provide a choice of programs in five or more different occupational fields. (NIE, 1980, p. VI-15) Some schools serve a few square miles of a city, but area schools may have dormitories to accommodate students who live hundreds of miles away, or may put shops and laboratories on wheels to take training to all parts of their districts.

More than 150 different occupations are taught, ranging from book-keeping to welding and from agricultural sales to X-ray technician. Classes are scheduled so that they are accessible to full-time and to part-time students. Shops and laboratories simulate conditions on the job as much as possible, and the theory of the occupation is related to its practice. Special efforts are made to assure access to the training wanted and needed by each student.

Placement on jobs or in advanced vocational training programs is the foremost goal. When economic conditions permit, placement may occur before and during training. For example, cooperative education students work half-time and their schooling is related to what they learn on the job. Because vocational education is never required and because it emphasizes placement, it must replace courses for which there is little demand and must seek out training needs that are not being met elsewhere. To aid in this process, advisory committees are used extensively.

HOW EFFECTIVE IS VOCATIONAL EDUCATION?

We know more about the effectiveness of vocational education than about any other type of education because it has been evaluated repeatedly. Dozens of studies agree that its trainees earn more per year, have less unemployment and are better satisfied with their work than similar workers who have not had this training. But the differences are small.

One reason for these disappointing results is that the studies are based on averages. The range of quality in Vocational Education is enormous, so a tally of the average program results does not describe what this type of education is or can do. In some programs nearly all of the graduates earn more than their instructor. In others, the dropout rate is high and the few who graduate are hired only as a last resort. When evaluators look only at averages, these extremes are overlooked. If the poorer programs could be improved or eliminated, naturally the average quality and results would go up also.

Wide Variety in Programs

Why do we have this range? Each community plans its own programs. Some have better planners; some have better cooperation between business, industry and the schools; some spend more money on vocational education; some have far more unfilled jobs and some have more opportunities for cooperative education than others. Conversely, some communities have a higher proportion of minorities and more persons with limited English-speaking ability. Some communities do a great deal for handicapped trainees, while others do almost nothing.

In addition to these variations from one community to another, there are variations by vocational field and by state. Some vocational subjects do not have enough qualified instructors, so less qualified people teach, or programs are closed. Some states insist on closing low quality programs, while others feel that almost any program is better than none. Some states design vocational education to attract employers from other parts of the nation and the world, while others do not.

VOC. ED.'S ROLES IN REINDUSTRIALIZATION

Vocational Education can aid reindustrialization by assisting in the training of three major groups for the work of the future: training young people for work, retraining present employees and retraining those who are re-entering the labor force. Only the first of these has received significant attention since the heyday of the GI Bill.

Training Young People for Work

We will soon face a shortage of young workers. From 1936 to 1961 (with the exception of the World War II years), the number of children born in the United States increased every year. The annual births peaked in 1961 when 4.3 million children were born. This baby boom caused the number of young people of working age to increase steadily from about 1950 to the present. This certainly has been a major factor in problems such as rising youth unemployment and increased crime rates.

For the decade and a half after 1960, the number of births decreased sharply, reaching a low of 3.1 million per year (Department of Commerce, 1980, p. 61). This is 600,000 more births than we had during the depth of the Depression, but as a percentage of the population, it is far lower. As a proportion of the labor force, it is lower still. One effect of this decrease in births is that the number of 20-year-olds (those born in 1961) began to go down in 1981. And the number of young workers will decrease for 15 years. I believe that this will result in a severe shortage of young workers by 1990.

To further complicate the picture, the birthrate has declined much faster for whites and for middle-class families than for the population as a whole. This is almost certain to make it easier for white youth to get jobs. And, because the gap between opportunities for white and minority youth is likely to increase, we can expect envy and added frustration among the latter, particularly if they have had no training.

There are four major possibilities which may invalidate my prediction of a shortage of young workers. One is that the economy could collapse. Another is that we could have a continuing, large flow of immigrants who will be eager to take the jobs normally held by young workers. Certainly we have had a major recent influx of immigrants, legal and illegal. Although it seems likely that there will be pressure to allow both types of immigration to increase, the keys to the actual amount of immigration are likely to be (1) how many acceptable jobs will be available in less developed countries (What, for example, will happen to the oil-fueled economy of Mexico?) and (2) how well unskilled alien workers are able to adapt to the continuing trend toward higher technology in work in this country.

A third reason that fewer young workers may be needed could be that they will be replaced by robots and other computer-controlled devices that will work more efficiently. I would fear the effects of this revolution more if I had not lived through repeated predictions of similar effects which have never materialized. One of my favorite stories is of Tom Watson, the former president of International Business Machines (IBM). He was so remorseful about the mass unemployment which he felt would result from the introduction of IBM's new computers in 1960, that he gave Harvard $10 million to find ways of relieving the misery. Harvard had some difficulty in studying this problem which did not exist. But the federal government had less difficulty in converting the Manpower Development and Training Act (MDTA) of 1962 from its original goal of retraining the predicted thousands of technologically unemployed who did not exist. MDTA became a program for aiding the poor, who certainly did exist.

Women in the Work Force

The fourth possibility is that the number of women in the labor force will continue to increase dramatically. At first glance, this would appear likely.

Certainly the proportion of adult females who are in or are looking for paid work increased from about 32 percent in 1947 to 52.2 percent in 1981 (Department of Labor, 1981, Table A-1). Even though we created about one million new jobs to employ every young worker plus the many women who chose or were forced by economic necessity to seek paid work, it is an oddity that the percentage of adult males seeking employment decreased every year from 1948 to 1981 (from 87 percent to 77 percent), at the same time that the rate for females increased so dramatically (Levitan, 1981).

Continued inflation may, of course, force even more women into employment (along with retirees of both sexes). In some countries, 60 percent of the women work (Levitan, 1981). I do not agree, however, with those extrapolators who think that before long there will be a higher proportion of females than males in the labor force. Indeed, I (and no one else, so far as I know) think that in the United States, as more employed women reach early retirement age and as more conservative groups gain power, the proportion of women seeking employment actually will go down. If you were to press me for figures, I would guess that the peak will occur at about 55 percent, before 1990. If so, this would add to our shortage of youth workers, rather than decrease the problem.

If the economy stays reasonably robust, I believe (for the reasons stated above) that we will not have major increases in immigration and that technology and older women will not take over most of the jobs typically done by new entrants to the labor force. If so, it seems clear that we will have a major shortage of young workers.

What Happens When a Shortage Exists?

Employers have become accustomed to having a large number of young applicants for each good available job. The only jobs that have had shortages of applicants are those requiring specific training or those offering poor working conditions. When many young people apply for jobs, the employer can choose the best, train them and expect that they will be employed long enough to recoup the costs of employment and training. But when there is a shortage of young workers, even the good jobs have few seekers. This means a lower selection ratio and more turnover. Consequently, employers are less willing to invest in training and are likely to begin demanding that government aid them by providing training to current and prospective employees. At the same time, government will push employers to spend more on training.

Germany, which had a severe shortage of young workers during the 1950s and 1960s, turned first to the recruitment of aliens to meet its work force needs. This had a number of unanticipated bad effects, so the country expanded the vocational training of German youth to a point far beyond what we have. Now Germany has a different problem. The "guest workers" had so many children that the nation began to have serious youth unemployment. This led to requiring employers to provide more training slots than there are youth, in order to take young people off the street.

I predict that our shortage of young workers will have similar effects. We have been encouraging substantial immigration (though not as overtly as the Germans did). We have been expanding the quantity of vocational education. The next step will be to improve the quality of vocational education and to match it to the needs of the reindustrializing America. If that does not produce enough training of high quality, government may go even further in dictating to employers what training they must provide and to whom. The emphasis will be on the training of youth, even though the social need for the retraining of adults may be even greater.

Retraining Present Employees

Investment in more efficient procedures, processes and equipment is a basic tenet of reindustrialization. This will necessitate job redesign and the retraining of already-employed workers on a scale that has not been approached since World War II. Whole industries may be abandoned when the subsidies that support them are removed. Their workers will need to be retrained for jobs in growing, efficient industries. It seems certain that there will be continued increases in the demand for skilled workers who can install, adjust and repair the more and more complex equipment that is being used in all forms of work.

Who will do the training? Much of it will be done on the job. But we now know that on-the-job training (OJT) is not very efficient if the flow of trainees is large. When the ratio of trainees to workers gets too high, workers spend too much time instructing trainees, and both the quantity and quality of work suffer. OJT is much more effective, for most of the trouble-shooting, repair and creative jobs, if it follows or is accompanied by instruction in the theory of the work, conducted in a classroom or laboratory. This is the type of training that vocational education can do best.

Reindustrialization poses a problem that is nearly equal to the challenge of conversion from peacetime to wartime industry. We met that challenge successfully during World War II, with vocational education playing a major role in the massive retraining of workers, and we can do it again.

Retraining Those Re-Entering the Labor Force

The largest group of workers who re-enter the labor force are women who have left paid work in order to raise a family. Another significant group of women (and many men) have been forced out of employment by a geographical move to facilitate the career of their spouse. Still others have been forced out by bad health.

It has always been true that the longer one has been away from paid work, the more likely that one will need substantial retraining. But reindustrialization is certain to increase further the amount of retraining needed by re-entrants, because it will cause their jobs to change more rapidly while they are away. Vocational education has made substantial progress in aiding homemakers who are returning to paid work, but much remains to be done, for them and for other re-entrants.

A similar need for retraining occurs as a result of early retirement. Almost a fourth of adult males are not working and not looking for work, and an increasing proportion of them are in their forties and fifties. Some have been forced to retire early, but an increasing percentage have elected to leave work because of the structure of their retirement plans. These plans continually reduce the difference between retirement pay and working pay, so that many workers over age 55 can receive almost as much money in retirement as they do in full-time work.

Once they retire, however, the situation may look less inviting. Inflation may cut their purchasing power. Many of these people wish they knew how to get back to work.

Many retirees need retraining to re-enter work, and, again, the longer they have been retired, the more retraining they need. Some can use their current skills but need to know how to become entrepreneurs. Others need to know how to adapt their skills to work in new settings, perhaps even in volunteer work. Others need to rebuild their self-concepts or need assertiveness training.

As reindustrialization progresses, it will be more difficult for retirees to return to work without retraining. It makes sense to build on their current skills whenever possible. Vocational education can assess these skills and build individualized retraining programs based on each trainee's needs.

WHAT NEEDS TO BE CHANGED?

Just as the economy needs revitalization, so does vocational education. Although it is basically sound, it has numerous deficiencies that must be remedied in order for it to be of maximum service to the nation and to its citizens. There are deficiencies in content, in the types of people served, in equipment and facilities, and in staff:

1. Content (What Is Taught)
    a. Inadequate variety of programs in rural areas.
    b. Too much content taken from the most obsolete half of business and industry instead of from the most up-to-date half
    c. Too much content based on obsolete practices rather than on current and future work
    d. Too little emphasis on developing entrepreneurs
2. Individuals Served (Who Is Taught)
    a. Too little service to adults
    b. Too little emphasis on serving people with special needs, that is, the handicapped, those with limited English, convicts and the poor
    c. Too few programs for the gifted
    d. Restrictions on who can enroll (because classes are offered only during the day or during the early evening, only to full-time students, only to those who enroll in September

243

3. Equipment and Facilities (What Is Used in Teaching)
   a. Considerable amounts of out-of-date equipment
   b. Some obsolete buildings, particularly in large cities
   c. Some buildings in the wrong places
   d. Some buildings used only from 8 a.m. to 4 p.m.
4. Staff (Who Does the Teaching)
   a. Many instructors who are technically obsolete
   b. Some instructors who do not know how to organize, present or evaluate what they teach
   c. Too many administrators who do not understand vocational education
   d. Many counselors who lack knowledge of the work world
   e. Salaries that are too low to attract qualified instructors in some fields
   f. Inadequate programs for training staff and keeping them up-to-date.

WHAT DOES NOT NEED TO BE CHANGED?

Many of the critics of vocational education suggest changes which would not be improvements. Contrary to their recommendations:

We should not remove all vocational education from the secondary school. More than two-thirds of the high school students take one or more vocational education courses. It is true that the more expensive postsecondary vocational programs increase the earnings of graduates more than the high school programs do. But, if there were no vocational education in the high school, adolescents would lose opportunities for career exploration; the drop-out rate would jump, which would decrease the amount of general education, and we could not accommodate the increased demand for post-secondary vocational education.

We should not transfer all vocational education from schools to employers. Most small employers cannot do substantial amounts of training, except through cooperative education. Large employers are effective trainers, but all employers tend to shut down training when they are not expanding. Everyone agrees that the most economical time to do training is during economic recession. If employers will not do it, then who will? Moreover, employers provide little general education to accompany their skill training. Schools, on the other hand, usually insist that vocational education students spend half or more of their time in general education. Finally, employers rarely are interested in providing training for employees who have their own reasons for wanting to change occupations. Schools, on the other hand, should be attuned to the needs and wishes of their clientele.

We should not fund only those programs for which there are immediate job vacancies. This would close all programs during a recession. A far better choice is to fund programs in which trainees are willing to invest their time. It is true that some students will invest in useless training, but students (and their parents) seem to have as good a track record as labor economists in predicting which training will pay off. And, they know far better than anyone else what is interesting to them. The customer is right, at least in the long run.

We should not judge programs as if they would or should enroll students on a quota basis, taking into account sex, race and ethnicity. Obviously, there should never be artificial barriers to enrollment, but choice of occupation should not be legislated.

RELATIONSHIP WITH CETA

The relationship between the Comprehensive Employment and Training Act (CETA) programs and vocational education remain anonymous. During its first 40 years, vocational education professed an almost sole concern for increasing individual productivity. Not until the Vocational Education Amendments of 1968 did it make its widespread attempts to serve the disadvantaged and handicapped. Even today, most of the 25 percent of students who drop out of school before high school graduation do so before they have an opportunity to enroll in vocational education. Most of these dropouts are poor and disadvantaged. But in spite of its failures to serve the dropouts, and in spite of its stated pre-1968 goals to serve only those "who could profit from training," secondary school vocational education has actually served those who were not interested in or were rejected by the college preparatory curriculum. Consequently it has attracted students who tend to be below average in verbal ability and in socioeconomic status.

Similarly, the Manpower Development and Training Act (MDTA) of 1962, the precursor of CETA, began with an interest in productivity. Its stated purpose was the retraining of workers who were unemployed because of technological change. But by the mid-1960s, MDTA was devoted almost entirely to unemployed young adults, particularly to urban minority youth who tended to have verbal ability and socioeconomic status levels similar to the lower half of those served by vocational education.

Vocational education began outside the educational establishment, under a separate federal board and became part of the U.S. Office of Education during the 1930s. Even today, several states have separate state boards for education and for vocational education. Nevertheless, vocational education has provided most of its training through the public secondary and postsecondary schools. CETA, on the other hand, generally has preferred to purchase training rather than to provide it. And, it has tended to choose the training which is provided by employers, community-based organizations (CBOs) and proprietary schools, rather than by the public schols.

At Arm's Length

Until the mid-1970s, CETA and vocational education generally kept an arm's length relationship. For example, CETA carefully avoided serving students of high school age, unless the high school principal specifically released the individual trainee. On the other hand, few public schools were interested in a close relationship with CETA, in part because they were struggling with the highest enrollments in their history.

In recent years, however, things have begun to change. Most public schools are worried about declining enrollments. And Congress encouraged joint planning and earmarked 22 percent of Title IV funds for The Youth Employment and Demonstration Projects Act of 1977 (YEDPA) programs to be conducted by local education agencies. To everyone's surprise, most prime sponsors spent far more than the required minimum on joint activities. Clearly the time has come for more collaboration between CETA and vocational education, not just at the local level, but at the state and national levels as well.

IMPEDIMENTS TO COLLABORATION

At the federal level, vocational education is fragmented within the Department of Education. What is needed is an "education and work" unit that can bring together vocational education, bilingual vocational education, career education, vocational education for special needs students, industrial arts, entrepreneurship education, experience-based education and other related programs. Once this is done, perhaps dialogue with the Department of Labor can be more fruitful.

At the state level, the balance-of-state CETA organization is generally weak. Consequently, CETA service to the rural poor is rarely satisfactory, and communication with the state vocational education establishment leaves much to be desired. Perhaps those states that have strong area and postsecondary vocational and technical programs serving all parts of the state should be allowed to turn to them for operation of the balance-of-state CETA programs.

Needed: Adoption of Common Goals

The greatest barriers to collaboration, however, are related to goals, rather than to organization. The national thrust toward reindustrialization demands an emphasis upon increasing the productivity of all workers. The impending shortage of young workers makes this emphasis even more essential. Vocational education, particularly in the postsecondary schools, knows how to develop productivity. CETA needs to adopt productivity as a goal.

Conversely, CETA has emphasized service to the most disadvantaged workers, while much of vocational education has adopted this goal only reluctantly. The increasing gap between opportunities for young white and young minority workers (based on differential numbers of births) demands that vocational education join CETA in whole-heartedly attacking this problem.

Both CETA and vocational education have just begun to learn how to develop workers who have handicaps. We now have the technology to move almost all handicapped people from institutions and sheltered workshops into competitive employment, but the new techniques need to be put to work. CETA and vocational education are the logical systems to do it.

Vocational Education and Reindustrialization

A little-noticed change in Congressional procedures may be the catalyst to force greater dovetailing between CETA and vocational education. *Reconciliation* requires that the Senate Subcommittee on Education and Employment divide a fixed appropriation among all of its activities. Thus, a dollar allocated to CETA is subtracted effectively from vocational education, and vice versa. This could lead lobbyists for the two groups to attack each other, but it is likely to lead the committee to demand more coordination between the two programs.

WHAT SHOULD BE DONE

At present, about 25 percent of federal vocational education funds must be spent on improvement of vocational programs (staff training, equipment purchases, buildings, research, development and curriculum improvement). Most of the remainder is spent on program maintenance (salaries, supplies), which should be the responsibility of state and local agencies. Federal support for program maintenance should be shifted, over a four-year period, to program improvement. Block grants, if they must be used, should be restricted to vocational education program improvement (rather than program maintenance) activities.

Equipment is very expensive in many vocational fields. For example, it costs a minimum of $200,000 to equip a vocational machine shop. Consequently, many such programs use equipment that came from World War II surplus and is 40 years old. Advanced training must usually be done on the job, but introductory training can be done effectively on equipment five years old. If industry could depreciate fully all equipment that is donated to and used by vocational programs, it would be more likely to buy modern equipment to replace it (thus aiding reindustrialization). Second-hand equipment is not a total answer, of course, but the availability of five-year-old tools would improve the quality of vocational equipment dramatically.

Putting R&D Funds to Best Use

Much research and development (R&D) money has been used to find better ways of collecting data to prove that previous programs of vocational education have been worthwhile. For example, millions of dollars have been spent on follow-up studies that give essentially the same results: programs conducted two or three years ago paid off, but did not pay off heavily. The time has come to concentrate R&D funds on improving present and future programs. We need to know when to use on-the-job training and when to use formal classroom and laboratory instruction. We need to develop specialized equipment for instruction. For example, many of the functions of a million dollar numerically-controlled machine tool could be taught on a specially designed plotter at far lower cost. Many trouble-shooting tasks and complex industrial processes could be simulated on microcomputers if existing programs were adapted for school use. The very modest federal vocational education R&D budget of $10 million should be quadrupled and a substantial portion of these funds expended on the improvement of vocational instruction. Regional R&D centers should be established to aid state program improvement efforts and to supplement the work of the National Center for Research in Vocational Education.

We must develop a system for updating vocational staff members. The more rapidly business and industry change, the more rapidly vocational instructors become obsolete technically. To remedy this, schools hire instructors from business and industry. Often, these instructors have no idea of how to teach their skill or how to evaluate the amount that has been learned. Moreover, many of them bring from the job certain biases which interfere with instruction of minority groups and women. Similar problems exist with vocational counselors, administrators and teacher educators. The identification of vocational staff who need updating, the provision of adequate ways to accomplish this and the development of incentives for staff improvement are major tasks that deserve high priority (Evans, 1980).

Traditionally, the content of vocational education has been based on local surveys. As the mobility of skilled workers has increased, that is no longer adequate. The welding industry is working with vocational educators to develop a curriculum that will train welders to work anywhere. Similar consortia should be encouraged in other businesses and industries.

Allow Professional Training

Vocational education typically has served students who are below average in verbal ability and who come from working-class homes. Some community colleges and technical institutes are developing technical education that challenges students who have high verbal and computational skills. More and more, these programs are enrolling the most capable high school graduates as well as unemployed and underemployed college graduates who need training that is salable. Vocational education law prohibits the training of people for professional work. This restriction should be removed, so long as the training can be accomplished in less than three years of postsecondary training.

Rural residents rarely have access to vocational education in a broad variety of occupations. Their high schools typically offer only agriculture, business and home economics. Community colleges with the largest numbers (and the widest variety) of programs tend to be situated in urban areas and generally do not have dormitories for students. In many states, discrimination exists against students who live outside specified districts. The goal of every state should be to have a system of postsecondary vocational and technical education that is available equally to each of its residents, rather than to give preference to some on the basis of where they live.

In most parts of the country, the declining adolescent population will close many high schools. Fear of losing their jobs causes high school staff to decrease the number of students that they will send to area vocational schools. In turn, this leads to lower enrollments and higher costs per student in area schools. In many states, the area schools are about to collapse, but in others they seem to be thriving. Why? How can we use the area vocational school as the nucleus for a large, comprehensive high school to replace small schools with limited programs and declining enrollments? A major national study of this problem is needed immediately, followed by remedial action.

Refine Evaluation Model

Most evaluations of vocational education are based on the premise that full-time students are in one of three curricula: vocational, general or college preparatory, with little overlap among curricula. Recent research shows clearly that this model is inadequate (Copa & Fosberg, 1980). In fact, many students from other curricula take one or more vocational courses. Part-time students may enroll in a four-hour short course or in a 144-hour course lasting all year. Most data collection systems count each of these as one course. The costs of vocational education should be based on the number of hours spent in it, instead of counting courses, or even worse, labeling a student as being either vocational or non-vocational. And, the amount learned should be judged in terms of competencies and job satisfaction, rather than courses or programs completed.

Linkages to local private industry councils (PICs) should be strengthened rather than placing total reliance on coordination of government efforts. State advisory councils should draw at least half of their members from business, industry and labor.

It has been charged that vocational education has been a major factor in keeping the annual pay of women below that of men, because 13 of 17 "traditionally female occupations" are taught in vocational education (Report, 1980, p. 5). A study of the effects of eliminating female enrollment in these 13 occupations would be illuminating, but what is really needed is a study of the reasons why people choose to receive training in sex stereotyped fields.

The Department of Education (or its successor) should organize an "education and work" unit which would include vocational education, career education, bilingual vocational education, vocational education for the handicapped, entrepreneurship education, experience-based education and other related areas that now are scattered throughout the department. This unit should begin immediate discussions with related groups in the Department of Labor to identify ways in which their programs can complement each other at the federal, state and local levels.

CONCLUSIONS

The recent increase in the size of vocational education has not been accompanied by a uniform increase in quality. In fact, some parts of vocational education have stood still while business and industry have changed markedly, as have the characteristics of the trainees to be served. Substantially improved quality in some parts of vocational education is essential if it is to play a key role in reindustrialization. The goal, of course, should be uniformly high quality.

There are four keys to quality in vocational education: content, trainees, facilities and staff, in other words, what is taught, to whom it is taught, what is used to teach it and who teaches it. These four are dependent on each other, for if one is gravely deficient or is particularly strong, the others are hampered or enhanced. If all four are first rate, there is no problem in preventing dropouts, in placing the graduates in satisfying and meaningful work and in aiding the reindustrialization of our nation.

The quality of vocational education is affected most by what is done at the local level. Local supervisors, instructors and advisory committees affect quality markedly. Some states have proved that they, too, can act in ways that improve quality. The principal efforts of the federal government have been two-fold: to assist the states to maintain existing programs and to ensure that funds have been spent in accordance with the letter of the law. The federal establishment has made small, but significant, contributions toward R&D and staff development. However, for a variety of reasons, it has become less and less involved in improving quality.

This chapter suggests ways in which the federal government can act and can assist the states in the revitalization of vocational education. The principal change suggested is that Congress cease supporting the status quo and move toward encouraging improvement of vocational education programs. Without changes such as those suggested here, the reindustrialization of the nation will be more difficult, more expensive and more time consuming.

REFERENCES

Combs, J., & Colley, W.W. Dropouts: In high school and after school. *American Educational Research Journal,* 1967, *3,* 343-363.

Copa, G., & Forsberg, G.D. *Measuring the employment and further education efforts of secondary vocational education in Minnesota.* Minneapolis, Minn.: R&D Center for Vocational Education, University of Minnesota, 1980.

Evans, N. *Reauthorization and vocational teacher education.* Urbana, Ill.: University of Illinois, Bureau of Educational Research, 1980.

_____. Reauthorization and the redefinition of vocational education. *VocEd—Journal of the American Vocational Association,* January 1980, pp. 30-34.

Flanagan, J., et. al. *The American high school student.* Pittsburgh, Pa.: Project TALENT Office, University of Pittsburgh, 1964.

Gallup, G. The public's attitudes toward the public schools. *Phi Delta Kappan,* September 1978, pp. 33-45.

Levitan, S. Personal communication. Washington, D.C., 1981.

National Association of State Directors of Vocational Education. *Position statement of the National Association of State Directors of Vocational Education.* Indianapolis, Ind.: Author, 1980.

National Institute of Education. *The vocational education study: The interim report.* Vocational Education Study Publication No. 3. Washington, D.C.: U.S. Department of Education, 1980.

Report on Educational Research. November 26, 1980, p. 5.

U.S. Department of Commerce, Bureau of the Census. *Statistical abstracts of the United States.* Washington, D.C.: Government Printing Office, 1980.

U.S. Department of Labor, Bureau of Labor Statistics, *Employment situation.* Washington, D.C.: Author, March 1980.

This article was originally prepared for the National Center for Research in Vocational Education. A reprint may be obtained for $2.20 from the Publications Office, The National Center for Research in Vocational Education, The Ohio State University, 1960 Kenny Road, Columbus, Ohio 43210.

VOCATIONAL EDUCATION IN THE ECONOMIC DEVELOPMENT ENTERPRISE: POLICY OPTIONS

Leonard A. Lecht

FORCES MAKING FOR CHANGE

Planning in vocational education is often identified with the information provided in the annual plans submitted by education agencies to obtain funding from federal, state and local government sources. More fundamentally, planning involves looking ahead and anticipating changes in the larger society in the next five or 10 years. These changes can influence course offerings, enrollments, financial support and careers for the students in the vocational programs.

Three major developments in the coming decade can be expected to assume a larger role as agents of change in vocational education. They are:
1. Changes in the demographic profile and in retirement practices;
2. Regional shifts in economic activity and employment;
3. Renewal of the industrial sector as a key ingredient in the economy's growth.

Each of these developments can be expected to involve adaptation to change by state and local vocational education agencies. More specifically, they imply that more older persons and fewer 16-to-21-year-olds will be enrolled in vocational programs. Vocational education will be more closely linked with state and local economic development programs. The programs offered will assign a substantially greater emphasis to training persons to operate, maintain and repair the more complex new technology and products that will characterize the economy in the 1980s. Vocational education agencies frequently will be well suited to respond to these changes because of their past involvement in both employability development and in adult, technical and continuing education.

A consideration of these developments in greater detail can indicate the problems and opportunities they will create for the larger society and the implications for planning in vocational education.

CHANGES IN DEMOGRAPHY AND RETIREMENT

Analyses of changes in the labor force in the 1970s have focused on the influx of women and 16-to-24 year-olds as the major influences on the shifts in the makeup and growth rate of the labor force. Considerably less attention has been given to a third major development—the withdrawal of older men from the labor force to retire at earlier and earlier ages. Continuing inflation, greater longevity and changes in public policy and social attitudes can be expected to reverse the trend to early retirement in the 1980s. Older persons will become a considerably more significant element in the market for vocational programs if their needs and the need for sustaining enrollments in vocational education receive a priority in the coming decade.

A multiplicity of incentives has been responsible for the sharp decline over the past generation in the percentage of men in their 60s, and even mid-50s who remain in the labor force. The decline shows up in the proportion of the men in the 65-and-over group who remain employed or who look for work and, more recently, in a similar decline among 60-to-64-year-olds (see Table 1).

Table 1
PERCENTAGE OF MEN 60 AND OVER
IN THE LABOR FORCE, 1947 to 1978

| Year | Percent in Labor Force | |
	65 & over	60 to 64
1947	48.0	—
1950	46.0	79.5
1960	33.0	78.0
1970	27.0	75.0
1978	20.5	62.0

Source: Derived from *Employment and Training Report of the President,* 1979, p. 236; President's Commission on Pension Policy, *Variety of Retirement Ages,* 1980, p. 7.

Shortly after World War II, close to half of all men in the 65 and older group were in the work place. By 1978, only one-fifth of the men in this age group were still employed or looking for work. The striking recent change has been the drop in participation by men in the 60-to-64-age group. This shift has been facilitated by the 1961 Amendments to the Social Security Act permitting retirement at age 62 with only modest reductions in benefits.

Support for Early Retirement
The propensity for men to retire at earlier ages has received widespread support from business and labor. Employers have come to regard retire-

ment, and often early retirement, as an important aid in hiring and promoting younger persons. These younger persons were assumed to be more productive and to possess more up-to-date skills than the older persons they replaced. Unions have responded to technological and other changes threatening their members' jobs with demands for generous and largely employer-financed pensions for their older members, coupled with work guarantees for their younger ones. Older persons, it was taken for granted, would prefer to retire if they were assured an adequate retirement income. Since all the parties concerned were assumed to gain by retirement, the benefits provided have gone through successive liberalizations. The age at which persons could retire with minimal losses in benefits has been shifted downward by law, collective bargaining and company policy.

A tendency as clear-cut as the recent trend for men to retire at or before age 65 would appear to be so firmly established that the prospects for its reversal in the near future might be regarded as remote. Yet continuing inflation, sharply rising retirement benefits costs, changes in the demographic profile and the preferences of older people are facilitating a shift in public policy and in personal decisions to retire. The shift is away from encouraging older employees to retire and toward encouraging them to remain at work for more years. The recent amendments to the Age Discrimination Act, outlawing mandatory retirements for most employees before age 70, symbolizes these changes.

Pensions and Inflation

For the Social Security system and other federally-funded retirement systems, inflation primarily affects program costs because it raises wage levels and also because the monthly benefit payments are increased at least once a year by the same percentage as the increases in the Consumer Price Index. The benefits in private pension systems and in most state and local government systems for public employees such as teachers are seldom adjusted, or "indexed," to keep pace with changes in the cost of living.

Inflation figures in these systems primarily because it increases the wage level on which the benefit payments are based. It also erodes the purchasing power of older persons after they have retired.

For the Social Security System, each percentage point increase in the Consumer Price Index has been estimated by the U.S. Congress to add $1.1 billion to the outlays for the largest component of the system, the Old Age and Survivors insurance benefits (U.S. Congress, 1979). The role of inflation in diminishing the purchasing power of a pension not indexed to changes in the cost of living can be illustrated by a projection of the purchasing power through 1995 of a $1,000-a-month pension granted in 1980 (see Table 2). The projection shows the losses in purchasing power, assuming alternatively a 10 percent and a 5 percent average annual increase in the Consumer Price Index.

Table 2
PURCHASING POWER OF A $1,000 MONTHLY PENSION
ASSUMING ALTERNATIVE RATES OF INCREASE
IN THE CONSUMER PRICE INDEX, 1980-1995

Year	Purchasing Power in 1980 Dollars	
	10% Annual Price Increase	5% Annual Price Increase
1980	$1,000	$1,000
1985	620	780
1990	390	610
1995	240	480

Source: *Social Security Bulletin,* November 1978, p. 1.

With inflation, as measured by the Consumer Price Index, averaging 10 percent a year, a pension that was not indexed would have lost five-eights of its purchasing power by the end of the fifth year. At the end of 15 years, the loss would be slightly greater than three-fourths. The assumed 10 percent inflation rate is something less than the comparable rate of inflation, say to 5 percent a year. At such a rate, slightly more than half of the original purchasing power represented by the pension would have been lost by the fifteenth year.

Private pension plans now cover approximately half the labor force and state and local government plans several million more. These pension systems, often coupled with Social Security, have come to enable many middle-class older persons and blue-collar workers to retire in modest comfort. Inflation will frequently induce employees depending on these pensions to postpone their retirement in the hope of maintaining their income and building up a larger pension reserve for when they do retire.

For the federal government, outlays for retirement systems and other income supports for older persons amounted to $170 billion in the 1979 fiscal year—representing more than a third, 34.5 percent, of the federal government's expenditures in that year (Lecht, 1981). Efforts to restrain the growth in the federal government's budget in the 1980s can be expected to slow down the growth in these massive outlays by encouraging older persons to remain in the labor force for a longer period.

Labor Force Fluctuations
Changes in the age make-up of the population in the next decade will supplement the effects of inflation in increasing the number of older persons

256

in the labor force. Gains in life expectancy, formerly concentrated in younger age groups, have come to characterize older persons as well. The improvements in the treatment of heart disease in the past 20 years represent an instance. At the other end of the age spectrum, declining birthrates since the mid-1960s will sharply reduce the size of the 16-to-24-year-old group in the population and in the labor force in the next 10 years (see Table 3).

By 1990, the Census Bureau's (intermediate) projections anticipate that there will be five million more persons who will be 65 and over. There will be some six million fewer people in the 16-to-24-age group. The bulk of the population and labor force increase will take place in the 25-to-44-year-olds, the "baby boom" generation of the two decades following the end of World War II.

Table 3
PROJECTED POPULATION GROWTH, 16-to-24-Year-Olds and Persons 65 and Over, 1980 to 1990

Age Group	Estimated Population (in millions)		Percent Change 1980 to 1990
	1980	1990	
16 to 19	16.7	13.5	−19.0
20 to 24	20.9	18.0	−14.0
65 & over	24.9	29.8	+19.5

Source: *Employment and Training Report of the President,* 1979, p. 353. The projections represent Census Bureau intermediate fertility estimates.

Labor force growth in the 1980s will undergo a marked slowdown as fewer young people come to be added to the work force. Over three-fifths of the growth that does take place is expected to be made up of women.

In many of the less highly skilled positions—the bulk of the jobs held by older or younger people—the pressures to retire will diminish as many fewer young people recently out of school are added to the labor force. For persons past 65 who continue working, important issues will remain to be resolved. These include, among others, the problem of fringe benefit cost to employers, the higher wage rates due to seniority for many older employees and the frequent needs for further education and training to upgrade obsolete skills or to acquire new ones. Other problems will arise because older workers often prefer to work on a less than full-time basis and on a more flexible arrangement than the 40-hour week or 52-week year.

The consideration of economic factors stresses the role of rising pensions costs, inflation and demographic changes as the strategic influences that will make for long-term changes in labor force participation by older persons. The preferences of older people who have retired or who are in the age group approaching retirement will also influence the decisions to retire or to continue working. The Harris Survey for 1979, for example, reports that:

1. 46 percent of those already retired would prefer to be working;
2. 48 percent of the persons surveyed in the 50-to-65-age group wished to continue working after age 65.

Close to half of the persons in the age group approaching retirement or who had already retired would prefer to be working. More essentially, the evidence from the Harris surveys and related studies shows that older persons seek greater freedom of choice in selecting among the options to continue working or to retire, to retire or to return to school, to work full-time or part-time, to earn income from work or to participate as a volunteer.

Enrollment Shifts

The changes that will influence population growth in the 1980s will frequently make it more difficult for educational institutions, including vocational institutions, to maintain enrollment. The decline in the population of young persons has become apparent to high school and postsecondary school educators as enrollments and requirements for teachers and facilities have tapered off. In the absence of a far-reaching shift in the percentage of the traditional school age population enrolling in vocational programs, demographic developments among the younger age groups indicate a prospect for serious losses in enrollments in the 1980s. The impact of the population decline in these age groups would be offset, and important economic and human needs served, if the vocational education system were to undertake changes that would increase its appeal to new audiences. Older people in their 50s and beyond make up an audience for vocational programs and one that can realistically be expected to grow over the next 10 years.

There has been growth in the educational programs for older persons. But older persons remain underrepresented in educational programs including adult and vocational education. For instance, only 7 percent of the persons in fiscal year 1979 who were enrolled in courses receiving support through the adult education state grant programs were 55 or older. This represented a decline from 12 percent in the 1966 fiscal year. The largest single group of enrollees in these programs in 1979 were 16-to-24-year olds. They made up over two-fifths, 41 percent, of the enrollees (National Advisory Council on Adult Education, 1980).

The limited information available shows that older persons make up an important potential audience for vocationally oriented programs. For example, a recent survey of "would-be learners" in the 55-to-60-age group reported that vocational subjects were the leading preference among choices of study, as shown in Table 4.

"Would-Be Learners"

Vocational subjects were listed as a first choice almost as frequently as the next two leading candidates added together, hobbies and recreation, and general education. The would-be learners group includes both those who primarily regard the programs as preparation for a second career or an opportunity to upgrade obsolescent skills, and those who were seeking to acquire a useful repair skill such as auto mechanics, or a hobby such as woodworking.

Table 4
DISTRIBUTION OF "WOULD-BE LEARNERS"
PREFERRED CURRICULAR CHOICES, 55-to-60 Age Group

First Choice	Percent Indicating Choice
Vocational Subjects	30
Hobbies, Recreation	17
General Education	16
Home and Family	13
Personal Development	8
Religion	7
Other	9
Total	100

In practice, the preferences of the would-be learners are only partially reflected in the enrollments of older persons in educational courses, and the largest enrollments recently have been in subjects related to hobbies and recreation. The vocational programs that would attract the would-be learners would have a different orientation from the current programs. They would build on work and interpersonal skills that are already present and that have been in use in the past.

Persons in their 50s and older typically have less interest than young persons in formal courses or degrees. They require a different kind of guidance and placement assistance than a young person seeking to gain entry to the world of work. Older persons often have work histories in declining industries or occupations, or their work skills have become obsolete because of technological change. Their opportunities for continued employment may depend on modifying or expanding existing skills to make them useful in different job contexts. Former typists, for instance, can be taught to qualify as word processors. A soon-to-be retired production foreman in the footwear or ladies garment industry could build on his or her managerial experience and acquire the skills needed in an expanding field, say in supervising operations in a hospital laundry.

The vocational education system is strategically situated to make the shift to serving nontraditional groups of students such as older persons or homemakers who wish to return to the labor market. The extent to which the potential for attracting these students is realized in the 1980s will depend on the steps taken by educational institutions to adapt their programs to the interests of older students with different needs and perspectives from the younger students now being served by the vocational programs.

REGIONAL SHIFTS

Regional shifts in employment and economic activity have made for slow growth in job openings in the Northeast and Middle West and for rapid growth in the South and Far West. Slow growth, and sometimes decline, has been especially characteristic of the older manufacturing centers as in Michigan and Ohio. Vocational education systems can contribute to economic development in both the rapid and the more slowly growing regions.

In the rapidly growing areas, local vocational education agencies can help to maintain the momentum of growth by increasing the supply of trained personnel needed for expansion by firms already in the area or to attract new firms. In the more slowly growing areas, vocational programs can contribute to development by providing trained workers to relieve the bottlenecks of specialized work forces that often cause employers to relocate. They can also provide trained replacements for attrition losses in industries in the areas that are not expanding.

Manufacturing Areas: Low-Growth Rates

The regions with the high concentrations in manufacturing have been characterized by below-average employment growth in the past 10 or 15 years. The regions with the more rapid increases in employment have been the areas in which the concentration in manufacturing, up to now, has been relatively less. This relationship can be seen by comparing the percentage of the economy-wide value added by manufacturing in different regions in 1976 with the percent change in employment from 1968 to 1978 (see Table 5).

Table 5
PERCENTAGE OF TOTAL VALUE ADDED BY MANUFACTURING AND EMPLOYMENT GROWTH BY REGION

Region	Percent of Total Value Added by Manufacturing in 1976	Percent Increase in Employment, 1968 to 1978
All regions	100.0	24.3
New England	6.2	16.4
Middle Atlantic	17.8	8.7
East North Central	27.5	15.4
West North Central	7.0	27.4
Mountain	2.3	57.9
Pacific	11.7	34.5
East South Central	6.1	23.8
West South Central	8.6	40.2
South Atlantic	12.8	31.7

Source: *Monthly Labor Review,* March 1980, p. 14; *Statistical Abstract,* 1978, p. 800.

The East-North Central and Middle-Atlantic states were responsible for close to half, 45 percent, of the economy-wide value added by manufacturing in 1976. In both areas, the percentage increases in employment during the 1968 to 1978 period were at least a third less than the national increase. The areas with the large percentage increases in employment, the Mountain and West-South Central states, were responsible for about a tenth of the total value added by manufacturing in 1976. This pattern reflects the decline in employment in the old manufacturing centers rather than a reluctance in the more rapidly growing areas to increase the importance of manufacturing in their local economies. Accordingly, there has been a steady decline in manufacturing in the Northeastern and North Central regions. At the same time, there has been a substantial increase in the role of manufacturing industries as sources of employment in the South and West. These shifts help explain the lack of openings in the traditional semi-skilled blue-collar jobs in manufacturing that had provided entry-level positions for many young people in the Northeastern and North Central states in the past.

Regional Migration

The regional patterns of employment and economic growth have become reflected in a similar pattern of regional migration. The Northeastern and North Central states have been the losers in this migration while the South and West have been the gainers (see Table 6).

Table 6
PERSONS MOVING TO AND FROM
EACH MAJOR REGION, 1973 to 1976

Major Region	Migrants (in 000)		Outmigration as a Percentage of Inmigration
	into region	out of region	
Northeast	1,058	1,829	173.0
North Central	1,935	2,400	124.0
South	3,254	2,407	74.0
West	2,106	1,718	81.5

Source: *Monthly Labor Review,* March 1981, p. 15.

While some persons have moved for non-economic reasons, such as the desire for a change of climate, the primary reasons have concerned employment and economic opportunities. The regional migrants, on an average, have been better educated and younger than the non-migrants. The highest rate of interstate migration took place at age 23. This tendency of young and better educated persons to migrate to the South and West adds to the factors facilitating the development of high technology manufacturing industries in these areas.

The regional shifts have been accompanied by corresponding changes in economic activity and employment in the larger cities within the different regions. Losses of population, high unemployment rates and job losses in the industrial base have been characteristic of the larger cities of the Northeast and Middle West in a belt extending from Boston to St. Louis. Correspondingly, there have been large gains in population and manufacturing jobs in the large cities of the South and West such as Phoenix and Houston. These patterns of central-city decline and growth have been partially associated with the regional shifts. They also stem from the movement of population and economic activity to the suburbs. The overall effect of both sets of changes has been to increase the older central cities' concentrations of unemployed and disadvantaged persons. These persons have limited job opportunities in the manufacturing industries that would have employed many of them in an earlier period (see Table 7).

Table 7
POPULATION CHANGE AND CHANGE IN
MANUFACTURING EMPLOYMENT
GROWING AND DECLINING CITIES, 1972 TO 1977

City	Region	Population Change 1970 to 1980 (in 000)	Change in Manufac- turing Employment 1972 to 1977
Growing Cities			
Dallas	South	+52	+5,500
Honolulu	West	+131	000
Houston	South	+273	+39,400
Los Angeles	West	+138	+35,500
Phoenix	West	+192	+6,000
San Antonio	South	+75	+3,900
San Diego	West	+173	+8,200
Declining Cities			
Baltimore	South	−123	−17,900
Boston	Northeast	−79	−8,100
Buffalo	Northeast	−106	−6,800
Chicago	North Central	−400	−64,600
Cincinnati	North Central	−70	−8,800
Cleveland	North Central	−178	−10,400
Detroit	North Central	−322	−27,100
Milwaukee	North Central	−84	−14,900
Minneapolis	North Central	−64	−5,900
New York City	Northeast	−880	−147,800
Philadelphia	Northeast	−270	−45,100
Pittsburgh	Northeast	−96	−7,000
St. Louis	North Central	−174	−3,600

Source: Kamer, Pearl, *Municipal Finance: How Deep the Crisis,* Metropolitan Economic Association, 1981 (mimeo).

All of the growing cities are in the South and West. Honolulu is included in the Bureau of the Census' West region, although it is outside the continental United States. All of the declining cities, except Baltimore, are in the Northeastern or North Central regions. Baltimore, of course, is a border city and its economic make-up more closely resembles the old manufacturing and port cities of the Northeast than southern cities such as Atlanta or Houston.

Though part of the population gain of the growing cities has come about because of the annexation of surrounding suburbs, the increases primarily represent growth for reasons other than an expansion of the city's boundaries to include more land and people.

National Significance

Many important national issues are involved in the regional shifts and in the growth and decline of the large cities within the different regions. The older regions can expect a loss of political influence as population losses lead to a reapportionment of congressional seats. The newer regions will gain political weight for the same reason. Labor unions will often face difficult problems as employment grows slowly or declines in the older regions and industries that had provided their membership base. In areas where unions have historically been weak, employment will be growing rapidly.

National policy increasingly becomes viewed from the perspective of the anticipated impact for the fortunes of different regions. For instance, plants recommended in the budget messages of the recent administration can be expected to hasten the decision of some firms to move from the Northeast to the South by providing tax write-offs that make the moves less costly than they would otherwise be. National policy for dealing with unemployment is faced with two alternatives. One must consider whether to encourage the movement of people to where the growth in jobs is taking place, or whether to undertake measures that would increase the jobs available in the Northeastern and North Central states with high unemployment rates.

Effect on Vocational Education

The regional and urban shifts will present problems and opportunities for local vocational education agencies. In rapidly growing areas such as Phoenix or San Diego, any decline in enrollments because of falling birthrates in the past 15 years will be at least partially offset by the effects of rapid population growth in increasing the number of young people in their areas. In the older cities, the losses of enrollments because of the decline in birthrates has been augmented by the movement of many families, especially young families, to the suburbs or to the more rapidly growing regions.

The vocational education systems in both the slow and rapidly growing regions can enhance their prospects for growth if they become active participants in state and local economic development efforts. These include efforts by government agencies, local chambers of commerce and similar organizations.

One of the attractions emphasized by many development agencies in seeking to attract new firms to their areas has been the availability of a labor supply possessing the skills required by the new firms. Often the skills include making use of the new technology organized around computers, microprocessors and similar applications of automation to industry. Development programs in other areas will focus on advanced technologies to obtain energy, usually oil or natural gas, from sources that were not economically feasible when oil prices were lower. Instances include extracting oil from shale rock or shipping coal by pipeline in the form of a slurry.

Economic growth in energy resource regions will lead to an expansion in business and consumer service industries which, in turn, will require many employees who are trained in technical and business skills. Vocational education agencies in the high-growth areas can provide the trained personnel to operate the more complex technologies, or to provide the business and consumer services that usually accompany growth.

Growth in Service

In the more slowly growing areas, local economic development agencies will seek to strengthen the healthy economic cores these areas typically possess. The recent growth in business services, international finance or tourism in New York City illustrates this type of development. Shortages of trained and educated clerical, administrative and technical workers have been one of the factors encouraging large firms to move their headquarters away from large central cities. Growth in finance or tourism in these cities has created many jobs in data processing, and for administrative employees, travel and recreation specialists, word processing operators and those who repair business machines. Revival in financial, legal and other business services has also meant revival in related goods-producing industries employing skilled workers such as printing and publishing or construction. In the past, many of the more desirable jobs in these fields were held by commuters because center-city residents lacked the necessary skills. Vocational education agencies in the cities can train many persons who would otherwise be bypassed by growth in the central cities.

In both high and low-growth areas, vocational education programs will continue to serve disadvantaged groups by providing them with the employability skills needed for more specialized training or to obtain and hold an entry-level job. The unemployment rate for blacks and other non-whites, for example, has been approximately double the white rate in both high and low growth areas. In Houston and Dallas, to cite two instances, the unemployment rates for whites in 1979 were in the 2.9 to 3.6 percent range. Unemployment rates for non-whites in the two cities were in the 6.4 to 6.9 percent range (U.S. Department of Labor, 1980).

Added Dimensions for Planning

Vocational education agencies have historically concentrated on the local area when planning career opportunities and personnel needs. The local labor market has frequently been identified with the political jurisdiction served by the educational system, usually a city. This kind of planning assumes that the graduates will very largely obtain employment in the local political unit. It also assume that schools have a special obligation to serve the local area that provides the bulk of their funds. This approach has lost a good part of its validity in the recent past and it is likely to lose more in the coming decade. The local labor market has come to extend far beyond the political city's borders as employers and jobs have moved to the suburbs or further away within the region. In many fields, especially more specialized fields requiring postsecondary education, the relevant labor market has become a regional or a national market. Planners in vocational education can serve students, employers and the nation more effectively by considering regional and national, as well as local, career opportunities in developing their programs.

STRENGTHENING THE INDUSTRIAL ECONOMY

A combination of high inflation rates, high unemployment rates and slow productivity growth have characterized the American economy in the past five years. Considerations growing out of the "stagflation" have become an important influence in changes in national policy and, more specifically, in economic policies intended to revive the economy's industrial base. These developments will have many implications for planning in vocational education in the 1980s. They will increase career opportunities in technical and service fields and in new growth industries, while reducing opportunities for semi-skilled factory operatives and changing the job content in many existing fields.

The American economy underwent major structural changes in the 1970s. These changes will continue, and probably accelerate, in the 1980s. Some segments, primarily the energy and high technology industries, have been expanding rapidly. The industries that have been growing slowly or declining have included many of the old manufacturing industries in which the United States was the world leader until recently. They include such important industries as automobiles, steel, rubber, consumer electronics and selected non-manufacturing industries such as the railroads.

Losses to foreign competitors such as the Japanese or the West Germans have highlighted the problem of the old manufacturing industries. Japan, for instance, has become the world leader in the number of automobiles produced and in the production and utilization of industrial robots. While productivity levels per hour worked have been higher in the United States, productivity *growth* has frequently been higher among its competitors. Continuation of the productivity growth differentials for another five or 10 years would mean that productivity levels, say output per hour worked, would reach or exceed the levels in comparable American industries. The problem of slow productivity growth in the industrial economy in the United States and the more rapid growth in other nations is summarized in Table 8.

Table 8
ANNUAL AVERAGE PERCENT CHANGE IN OUTPUT PER HOUR MANUFACTURING INDUSTRIES, 1970 TO 1979

Country	Annual Percent Change	
	1973 to 1979	1978 to 1979
United States	1.4	0.8
France	4.8	4.7
West Germany	5.3	5.2
Japan	6.9	8.1

Source: *Monthly Labor Review,* December 1980, p. 33.

Rising Labor Costs

Slow productivity growth accompanied by substantial increases in wage rates and fringe benefits have become translated into high and rising labor costs in many manufacturing industries. This development has encouraged a shift in manufacturing from the United States to other nations, including many newly industrializing countries. Multinational corporations have facilitated the development of manufacturing "export platforms" in places such as Hong Kong, Mexico, South Korea or Taiwan. Electronics manufacturers in the United States, for example, frequently have components assembled in Mexico, Malaysia, Taiwan or Singapore.

Quality control considerations have oftentimes been a factor in loss of markets to foreign competitors. Japanese exports of semiconductors to the United States rose from $20 million in 1973 to over $250 million in 1979. One reason for the rapid growth was that the rejection rates for the Japanese produced units imported into the United States were one-half or less the comparable rates of the domestically produced equivalents (U.S. Congress, 1980).

All of these developments have been accentuated directly or indirectly by the steep increases in energy prices since 1973. Escalating energy prices have made much of the industrial plant and equipment obsolete. This is especially so in older industries, because use of the plant and equipment required large quantities of energy.

The Response: Restructure

The response by affected U.S. industry to foreign competition, slow productivity growth, rising labor costs and high energy costs has been to engage in large-scale capital outlays to restructure the industrial plant. The capital outlays are intended to increase productivity and, often, to produce products that require less energy for their use. General Motors, for example, anticipates spending some $40 billion in the coming decade to build new plants and re-equip existing plants. Such efforts would help to reduce costs and to produce a new generation of smaller and more fuel efficient motor vehicles *(Wall Street Journal,* 1981).

These massive capital outlays will frequently introduce a more complex technology involving the use of automated and computerized processes in manufacturing. Industrial robots provide a good illustration of the new technology (Ayers, 1980).

The Institute of Robotics estimates that some 3,200 robots were in industrial use in the United States in 1980. They were used mainly for painting and welding automobile bodies or in foundry-type operations. General Motors plans to add 2,000 robots to its current 300 machines by 1983 and as many as 14,000 by 1990 *(Business Week,* 1981, p. 98). The Institute of Robotics foresees the possibility that robots will become a $2 billion a year industry by 1990 *(Wall Street Journal,* 1980).

The long-term prospect for robots points to their use as part of advanced computerized systems that both design equipment and direct production. The robots that will figure in these computerized automated design and manufacturing systems will be programmable and will have the capacity to sense and react to their environment as well as to perform repetitive operations.

Robots represent one important example of the rapidly expanding new high-technology organized around the use of microprocessors and computers. Use of this technology has mushroomed as computer costs have declined. For instance, the cost of storing one unit of a bit of information in a semiconductor memory fell by 98 percent in the past 10 years *(Business Week,* 1981, p. 96). Much of the capital outlays in restructuring the nation's manufacturing plant will make use of "smart" machines involving the new microprocessor technology. These applications of scientific knowledge drawn from physics and chemistry are likely to be joined in the next two decades with far-reaching applications of biological research in genetic engineering.

Productivity Increases

The incentives to make use of advanced computerized technology such as robots in the 1980s will stem from the quality control, as well as the increases in productivity the new technology makes possible. For example, in painting automobile bodies in the past, according to a General Motors spokesperson, only about 30 percent of the paint remained on the car. The rest was lost in the powerful exhaust systems that protect workers from paint fumes or in some other way. By programming robot sprayers, it has become possible for General Motors to get more than 50 percent of the paint on the cars *(Wall Street Journal,* 1981). Aside from their technical advantages, the robots cannot join unions, go out on strike, take coffee breaks, become alienated from work or require costly environmental, health and safety protections to reduce hazards in the workplace.

The new technology will continue and probably accelerate the slow growth or declines in employment for semi-skilled workers in manufacturing industries. This tendency is illustrated by the experience in the automobile industry since the end of World War II. In 1948, some 713,000 auto workers in the United States and Canada produced 5.96 million automobiles, trucks and buses. In 1978, 839,000 auto workers produced nearly 14.26 million motor vehicles (United Auto Workers memo, 1980). Seventeen motor vehicles were produced per automobile worker in 1978, as compared with a little more than eight vehicles in 1948. Many developments similar to those in the automobile industry have led to considerably slower growth in the past generation for production workers in manufacturing than for total non-agricultural employment (see Table 9).

Table 9
TOTAL NON-AGRICULTURAL EMPLOYMENT AND EMPLOYMENT FOR PRODUCTION WORKERS IN MANUFACTURING, 1948 TO 1979

Year	Total Agricultural Employment (in millions)(Index 1948=100)		Employment for Production Workers in Manufacturing (in millions)(Index 1948=100)	
1948	44.9	100.0	12.9	100.0
1960	54.2	120.7	12.6	97.5
1970	70.9	157.9	14.0	108.8
1979	89.5	199.4	15.0	116.3

Source: *Employment and Training Report of the President,* 1979, pp. 319, 320; *Employment and Earnings,* January 1980, pp. 204-205. The figures listed refer to payroll employment.

Absorbing Workers into Employment

Total non-agricultural employment nearly doubled in the generation after World War II. Jobs for production workers in manufacturing increased by about a sixth. More recently, during the 1970s the overall non-agricultural employment grew by 18.5 million. The comparable increase for production workers in manufacturing was one million. The absence of more substantial job growth in manufacturing in the past decade has made it difficult for the economy to absorb into employment the larger number of women entering the labor force or the generation born in the late 1950s or early 1960s. The significance of the greater capital outlays for a more complex technology in the 1980s is that it is intended to bring about a renewal of the industrial economy without a comparable increase, and in many cases with a decrease in requirements for semi-skilled and unskilled blue-collar labor.

The displacement created by the computerized technology that will be introduced in manufacturing industries in the 1980s will be concentrated in one occupational group—semi-skilled operatives. Over three-fourths, 77 percent of the 11 million persons employed as operatives in 1979, excluding operators of transportation equipment, were at work in manufacturing industries. The new capital investments will create many jobs, but they will be concentrated in professional, technical and skilled areas in designing and producing the equipment, or in operating, maintaining and repairing it. Few of these positions could be filled, say by a displaced automobile worker, without considerable additional training.

The Service Sector

Although concern with the economy has focused on renewing the industrial base, the bulk of the job growth in the 1980s is expected to take place in service industries. In addition, there is a rapidly growing and hidden service sector in manufacturing industries made up of persons who provide data processing, financial, legal, public relations and advertising and other business services that would otherwise be purchased from firms in service industries. Many service firms will be introducing more extensive use of the microprocessor technology and related advances. However, growth in service industries is expected to be sufficiently rapid to more than offset the displacement effects of the new technology. These patterns of job growth are illustrated by the Bureau of Labor Statistics' projections of employment growth by industry between 1977 and 1990 (see Table 10).

The Bureau of Labor Statistics' projections look ahead to a future in which employment in manufacturing grows more slowly than total employment. The growth in manufacturing represents the combined effects of slow growth in the older manufacturing industries and more rapid growth in the new high-technology industries. Three-fifths of the overall increase is expected to take place in two economic sectors, services and trade. Changes unanticipated in the projections, such as rapid development of new energy sources, could make for larger than expected increases in employment in energy industries and in the manufacturing industries that are heavy users of energy. But the predominant theme in the projections is the expectation of a continuation in the shift to a postindustrial society as the major factor affecting employment in the 1980s. This change will be compatible with the development of many career opportunities associated with the new technology that is contributing to industrial revival.

Table 10
EMPLOYMENT FOR SELECTED MAJOR INDUSTRIAL SECTORS, 1977 AND PROJECTED 1990

Sector	Employment (in millions)		Percent Change 1970 to 1990
	1977	Projected 1990	
Total Civilian	93.7	118.6	26.6%
Manufacturing	19.8	23.9	23.0%
Transportation, Public Utilities	4.8	5.7	16.9%
Wholesale and Retail Trade	20.9	27.4	30.9%
Finance, Insurance, and Real Estate	4.9	6.7	37.0%
Services*	17.7	26.7	51.3%

*Excluding private household workers.
Source: *Employment and Training Report of the President,* 1979, p. 362.

Much of the cost saving from making use of the new technology represents the savings that result because of continuous operation. Industrial robots, for example, are currently estimated to involve an initial unit capital outlay in the $70,000 to $80,000 range *(Business Week,* 1980). Much of the saving that is anticipated from the investment would be lost if the machines were out of use frequently for maintenance and repairs.

In the initial introductory phases, repairs to complex technology such as robots are often made by the "superstars," persons with graduate degrees in science or in engineering who have specialized in the field. With more widespread use of automated and robotic technology, there will be changes in the training needed to qualify for employment in repairing, servicing, operating and maintaining the equipment. Many of the persons now being trained as engineers in fields related to the new technology will pass on their knowledge to others in universities, community colleges, technical institutions and other postsecondary schools.

A Useful Background

The emphasis on industrial renewal in the 1980s will place greater and new demands on vocational education. Courses in electronics will provide the basic foundation for training in the fields related to the new technology. In other instances, persons with a vocational training background in more specialized aspects of automobile mechanics will find their training

271

a useful background for further training in the new fields. The level of complexity involved in the automated technology suggests that the bulk of the training will be given in postsecondary institutions.

Many of these institutions already have extensive expertise in electronics technology. Work-study and cooperative education programs can provide an effective way to give students a working familiarity with the advances coming into use in industry. Vocational programs in the secondary schools can arouse student interest by providing basic training in these areas and by employability development courses that familiarize students with the work world. The vocational programs will often serve as a basis for specialized training in industry in much the same way that Xerox or IBM currently trains employees to service and repair equipment.

So far, the high cost of the equipment required to train persons in the new technology has served to defer private proprietary schools from assuming a major role in training. None of the member schools of the National Association of Trade and Technical Schools, for example, offer courses in robotics. As with other automated equipment, it is likely that equipment costs will decrease with greater volume of production. A reluctance by the public vocational institutions to train persons for the jobs that will grow out of industrial revival in the coming decade will have the effect of encouraging private proprietary institutions to take on a larger role in this field.

A NEED TO ADAPT TO CHANGE

Much has been made in the past of the need to identify new occupations that might be suitable fields for training. The experience with robots and related automated technology frequently illustrates another tendency. This is the tendency for the job content to change in existing occupations in response to advances in technology. The changes in the content of machinists' jobs resulting from the introduction of numerically controlled machine tools illustrates these developments. In the coming decade, the job content of many electronic technicians' jobs will come to include a working knowledge of advances in fields such as robotics. Programmers and designers will discover their job skills undergoing change with the more widespread integration of computer-assisted design and computer-assisted manufacturing. On a lesser technical level, the duties of the typist have taken on a new dimension with the advent of the word processor.

Vocational education systems, like other institutions, must adapt to change if they are to serve their students, the larger society and their own need to grow. Planning in vocational education can supply an early warning system to increase sensitivity to changes in the coming decade that will require a response by vocational educators. The priority for renewing the nation's industrial base, like the demographic changes and the regional shifts, illustrates underlying long-term developments that will figure prominently in the agenda for planning in vocational education in the decade ahead.

REFERENCES

Ayers, R.U. *A preliminary technology assessment: Industrial robots and CAM.* Pittsburgh, Pa.: Carnegie-Mellon University, 1980.

Business Week, June 9, 1980.

Business Week, June 1, 1981.

Louis Harris and Associates. *1979 Survey of American attitudes toward pensions and retirement.* 1979.

Lecht, L. *Expenditures for retirement and other age related programs: A major shift in national priorities.* New York: Academy for Educational Development, 1981.

National Advisory Council on Adult Education. *A history of the Adult Education Act.* Washington, D.C.: Author, 1980.

United Auto Workers Union, Research Department. *Memo,* October 20, 1980.

U.S. Congress, House of Representatives, Committee on Ways and Means. *Options for financing social security programs.* Washington, D.C.: Government Printing Office, 1979.

U.S. Congress, House of Representatives, Committee on Science and Technology. *Seminar on research, productivity, and the national economy,* no. 127. Washington, D.C.: Government Printing Office, 1980.

U.S. Department of Labor, Bureau of Labor Statistics. *Geographic profiles of employment and unemployment,* report 619. Washington, D.C.: Author, 1980.

Wall Street Journal, November 28, 1980.

Wall Street Journal, February 3, 1981.

This chapter was originally prepared as a presentation at the State Vocational Directors meeting and is used with permission of The National Center for Research in Vocational Education. Reprints may be ordered for $2.20 (indicate OC 74) from the Publications Office, The National Center for Research in Vocational Education, The Ohio State University, 1960 Kenny Road, Columbus, Ohio 43210.

MULTI-AGENCY SYSTEM LINKAGES AND COORDINATION

Clyde Maurice

Agencies and institutions establish linkages or coordinative relations for a variety of reasons. Among them are the need to eliminate boundaries and bridge gaps; the desire to improve the delivery of service; pressure to reduce duplication and prevent administrative overlap; the need to enhance the efficient use of resources and the need to establish coalitions so that bargaining power can be increased. But these reasons, although frequently cited, are only superficial justifications that mask more basic problems. Agencies' attempts to cooperate are usually undergirded by circumstances that serve as driving forces propelling agencies to establish cooperative ties.

INTRODUCTION

The vocational education community is presently bombarded by such forces. An atmosphere of fiscal conservatism exists at the federal, state and local levels. Enrollment has stabilized or is continuing to decline in most geographic regions, and there is increased competition from public and private agencies for the use of limited resources that have traditionally supported the vocational education enterprise. These and other similar forces will continue to exist. It is essential that practitioners in vocational education acquire skills that will enable them to cope with such forces so that survival can be ensured.

One strategy for coping is by initiating and maintaining effective coordination and cooperation. But now and in the future, coordination can no longer be considered a superficial exercise. Rather, it must be viewed as an essential instrument for survival and a major challenge to the vocational education enterprise.

The primary purpose of this chapter is to note some considerations and strategies that will enable vocational education practitioners to pursue, establish and maintain successful coordinative relationships. A concomitant and more hidden purpose is to assert the importance of establishing cooperative ties as a viable alternative for coping with circumstances that will continue to affect vocational education.

The rationale underlying these purposes is that vocational education practitioners must be prepared to meet the challenge to coordinate and capitalize on opportunities for establishing linkages for the future. If successful coordinative relationships must be established, then it is essential to

275

understand the characteristics of coordination which underlie its success and the mechanisms that can be implemented to create and nurture the bond between agencies.

The chapter is divided into four sections: (1) *The concept of coordination*—examines definitionally and conceptually the meaning and dimensions of coordination; (2) *Coordination in vocational education*—provides an overview of a structure for thinking about coordination in vocational education; (3) *The basic necessities for successful coordination*—identifies some factors that have significant effects on coordination and are considered the basic conditions that must exist for establishing and maintaining successful coordinative relationships; and (4) *Making coordination work: some strategies*—highlights some mechanisms that have been successfully used to create and maintain linkages between agencies.

THE CONCEPT OF COORDINATION

The term coordination is deceptively simple. It is used (or abused) so often, that its real value remains obscure or unnoticed. Esterline (1976) noted his fear that coordination is becoming a vague, imprecise and probably useless term. Cohen (1977) recognized that it is a complex phenomenon that is difficult to implement and when implemented, prone to failures. But the concept of coordination clearly communicates its inherent use for maintaining organizational effectiveness.

Coordination is defined by Webster as "bringing together into a common action, movement or condition; to harmonize; to act together in a smooth concerted way." This perspective on coordination refers to commonality of purpose, unity and concert in action. It reflects coordination as an orchestrated, articulated system bound together by unity of purpose. But this unity may not always be necessary, and in practice, such unity may not be truly characteristic of the variety of coordinative relations that exist.

A Process of Exchange

Coordination can also be interpreted as the process of exchange (Levine & White, 1960; Esterline, 1976). Here, coordination is defined as the exchange of needed resources between two or more organizations. In this context, resources are used in a most general sense to mean money, personnel or equipment, or less tangible items such as information or advice. Merely exchanging items for some purpose—any purpose—denotes an act of coordination. Even securing the consent of one agency fits within the exchange perspective of coordination. Although some degree of cohesiveness may exist, commonality of purpose is unnecessary. This perspective allows the concept of coordination to encompass a wide scope of organizations that potentially can be defined as participants in a coordinative relationship.

Coordination, then, is an organized effort. It involves more than one party. In its simplest sense, it can mean mere exchange and refer to a wide range of organizations. Or it can be restricted to refer to a cohesive, interrelated system of organizations working toward similar or common purposes. The complexity of coordination in its true sense becomes readily apparent when one considers the negotiation, integration and accommodation necessary to achieve interorganizational or interunit cohesiveness. Bargaining must take place to reconcile differences, and adjustments become necessary to address the disparities between structure, processes and ideologies.

As manifested in public agencies, coordination exists at three activity levels: the policy level, the administrative level and the service delivery level (National Institute for Advanced Studies, 1977). At each of these levels coordination takes many different forms which may require different degrees of cohesiveness and, hence, different forms of integration and accommodation.

Voluntary Coordination

Little cohesiveness is usually required when coordination is the natural outgrowth of the needs of specific agencies or units. Here, a relationship is established so that required agency functions can be accomplished. For instance, data are requested from an external agency because they are needed for reporting or justification purposes. The effort is voluntary and there are no sanctions or penalties for noncoordination. The relationship is based on the sole realization that in order to provide adequate service, or to accomplish a specific function, the support of some external agent will be necessary. Esterline (1976, p. 6) has referred to this type of coordination as voluntary coordination or coordination by mutual adjustment. This kind of coordination usually involves a wide variety of organizations voluntarily deciding to exchange commodities or service.

Hierarchical Coordination

Hierarchical coordination (Esterline, 1976) is more restrictive in scope and organizational freedom. Here, a hierarchical relationship exists between agencies that are coerced into coordinating. The state division of vocational education may require local agencies to submit certain types of information on a continual basis, or local agencies may have to request permission to perform certain activities. Typically, this vertical coordination requires a central authority, relationships that are predefined, and established and formalized procedures for interaction.

Horizontal Coordination

Horizontal coordination, on the other hand, is a composite of selected characteristics from hierarchical and voluntary coordination. Here, although coordination is not hierarchical, it is rigidly defined through existing legislation and operational policies that attempt to relate specific agency functions. Horizontal coordination usually takes the form of various interagency linkage devices such as coordinating councils, fund-transfer mechanisms, policy coordination requirements or external review procedures. The state plan group for vocational education is one such example.

The group is required by law and is comprised of representatives of seven state agencies that can potentially contribute to vocational education planning.

Two critical features emerge as dimensions of coordination in public agencies: (1) whether the relationship is voluntary or mandated and (2) whether participating agencies complement each other in accomplishing a broadly defined goal. Linkages are not casually established. Whether coordination is required by law or voluntarily pursued, the object is usually the contribution such a linkage can make to some predefined organizational purpose.

COORDINATION IN VOCATIONAL EDUCATION

There are numerous groups, agencies and institutions that are directly or indirectly involved with the delivery of vocational education services. As a consequence, it is difficult, if not impossible, to fully describe the dimensions for coordination in vocational education or the myriad possibilities for linkages in the field. Nevertheless, it may be instructive to understand a general structure for coordination between vocational education and related agencies.

The hierarchical perspective of coordination in vocational education is exhibited in the relationship between the state division of vocational education (SDVE) and the various public local education agencies (LEAs) concerned with delivering vocational education services. The state division is a central authority; relationships with local agencies are defined within state and federal legislation, and formalized procedures exist for the interaction between these agencies. Each part of the total system provides support for the accomplishment of a common but broadly defined goal: the training of individuals for work roles. There, the primary agencies in the coordination network are LEAs and SDVEs.

Local Level Agencies

However, at both local and state levels, many external agencies or organizations play critical supportive roles in maintaining the effectiveness of vocational education. At the local level, advisory and craft committees offer valuable contributions for critical decisions. The school board and various local administrative councils provide policy guidelines. Comprehensive Employment and Training Act (CETA) prime sponsors, the local employment security office, the local chamber of commerce, local unions, individual businesses and industries and a variety of community-based organizations (CBOs) at the local level all play essential roles in vocational education coordination.

At the state level, there is the state board for vocational education, the state legislature, the state advisory council for vocational education, and the state plan group. In addition, there are other supportive agencies or groups such as the state occupational information coordinating council and the state employment services agency, among others. Whether linkages

278

are established voluntarily or by legal mandates, these and other related state agencies also have their place in the network of vocational education coordination.

The Network for Coordination

The network for coordination in vocational education can be graphically illustrated in a series of three concentric circles. The illustration represents different levels of cohesiveness within the vocational education inter-institutional system. Represented at the core of these circles are state and local vocational education agencies, namely, the state division of vocational education and a variety of local secondary and postsecondary vocational education institutions for which the state division has oversight. These agencies form the nucleus of the vocational education enterprise.

The next band illustrates the first level of supportive relationships. These relationships are usually state or federally mandated linkages at the state or local levels such as advisory committees, coordinating councils and committees and policy-making boards, among others. The outermost band represents voluntarily initiated relationships (state or local) which contribute to organizational goals and purposes. This band comprises the second level of supportive relationships contributing to the nucleus of the system.

While legislative mandated linkages are often utilized, other potentially valuable linkages usually go unexplored. The establishment of voluntary cooperative ties depends to a large extent on the ability to recognize avenues for coordination. To the uninitiated practitioner, doubts may exist as to the appropriate opportunity for establishing cooperative ties and the determination of whether potential relationships are feasible or not. The following section is intended to help clarify such doubts.

BASIC NECESSITIES FOR COORDINATION

When should a coordinative relationship be initiated? What is the basis for success in such relationships? What should an individual know about coordination before initiating or while trying to maintain a successful coordinative relationship? These questions are usually overlooked. Yet they are at the heart of understanding the intricacies of coordination that can determine success or failure.

There are at least nine necessities for establishing and maintaining satisfactory interorganizational relations. These necessities represent some of the basic conditions that seem to underlie coordinative relationships. If these conditions exist, then the probability of successful coordination is increased. If these conditions do not exist, however, serious questions can arise about the quality of the coordinative relationship. An explanation of each condition (or basic necessity) follows.

A Basis for Exchange

The decision of whether or not a coordinative relationship is established is never reached arbitrarily. One of the fundamental conditions for establishing interorganizational relations is a basis for exchange. Coordination requires that some sort of transaction take place between coordinating agencies. This transaction is usually expressed in terms of the resources each participant brings to the coordinative relationship (Kochan, 1975), since it is expected that each participant has something to contribute. The items or commodities transacted, or the items contributed to the relationship, comprise the basis for exchange.

There are a variety of exchangeable items. These include money, information, equipment, specialized personnel, clients or even political support. As long as there is something worth exchanging, there is the possibility for coordination. The coordination between vocational education and CETA at the local level, for example, is based on the exchange of financial resources by CETA to vocational education for the use of established vocational education facilities. Each agency has something of interest to the other. This is usually an initial step toward the establishment of cooperative ties.

A decision as to whether a relationship between agencies is appropriate must be preceded by some consideration of the items for exchange. And exchange, by definition, is never a one-way transaction. Something must be given in return for what is gained. Noting what one wants to receive must always be aligned with what one can give in return.

Mutual Benefit

The value of items of exchange is important. What one gives or receives may not be considered valuable enough to warrant entering a relationship. For this reason, the concept of mutual benefit is closely tied to the items that comprise a basis of exchange. If there is something to exchange, the concern then becomes whether there are benefits to be realized from the exchange.

The exchange perspective of coordination postulates that relations are formed between two or more organizations when each of them perceives mutual benefit or gains from interacting (Levine & White, 1960; Evans, 1966). The interaction is based on self-interest. Administrators will sometimes enter a relationship only when such action enables the agency in their charge to attain some of its subgoals. Hence the vocational education director will have ties with employers in the area to facilitate placement of graduates. Conversely, local employers will establish ties with LEAs to facilitate the availability of trained workers. In effect, the decision becomes a cost-benefit analysis—"What can my agency gain from the relationship, and what does the agency have to give up or contribute?"

The consideration of mutual benefits is especially important since organizations place a high value on autonomy (Aiken & Hage, 1968). As Esterline (1976) observes, autonomy makes it convenient for an agency to maintain contact with its environment—funding sources, clients and interest groups. With autonomy comes a certain degree of freedom. As a result, the attempt to attain benefits through an external relationship is an important decision for the agency, since some autonomy must be sacrificed in order to realize those benefits. Any form of interdependency encroaches significantly on organizational autonomy because of the constraints posed through obligations, commitments and contracts. For this reason, some agencies may choose to forego substantial benefits in order to retain autonomy. An example in vocational education is the choice of LEAs to forego the benefit of federal funding due to the restrictions imposed on expending the funds.

Although there are items to exchange, and although such items may be mutually beneficial to the participating agencies, coordination may still be perceived as inappropriate to the extent that it curtails organizational freedom. Continual assessment must be made to ascertain the needs and the resulting coordinative posture of agencies that are candidates or participants in an interagency relationship.

Organizational Awareness

Continual assessment requires a high degree of organizational awareness. Esterline (1976) referred to awareness as a "prerequisite factor" for the exchange of resources. Awareness refers to the degree to which agencies, or units within these agencies, are familiar with the services, goals or selected characteristics of other agencies or units. More specifically, awareness is the extent to which each agency is knowledgeable of the potential of other organizations to support its activities (Litwak & Hylton, 1962). Knowledge about other agencies or units enables each organization in the network to make an assessment of the potential for coordination and develop realistic expectations about what can be accomplished through the interaction. Possible items for which agencies (or units) must be mutually aware are listed below.

- *Output:* total range of items, services or products produced by external agencies or units, and the selected subset of these items that may contribute to one's own agency's functions.
- *Needs:* the requirements or subgoals of other agencies or units to which one's own agency can make a contribution.
- *Structure:* the administrative lines and legal framework defining external agencies' operations and authority.
- *Capacity:* the ability of selected agencies (units)—through staff qualifications, resource availability, client relationships or constituent support—to make some contribution to one's own agency's subgoals.
- *Domain:* the territory (defined geographically, through client characteristics, or through services provided) for which other agencies similar to one's own are responsible.

Familiarity with these factors will enable an objective assessment of the feasibility of coordination. But awareness also refers to "the degree of personal acquaintance between key staff in different agencies or units" (Esterline, 1976). Such acquaintances or interpersonal familiarity make external agencies more accessible, and as a result the ensuing relationships tend to be longer-lasting and more meaningful. It facilitates what Guetzkow (1966) calls organizational interpenetration, or boundary permeability. Awareness then, refers to acquiring familiarity with an agency's operation, as well as establishing personal acquaintances with representatives of that agency.

Mutual Respect, Confidence and Trust

Respect, confidence and trust are interdependent terms; one cannot be realized without the others. Total awareness of the characteristics of other agencies (units) is the initial step in gaining mutual respect, confidence and trust. Before a coordinative posture is developed, enough must be known about the external agency to lay an adequate foundation for mutual confidence. With such knowledge, there may be fewer unanticipated shortfalls, and the problems encountered may not be as jolting or disruptive, primarily because expectations are more realistic. But this is only the groundwork.

The respect, confidence and trust nurtured in the beginning of the relationship must be sustained. This sustenance is based on the quality of interaction and the degree to which realistic expectations are fulfilled. There are many factors which can undermine mutual respect, confidence and trust. A few of these factors are:
- A lack of timeliness in meeting mutual deadlines
- Poor quality output such as inaccurate information, incomplete reports, unrealistic advice and biased viewpoints
- Friction over territory, or lack of domain consensus
- Competition over common resource bases or clientele

Lack of trust results in an environment of suspicion, which is extremely unhealthy for fruitful coordination. Nurturing trust on the other hand can only be accomplished through honesty and understanding in pursuing cooperative ventures.

Access

The accessibility of agencies to each other is listed by Levine and White (1960) as one of three important factors underlying interdependence. Synonymous terms such as organizational penetration and boundary permeability (Guetzkow, 1966) are also used to refer to access. All of these terms complement each other to convey the meaning and importance of access to successful interorganizational relations. Although the term penetration may be an overstatement, agencies must be "penetrated" by other agencies to establish or maintain a relationship. Penetration in this context can be defined as the means whereby external agents reach the decision-making network within an agency to gain access to some of its resources. The more accessible an agency, the easier it is to penetrate. There are two major types of accessibility—physical and organizational.

Physical accessibility refers to the physical convenience of contacting the appropriate person within an agency. Some of the factors affecting physical accessibility include geographic distance between agencies and the availability of direct and regular communication such as telephone, newsletters or memos.

Organizational accessibility refers to inherent characteristics that tend to promote contact with the appropriate persons within the organization. Some of the factors impeding organizational accessibility are an organizational distance imposed by tradition of working independently; an organizational structure without appropriate assignment of "boundary" personnel for handling relationships; an absence of decision-making authority for persons in key coordinative roles; and policies or administrative guidelines that make it difficult to establish contact or maintain a relationship.

Some agencies willingly make themselves inaccessible in an attempt to preserve organizational autonomy. In most such cases, boundary personnel are used as buffers to help the institution insulate itself from the environment (Guetzkow, 1966; Thompson, 1967). This insulation is used to acquire the benefits of a coordinative posture, while still preserving organizational independence. Again, the need for autonomy results in a distinct pattern of coordinative behavior—a behavior that affects coordination through the denial of access.

In the final analysis, a relationship cannot be sustained without some convenient form of access to each participating agency. As access becomes more difficult, through geographical or institutional structure, the relationship will become more strenuous. Accessibility is integral to the evaluation of the feasibility or effectiveness of linkage arrangements.

Communication

Communication is the transmittal of information between agencies in a coordination network. It is important in maintaining coordinative relationships, since it keeps appropriate parties informed and aware of issues of mutual concern. Communication can be informal or formal; it can be occasional or regular; it can be conducted face-to-face through meetings, seminars or personal visits, or via telephone conversations, memos or reporting forms. There are two types of communication: internal and external. Internal communications enhance intraorganizational coordination, while external communication caters to the maintenance of external relationships. But these two types of communication are interrelated.

The number of external relationships affects the nature of internal communication. Evans (1966) noted that the number of agencies with which an agency interacts has significant consequences on its internal structure. For an organization to maintain external relationships, internal communication must be increased to accommodate the internal flow of information necessary to maintain an adequate linkage (Aiken & Hage, 1968). Since communication is increased with the intensity and number of cooperative ties, the need for internal adjustment in communication channels will be greatest when there are strong cooperative efforts or when a large number of organizations is engaged in cooperative relationships.

Organizational flexibility to make internal adjustments is essential to accommodate increasing communication demands. A typical organizational adjustment to promote effective communication is the decentralization of decision-making authority. This action avoids the long lines of communication for decision-making, which are usually very time-consuming and which have the tendency to distort information before decisions can be made. When internal communication channels are inadequate, the benefits of coordination are harder to accomplish. As a result, cooperative ties become less productive and eventually die.

Similarity of Attributes—Goals, Values

Compatibility for congruence are elemental concepts central to understanding coordinative behavior. In comparative approaches to interorganizational analysis, organizations are compared on certain attributes to assess the feasibility of interaction. Generally, similarity on a few critical attributes is considered a necessity for interorganizational relations. Miller (1958) found that differing philosophies are a deterrent to coordination, and Johns and Demarche (1951) cited congruency of objectives as a factor affecting interaction. Differing attributes such as philosophies and ideologies, goals and objectives, or even differences in organizational structure and agency expectations can negatively affect coordination. Similarity in these attributes increases the chances for establishing cooperative efforts.

Dissimilarity can be detrimental for many reasons. As differences between organizations increase, the need for compromise also increases. This results in greater emphasis on conflict-laden activities such as negotiation and accommodation. In addition, differences in goals and values can cause agencies to have varying levels of commitment to selected interorganizational goals. Similarity on these dimensions is the first step to unity in purpose and is a precursor to cooperation. But this is not always the case.

Evans (1966) predicts that the greater the similarity of goals and functions between two organizations, the greater the amount of competition between them. This is understandable since organizations with similar goals may have the same clients and resource base. Under such circumstances, some competition can be expected. Levine and White (1960) note that the tendency for competition is greatest when organizations with similar functions operate below their capacity. In an environment where there are enough clients and resources to meet the need of both organizations, competition is less keen and cooperation is possible. When resource bases are different, the possibility of competition may also be lessened.

Sometimes goals are not similar, but complementary. Under these circumstances competition is avoided, and the situation is much more conducive to cooperation between the respective organizations.

Opportunity

Stevens (1979), in discussing coordination between vocational education and CETA, identifies two distinct aspects of cooperative ties: "the opportunity to cooperate, and the incentive to do so." The opportunity is the existing condition, or set of circumstances, that causes one agency to initiate contact with the other. Though all the basic necessities for coordination may exist, if the opportunity to cooperate does not occur, coordinative relationships will not be established. It is essential to recognize and respond to such opportunities.

The opportunity to cooperate arises in a variety of ways: new demands may be made on an organization; resources can be scarce; personnel may be transferred from one agency to the other. However, the most frequent condition that creates such an opportunity in public agencies is the provision of legislation and policy guidelines. Both the Education Amendments of 1976 and the CETA Amendments of 1978 provide the opportunity for vocational education and CETA to coordinate. Although the opportunity is there, if other basic coordination factors (or necessities) are missing, impediments to coordination are encountered.

Incentive

Incentive or inducement to establish coordinative relationships is the basic necessity which differentiates between symbolic and productive coordinative activities. Symbolic coordination activities result from weak inducement to cooperate. One such inducement is that labeled by Cohen (1977) as "bureaucratic." The implementing agent for bureaucratic inducement is realized in the form of legislation or policy guidelines. Here, the requirement for coordination is imposed upon the agency, and the incentive to coordinate may be artificial and weak. Only administrative evidence is required to show coordination, and there is no compelling reason for agencies to realize the true benefit of cooperation. This led Stevens (1978) to conclude that the incentive for genuine cooperation is missing from CETA and vocational education legislation.

A more fruitful way of thinking about incentive is in terms of rewards. Here, the anticipated reward from cooperation serves as an inducement to establish cooperative ties. In genuine and productive coordinative efforts, the anticipated benefits to be derived from the relationship (or the items exchanged) is sufficiently rewarding to establish cooperative ties.

STRATEGIES FOR MAKING COORDINATION WORK

Considering the many conditions necessary for successful coordination, it is not difficult to understand why coordination efforts are "failure prone." It is much too easy to overlook some of the essential features. Yet understanding the concepts alone is not tantamount to implementating them at the appropriate times. Knowledge of specific means or facilitators to coordination more adequately serves implementation.

A facilitator to coordination is a procedure, activity or policy (or a combination thereof) which has the potential for promoting, maintaining or strengthening cooperative ties between agencies. Facilitators are the mechanisms through which the basic necessities for successful coordination are realized. Table 1 lists a series of facilitative mechanisms and notes the type of facilitation consistent with the factors previously discussed.

Table 1
FACILITATORS OF COORDINATION

Facilitator	Type of Facilitation
overlapping membership	• promotes awareness • provides a direct communication link-access • fosters the accommodation of differences in ideologies, etc.
personnel transfers	• promotes better understanding of each other's operation • fosters accommodation of differences
connector committees	• fosters accommodation of differences • provides direct communication linkages • serves as a buffer for interagency conflict
joint use of facilities	• trial provides a clear realization of mutual benefits • accommodates differences in programming and schedules • provides a common bond for joint action
centralized purchasing	• provides a clear realization of mutual benefits • promotes interagency awareness
permanent staff liaison	• provides direct communication linkages • promotes access
joint discussion and study groups for policies	• accommodates differences • promotes interorganizational awareness • provides a forum for joint action • provides a basis for mutual commitment • provides a means of interagency communication

Multi-Agency System Linkages and Coordination

joint maintenance of public information programs	• promotes awareness
delineation of constraints and identification of supportive resources for coordination	• identifies coordination barriers that need to be eliminated
identification, study and publicity of successful interagency experiences in coordination	• develops a support base to maintain a coordinative relationship
establishing non-threatening settings for interagency personnel to get to know one another	• fosters free and uninhibited communication between agencies
making all actors aware of the negative effects of dysfunctional operations and the advantages of coordination	• creates awareness of the scope and potential for coordination
encouraging mutual sensitivity	• enables each agency to understand the constraints and philosophies of the other, thereby breaking down barriers resulting from lack of knowledge
assisting participants in broadening their viewpoints	• educates participants about the scope for coordination-awareness
interagency study committees	• provides an opportunity for mutual problem-solving • provides an opportunity to understand the goals and limitations of others • provides a common information base for supporting activities
training about the role and functions of different persons and units in the system	• promotes awareness • fosters communication
external agency participation in the development of plans	• promotes awareness • promotes mutual sensitivity
initiation of clearinghouse review functions	• promotes awareness
interagency planning team	• promotes interagency awareness • synchronizes timelines

developing and distributing procedures for resolving inter-agency policy conflicts	• facilities interagency problem-solving
joint development of data bases, information systems, definitions and publication format	• provides a basis for communication • provides a common base for planning
use of common advisory structures or committees	• enables cross-communication • provides a common base of support • provides a forum for resolving differences
procedure for giving pertinent agencies an opportunity to have input in policy formation	• avoids the potential of noncoordination because of inadequate policies • provides an incentive for coordination
developing specific ways of establishing both formal and informal communication networks such as newsletters, meeting notices, activity schedules	• provides avenues to keep pertinent individuals aware and informed • prevents disruptions to smooth coordination because of a lack of critical information

CONCLUSION

The gains from interorganizational linkages in the future will be realized not only from the ability to utilize mandated linkages, but by the capacity to individually recognize avenues for establishing profitable relationships, and the sensitivity and responsiveness to nurture and maintain the vibrance of such relationships. Administrators in vocational education must be confident that the establishment of linkage arrangements and the initiation of cooperative ties are truly worthy endeavors. But, the basis for successful coordination must be understood and an array of alternative coordination mechanisms must be always at hand.

REFERENCES

Aiken, M., & Hage, J. Organizational interdependence and introorganizational structure. *American Sociological Review,* 1968, *23,* 912-930.

Cohen, D. Some theoretical notes from historical analysis. In *Intersectoral educational planning.* Paris: Organization for Economic and Cooperation Development, 1977.

Easterline, B.H. *Coordination: A conceptual model and practical consideration.* Paper delivered to the Education Commission of the States' National Seminar on State Capacity Building, December 1976.

Evan, W.M. "The Organization-Set: Toward a Theory of Interorganizational Relations." In J.B. Thompson (Ed.), *Approaches to organizational design.* Pittsburgh: University of Pittsburgh, 1966.

Guetzkow, H. Relations among organizations. In R. Bowers (Ed.), *Studies on behavior in organizations.* Athens, Ga.: University of Georgia Press, 1966.

Johns, R., & Demarche, D. *Community organization and agency responsibility.* New York: New York Association, 1951.

Kochan, T.A. Determinants of the Power of Boundry Units in an Inter-Organizational Bargaining Relation. *Administrative Science Quarterly,* 1975, *5,* 435.

Levine, S., & White, P. Exchange as a conceptual framework for the study of interorganizational relationships. *Administrative Science Quarterly,* 1960, *5,* 583-601.

Litwak, E., & Hylton, L.F. Inter-organizational analysis: Hypothesis on co-ordinating agencies. *Administrative Science Quarterly,* 1962, *7,* 395-420.

Miller, W.N. Interinstitutional conflict as a major impediment to delinquency prevention. *Human Organization,* 1958, 20-22.

National Institute for Advanced Studies. The development of alternative plans for improving coordinative and cooperative planning in the provision of services to handicapped individuals. In *Summary of the proceedings: The coordination of programs serving handicapped individuals.* Washington, D.C.: Department of Health, Education and Welfare, January 1977.

Stevens, D. W. *The coordination of vocational education programs with CETA.* Columbus, Ohio: The National Center for Research in Vocational Education, 1979.

YEARBOOK AUTHORS

Edward D. Berkowitz is the John F. Kennedy Fellow and assistant professor of history at the University of Massachusetts at Boston. During 1980 he served on the senior staff of the President's Commission for a National Agenda for the Eighties. Dr. Berkowitz is the author of several books and articles on social welfare history, including the recently published *Creating the Welfare State.*

Ellen Andrew Carlos, assistant project director for the American Vocational Association's (AVA) Economic Development project, has been with AVA for two years. Previously, she was a vocational educator in an area vocational-technical school for seven years in Pennsylvania. Among Dr. Carlos' recent publications are a monograph on the foundations of occupational home economics and various articles on the role of vocational education in economic development.

Kermeta "Kay" Clayton is assistant professor of home economics education at The University of Texas at Austin. Dr. Clayton, who received her Ph.D. from Texas Women's University, is the principal investigator for the Standards for Vocational Home Economics Education Project funded by the U.S. Department of Education.

Rupert N. Evans began teaching vocational education in a secondary school, after working in industry and the military. Since 1950 he has been with the College of Education, University of Illinois, where he has served as professor, department chairperson and dean. Currently he is professor of vocational and technical education, assigned to the Bureau of Educational Research. His research and writing have sought to improve teacher education and education about and for work. His Ph.D. in industrial psychology was earned at Purdue University.

Marvin Feldman is president of the Fashion Institute of Technology in New York City, a specialized college under the program of the State University of New York, which prepares students for creative and management careers in the fashion industries. Dr. Feldman has held positions with the Office of Economic Opportunity in the U.S. government, the Ford Foundation and served for 12 years in the field of university and secondary school administration and education with the state of California.

Eli Ginzberg is Hepburn professor emeritus of economics and director, Conservation of Human Resources, Columbia University. Dr. Ginzberg is also chairman of the National Commission for Employment Policy. He is the author of over 35 books.

Robert W. Glover is acting director of the Center for the Study of Human Resources and assistant professor at the Lyndon B. Johnson School of Public Affairs at the University of Texas at Austin. Dr. Glover received a Ph.D. in economics, with a speciality in labor economics and human resource development, from the University of Texas in 1972. He has served as chairperson of the Federal Committee on Apprenticeship since 1978. Dr. Glover's primary research interests are in apprenticeship, the construction industry, labor market discrimination and private sector training efforts.

Kenneth C. Gray is the assistant director of the division responsible for managing the regional vocational-technical school system in Connecticut. Dr. Gray holds degrees in economics, guidance and counseling and in vocational education. While studying at Virginia Polytechnic Institute, he developed skills in historiography, as witnessed by his original research concerning the role of manufacturers in the Smith-Hughes movement and a recent award-winning historical analysis of the role of job skills as a barrier to youth employment.

W. Norton Grubb teaches economics and statistics at the Lyndon B. Johnson School of Public Affairs, The University of Texas at Austin. In addition to their work on the relationship of schooling and work, he and Marvin Lazerson have written extensively on relationships among government programs, children and families. Their book, tentatively titled *Broken Promises: The State, Children and Families in Post-War America,* will be published by Basic Books in 1982. Professor Grubb is now examining the effectiveness of different vocational, CETA and private training programs to isolate the conditions that lead to successful programs.

Edwin L. Herr is professor and head, Division of Counseling and Educational Psychology at The Pennsylvania State University, University Park. Dr. Herr is the author or editor of 20 books and monographs and more than 180 articles. Two of his most recent books are *Guidance and Counseling in the Schools: Perspectives on the Past, Present and Future* and (with Cramer) *Career Guidance Through the Life Span: Systematic Approaches.*

Marvin Lazerson is an historian, and teaches educational history, educational policy and history of thought at the University of British Columbia, Vancouver. He has completed a book with Norton Grubb, tentatively entitled *Broken Promises: The State, Children, and Families in Post-War America,* which will be published by Basic Books in the Spring of 1982. His current work involves youth policy and the relationship between education and labor markets.

James A. Leach is an assistant professor in the Department of Vocational and Technical Education, University of Illinois at Urbana-Champaign. In addition to teaching small business management, he has conducted workshops and developed curriculum materials for the teaching of small business management, authored numerous articles on the topic and been an active small business consultant.

Leonard A. Lecht is an economic and human resources consultant. From 1974 to 1979, Dr. Lecht was director, Special Projects Research, for the Conference Board in New York City. He was director of the Center for Priority Analysis for the National Planning Association for 10 years, prior to which he was professor and chairman, Department of Economics, Long Island University. Dr. Lecht, who received his Ph.D. in economics from Columbia University, is the author of *Occupational Choices and Training Needs* and *Evaluating Vocational Education: Policies and Plans for the 1970's; Goals, Priorities and Dollars — The Next Decade.*

Morgan V. Lewis is a senior research specialist in the Evaluation and Policy Division of the National Center for Research in Vocational Education, The Ohio State University, a position he has held since January 1978. Prior to joining the National Center, Dr. Lewis served 13 years with the Institute for Research on Human Resources, The Pennsylvania State University. Dr. Lewis also received his graduate training in psychology at Penn State.

Clyde Maurice is an assistant professor in the Comprehensive Vocational Education Program at Florida State University. Dr. Maurice was previously a research specialist at the National Center for Research in Vocational Education, where he was involved in a national study to assess coordination in planning vocational education. Presently, he engages in research on interagency coordination and teaches courses on policy development and planning in vocational education.

Donna M. Mertens is currently a research specialist in the Evaluation and Policy Division of the National Center for Research in Vocational Education at The Ohio State University. She was previously the coordinator of evaluation for the Appalachian Community Service Network in Lexington, Kentucky. She obtained her Ph.D. from the University of Kentucky in the Department of Educational Psychology.

Egils Milbergs is currently associate deputy secretary for the U.S. Department of Commerce. His yearbook article is based on speeches delivered in the summer of 1980 when he was director of Group Development at Stanford Research Institute International in Menlo Park, California.

Melvin D. Miller is director, School of Occupational and Adult Education, Oklahoma State University, Stillwater. He recently completed a fellowship in the Advanced Study Center at the National Center for Research in Vocational Education. His chapter in this yearbook is based on research conducted during his fellowship and, in part, is drawn from his manuscript, "Principles and A Philosophy for Vocational Education," completed during his stay at the Advanced Study Center.

William Mirengoff is currently the director of the Employment and Training Evaluation Project for the Bureau of Social Science Research in Washington, D.C. He previously was study director of the Committee on Employment and Training Programs for the National Academy of Sciences, where he was the principal author of nine volumes assessing the economic, social and political impacts of CETA. Mr. Mirengoff has held several positions with the U.S. Department of Labor, including administrator of the Public Employment Program, director of Job Corps and director of Office of Policy, Evaluation and Research.

Brian Murphy is marketing education specialist at Onan Corporation, Minneapolis, Minnesota. He holds a B.S. in industrial education and an M.Ed. in career and technology education from Bowling Green State University. Mr. Murphy's experience includes postsecondary teaching, vocational curriculum development and industrial training. His specializations are in training analysis, design and development.

Robert E. Nelson is chairman of the Division of Business Education at the University of Illinois, Champaign-Urbana campus. Dr. Nelson has written extensively in the area of entrepreneurship and small business development. He has directed several projects to develop curriculum materials for teaching entrepreneurship and small business management. He has worked with the International Labour Organisation regarding various small enterprise projects being conducted in developing countries in Asia and Africa.

Krishan Paul is the director of the Economic Development Project at the American Vocational Association. Before assuming his present job, he worked in Tennessee for a number of years, first as director of research in the Department of Economic and Community Development and then as project director with the Nashville Urban Observatory. Dr. Paul worked previously as a research and development specialist at the National Center for Research in Vocational education, The Ohio State University. Among his recent publications are a book on occupational analysis and a number of papers and articles on the role of vocational education in economic development.

Beatrice Reubens is senior research associate, Conservation of Human Resources, Columbia University. Dr. Reubens, who received her Ph.D. in economics from Columbia University, is a consultant to numerous American and international agencies and a specialist in education and employment problems of youth on a comparative basis. She is the author of numerous articles and books, the most recent of which is *Bridges to Work*.

Paul J. Ringel received his doctorate from Teachers College, Columbia University, and was awarded the 1981 "Outstanding Dissertation Award" by the Society for the Study of Curriculum History. He is a teacher in the New York City public schools.

Dolores M. Robinson is an associate professor in vocational education at Florida State University, Tallahassee. She has worked with youth in the public school system in Atlanta, Georgia, and with unemployed youth through a CETA project. Her yearbook article is based on her work as a fellow at the Advanced Study Center of the National Center for Research in Vocational Education, The Ohio State University.

John Skinkle is an assistant professor at Texas A&M University. He graduated from the University of Minnesota in 1978 with a Ph.D. in vocational education. Dr. Skinkle teaches graduate courses on administration, evaluation and research in vocational education.

Sonja Haynes Stone is a member of the African and Afro-American studies faculty at the University of North Carolina at Chapel Hill. During 1980-81, she was a postdoctoral fellow at the National Center for Research in Vocational Education, The Ohio State University.

Paul Sultan completed his undergraduate work with honors in economics at the University of British Columbia and his graduate work in economics at Cornell University. He has taught at the University of Buffalo, the University of Southern California and the Claremont Graduate School, and, most recently, at Southern Illinois University, Edwardsville. He has had numerous visiting appointments. Dr. Sultan has written four books in the labor field, written some 20 articles and authored six monographs dealing with research issues in labor market performance.

Richard Swanson is professor of vocational and technical education at the University of Minnesota, Minneapolis. Dr. Swanson received his B.A. and M.A. degrees from Trenton State College and his Ed.D. from the University of Illinois. His research and development interests include training cost-benefit analysis, analysis of work behavior and training design.

INDEX

A

Addams, Jane, 37
Advisory Council on Vocational Education (1968), 117
Affirmative action pressures, 97
Afro-American Community, 71, 73, 77, 80
Agencies, multi-system linkages of, 275-288
Agriculture, 40, 60, 66-68
Alabama State Teachers Association, 75
Alexander, M.W., 41
Alienation, 55
Altruism, 53, 57, 71-80
AME Christian Recorder, 74
American dream, 6, 129
American Federation of Labor (AFL), 41, 45-46, 65
American Indians, 75
American Industries, 44, 129
American Revolution, 31
American Vocational Association, 225, 235
Anti-intellectualism, 117
Apprenticeships and vocational education, 83, 97-104, 130, 217-221, 235
Armstrong, Samuel Chapman (General), 39, 72, 80
Assertiveness training, 243
Atlanta University Conference on the Negro in Business, 75
Australia, 218
Austria, 217, 220-221
Authority, 6, 52
Automation, 49, 264, 271-272
Automobile industry, 259, 266, 269, 271
Autonomy, 59, 94, 280-281, 283
Avery College (Pittsburgh), 72
Avocations, personal, 50

B

Baby boom generation, 18, 21, 257
Barlow, Melvin L., 40, 63
Bellman, Richard, 50
Benefits, 52, 64, 255, 267
Berkowitz, Edward, 3, 15-21, 291
Bethune-Cookman College, 73
Bethune, Mary McLeod, 72-73, 75-81
Biculturalism, 71
Bilingualism, 118

Biology, 53, 268
"Black Cabinet," 72-73
Black leadership, foundations of, 71-81
Black-lung affliction, 55
Blacks, 39, 58, 124, 265
Black Thursday, 24
Block grant programs, 94
Blue collar workers, 137-138, 256, 261, 270, *see also* Working class
Bonus marchers (1932), 25
Bottlenecks of specialized work forces, 118, 260
Boulding, Kenneth, 7
Brazil, 10
Budget messages of the recent administration, 264
Bunche, Ralph, 71
Bureau of Apprenticeship and Training (BAT), 99
Bureau of Labor Statistics, 207, 270
Businesses, 66, 265
  minority owned, 181
Business and Industry Liaison Program, 235
Business services, 265

C

California, universities in, 15
Callaghan, James, 24
Calvin, John, 53-54
Canada, 218, 269
Candide (Voltaire), 54
Capital, 27-28, 51-52, 54, 267, 270
Capitalism, 27, 49-54
Capital punishment, 28
Career education, 116, 118-119, 121-122
Careers, 53, 109, 209, 211, 234, 253, 259, 265-266, 270
Carlos, Ellen A., 225, 227-236, 291
Carlyle, Thomas, 54
Carnegie Council, 217-218
Carter, Jimmy, 207
Catholic industrial schools, 38
Census Bureau, 257, 263
Central-city population issues, 262-265
Centralization, 5, 7
Chamber of Commerce (U.S.), 46, 75, 264, 278

Cheney, Howell, 46
Cheyney State Teachers' College, 72
Children, battered, 57
Cities, 29, 262-266
Citizens Committee Against Juvenile
    Delinquency and Its Causes (Philadel-
    phia), 76
Civilian Conservation Corps, 116, 118
Civil rights, 76
Civil Rights Act of 1964, 145
Civil War, 25, 39, 72-74
Classical economics, 29
Class stratification, 133
Clayton, Kermeta "Kay," 167, 189-193, 291
Clerical workers, 265
Climate, desire for change of, 262
Collective bargaining, 255
Commercial education, 46
Commissioner of Education (U.S.), 38
Commission on National Aid to
    Vocational Education, 46, 64-68
Committee on Agriculture and Forestry,
    45
Committee of Ten, 42-44
Commodities, production of, 55
Communication, 11-12, 283-284
Community-based organizations (CBOs),
    245, 278
Community colleges, 101, 143, 271
Community networks, 1-2, 8, 13, 86, 172
Community services, 20, 93
Community Work Experience Program, 19
Competency-based instruction, 197-204
Competition, 50, 52-53, 284
Comprehensive Employment and Training
    Act of 1973 (CETA), 18-20, 83, 85-86,
    88-95, 119-122, 125-126, 144, 147, 150-
    151, 161, 163, 197, 232-233, 245-247, 278,
    280, 287
    amendments to, 91, 285
    applicants under, 91
    evolution of, 85
    summary of titles of, 87
    Title I of, 119
    Title II of, 86, 91
    Title IID of, 94
    Title VI of, 90-91, 94
    Title VII of, 91
Comptroller General, 117
Computers, 10-12, 15, 30, 240, 268, 270,
    272, see also Microcomputers
Congress (U.S.), 18, 47, 63, 86, 88, 90-91,
    93, 144, 147, 182, 237, 246-247, 250, 255,
    264, see also Senate
Conservation of Human Resources Project
    (Columbia University), 144

Conservatism, 51-52, 102, 275
Construction industries, 265
Consumer electronics industries, 266
Consumerism, 6
Consumer Price Index, 255-256
Consumer service industries, 265
Consumption, 27, 49-51, 56, 60
Cookman Institute (Jacksonville, Fla.), 73
Cooperative Industrial Course (Fitchburg
    High School), 137-138
Cooperative ties in the vocational educa-
    tion community, 275, 279-280, 283-285,
    288
Coordination among agencies and
    institutions, 275-288
Cooperation, 233, 283-285
Cooperative education, 98, 103, 131, 137,
    212, 218, 239, 244, 272
Coppin, Fanny Jackson, 72-78, 80-81
Corporations, 5, 16, 52, 133, 267
Cost of living, 64, 255
Costs, 267, 270
Counselling, job, 211
Council of Economic Advisors
    (Kennedy's), 19
Countercyclical programs in CETA, 90
"Cowboy economy," 7
Crafts, 55, 155
Creaming, 90
Credentialing, 123, 126
Crime, 12, 116
Cubberly, Ellwood, 39-40
Culture, 52, 71-72
Curricula, 195, 212, 259

D

Darwin, Charles, 53-54
Data processing, see Computers; Micro-
    computers
David, Henry, 37
Davis, Charles, 44-45
Daytona Literary and Industrial School
    for Training Negro Girls, 73
de Beauvoir, Simone, 55
Decategorization, 86, 88
Decentralization, 7, 32, 86, 88
Decision making, 88, 102, 284
Deficit spending, 26
Degrees, academic, 259
Delivery systems for education, 1
Deluder Satan Act (Massachusetts Bay
    Colony 1647), 38
de Mandeville, Bernard, 53
Demand-side economics, 23, 25, 27, 29,
    183, 229
Democratic societies, 54

Index

Democrats, 18-19, 23, 86
Demographic profiles, 253, 255, 257, 272
Denmark, 221
Department of Agriculture (USDA), 181
Department of Economic Development (Oklahoma), 231
Department of Education (U.S.), 231, 235, 246, 249
Department of Labor (U.S.), 64, 85, 94, 97, 99-100, 103, 120, 149-150, 207, 246
Department of Vocational and Technical Education (Vo-Tech), 231-232
Dewey, John, 29, 38, 46, 122
Dictionary of Occupational Titles (Department of Labor), 198
Disadvantaged persons, 2, 19, 88, 90, 92-93, 118, 167, 203, 219, 245, 265
Disadvantaged workers, 17-19, 21, 172, 176, 245
Discipline, lack of, 59
Discrimination in the labor market, 126-127, *see also* Racism; Sex stereotyping
Displaced homemakers, 2
Distributive occupations, 68
Division of Special Schools for Industry Training (Oklahoma), 231-232
Doctrine of social efficiency, 40
Dolliver Davis Bill, 45
Dropouts, 64, 118, 147, 155-156, 161, 212
Du Bois, W.E.B., 71, 75
Duffy, Frank, 41

E

Earnings, 17, 153
Economic activity, regional shifts in, 253
Economic analyses, 54
Economic development, 227-236, 253, 264-265
Economic Development Project (Oklahoma), 231
Economic drift, 6
Economic growth, 5-6, 16-17, 115, 227-229
Economic opportunities, 262
Economic Opportunity Act of 1964 (EOA), 19, 85
Economic optimism, 6
Economic restructuring, 8
Economics, 53
  classical, 27
  demand-side, 23, 25, 27, 29, 183, 229
  supply-side, 3, 23-33, 50
Economic well-being, 17
Economies
  expanding, 16
  industrial, 10, 270

local, 261, 264-265
material-based, 10
regional, 16, 260, 262, 272
semi-autonomous self-sustaining, 52
subterranean, 51
Economy
  American, 15-16, 23-25, 147, 182
  changes in the, 3, 5-13
  degeneration of the, 8, 18
  Japanese, 5, 266-267
Education, 64, 66-67, 130, 135
  adult, 253, 258
  aims and methods of general, 64-65
  continuing, 156, 253
  costs of, 59
  higher, *see* Higher education; Post-secondary education
  industrial, 37-45, 47, 67, 72, 129-133
  liberal, 31, 66
  life adjustment, 117
  persons with superior, 262
  preventive, 212
  public, 68, 134
  remedial, 58, 212
  secondary, 157, 217-223, 272
  technical, 253
  for work, 1, 35, 109
Educational institutions, enrollment in, 258
Educational psychology, research in, 201
Educational systems, mass, 122
Education Amendments of 1976, 189, 285
Education Professions Development Act (EPDA), 190
Efficiency, 18, 266-267, 272
Egalitarian programs, 51
Elderly persons, *see* Older persons
Electrical engineering, 16
Electronic mail, 11-12
Electronics, 11, 267-272
Eliot, Charles, 37
Emergency Employment Act of 1971 (EEA), 85-86
Emergency Jobs Program Extension Act of 1976, 90
Employability Development Plans (EDPs), 91
Employability skills development, 115, 169, 195, 207-216, 253, 265, 272
Employees, 55, 59, 214, 255-256, 265
Employers, 55, 210-214, 266
Employer-sponsored training, 156
Employment, non-agricultural, 269
Employment agencies, 213
Employment and Training Administration, 85, 99
Employment and Training Report of the President (1979), 254, 257, 269, 271

Employment growth, 16, 260-261
Employment opportunities, 262
Employment patterns, regional, 260, 262
Employment rate, 260-261
Employment regulations, 2, 18
Employment Service (ES), 85, 88, 93
Employment statistics, 208, 260-261
Energy, 6, 264-265
  heavy users of, 270
  increases in prices of, 267
  new sources of, 270
  nuclear, 6
  renewable sources of, 7
Energy industries, 266, 270
Energy resource regions, 265
Engineering, persons with graduate
  degrees in, 271
English as a second language, 2, 167, 239,
  243
English language (as a school subject),
  59, 110, 237
Entrepreneurial opportunities, increasing,
  180, 182
Entrepreneurial skills, 13, 187
Entrepreneurs, 30, 32, 53, 167, 179-187,
  235, 243, *see also* Self-employment
  education and training of, 2, 33, 167,
  180, 185-186, 246, 249
Entry-level positions, 259, 261, 265
Environmental concerns, 6, 269
Environment for work, 60
Equipment
  design, production, operation, and
  maintenance of, 270-272
  obsolete, 267
Equalization of opportunity, 126
Ethical principles, 54
Ethnic populations, 132
Ethnic studies, 81
Europe, 52, 218, 223
Evaluation of training, 118
Evans, Rupert, 43, 47, 225, 237-251, 291
Exchange, process of, 276
Exploitation, 54
"Export platforms," 267

F

Fable of the Bees (de Mandeville), 53
Factories, 66
Failure to achieve, 50
Families, 12-13, 17, 56-58, 259, 264, *see
  also* Homemakers
Farmers' Conference, 75
Farm mechanization and technology, 50,
  60, 64
Fashion Institute of Technology, 30

Fast track, 15-16, 19, 21
Father Divine, 73
Federal apprenticeship regulations, 100
Federal Board for Vocational Education,
  64, 68
Federal government, 27, 68, 256
"Feed forward" signals, 37
Feldman, Marvin, 3, 23-33, 291
Feminism, 6, 15
Fiber optics, 11
Filene, Lincoln, 46
Financial resources and services, 52,
  265, 270
Firm-based programs of vocational educa-
  tion, 126
Fitchburg Plan, 135-137
Ford Administration, 23
Ford Foundation, 85
Foreign competitors, 6, 9, 52, 266-267
Foreign labor in U.S. industry, 130
France, 9, 11, 59, 218, 222, 267
Fringe benefits, 257, 267
Frugality, 53
Fulfillment in work, personal, 56, 58, 60
Full employment, 23, 26-27, 33, 125
Full Employment Act of 1946, 27
Funding, plans submitted to obtain, 258

G

Garraty, John, 25
*General Theory of Employment, Interest,
  and Money* (Keynes), 23, 26
Genetic engineering, 268
George-Dean Act of 1936, 116
George-Eilzey Act of 1934, 116
Germany, 5, 217, 220-223, 232-233, 241-242
  West, 9, 11, 59, 235, 266-267
  youth of, 241
Ghana, 75
G.I. Bill, 239
Ginzberg, Eli, 113, 143-147, 291
Giving Youth a Better Chance (Carnegie
  Council), 217-218
Glover, Robert W., 83, 97, 292
Golden, John, 38
Gompers, Samuel, 37, 65-66
Government, 5, 66, 68, 256
Gray, Kenneth C., 35, 37-48, 292
Great Britain, 24, 32, 38-39, 59, 222
Great Depression, 23-24, 119, 126, 240
Great Society, 51, 85, 145
Greed, 54
Greenewalt, Crawford H., 129
Greenwood, Katy B., 1-2
Gross national product (GNP), 24, 60, 180
Growth, 45

Index

industrial, 129, 132
in number of jobs, 52, 270
population, 262, 264
productivity, *see* Productivity growth
societal, 50
Grubb, W. Norton, 113, 115-128, 292
Guidance and placement assistance, 259

H

Hampton Institute, 39, 72-74, 77
Happiness, 5, 56
Handicapped persons, 2, 20, 118, 167, 203,
239, 243, 246, 249
Harris Survey for 1979, 258
Hayes, Al, 143
Health, environmental, 269
Health occupations, 145
"Hearings on Vocational Education," 45
Hearst, William Randolph, 26
Hedonism, 55-56, 66
Heller, Walter, 19
Helmeke, Kerry, 208
Herr, Edwin L., 167, 169-178, 292
Hierarchical coordination, 277
Higgens, Milton, 41
Higher education, 15, 57, 115, 122-123,
158-161, 212, 258, 271-272
High schools, 64, 209, 211-212, 215, 258
counselors in, 211
diplomas from, 59
dropouts from, 64, 147, 212, *see also*
Dropouts
students in, 59, 211
teachers in, 211
Hiring processes, 213
Hispanics, 58, 124
Hobbies, 259
Hoffman, Abbie, 49, 60
Homemakers, 2, 260, *see also* Families
Horizontal coordination, 277
Hubbard (Reverend, Auburn, New York), 38
Hughes, Dudley, 45
Humphrey, Hubert H., 19
Humanity and human ingenuity, 51, 53

I

Idealism, 57
Illiteracy, 58
Illinois Advisory Council on Adult, Voca-
tional, and Technical Education, 184
Illinois Wesleyan, 24
Immigration, 116, 129, 134, 241
Imperialism, 49
Improving the Work Skills of the Nation
(National Manpower Council), 143
Incentives, 18, 50, 53, 60, 254, 268, 285

Incomes, 27, 51, 58
Income supports for older persons, 256
Industrial base, 10, 266, 253, 270-272
Industrial education, 37-45, 47, 67, 72,
129-133, 135-138
Industrial growth, 129, 132, 270-271
Industrial history, 7, 54-55
"Industrial missionaries," 78
Industrial proletariat, 31, 133, 135
Industrializing nations, 267
Industries, 66, 68, 120, 227, 229, 259
goods-producing, 265
labor-intensive, 223
ladies garment, 260
new-growth, 266
non-manufacturing, 266
older, 266-267, 270
printing and publishing, 265
rubber, 266
service, 16, 123, 223, 266, 270
southern, 234
steel, 52-53
technical, 266
telecommunications, 10, 12
Industry-based training, 217
Industry-specific skills, 175-176
Industry Training Program (Ohio), 234
Infants yet to be born, 52
Inflation, 5-6, 9-10, 23-24, 241-242, 253,
255-256
rates of, 8, 79, 266
Information-based societies, 3, 5-13
Infrastructure, 228
Ingenuity, 53, 55
Injuries, risks of, 55
Institutionalized persons, 52
Institute for Colored Youth (ICY; Phil-
adelphia), 72, 74, 78
Institute of Robotics, 268
International competition, 60
International finance, 265
Interorganizational relations, 233, 281-283,
286
Interpersonal skills, 211, 214, 259
Interstate migration, 262-263
Interviewing for a job, 213
Investments, 51-52
*Issue Paper on Education, Training and
Assistance* (White House Conference on
Small Business), 182
Italy, 59
Ittner, Anthony, 41-42, 44

J

Japan, 5, 9, 11, 59-60, 217-218, 235, 266-267
Jefferson, Thomas, 32

Job applications, 213-214
Job Corps, 87, 170, 172
Job counseling, 211
Job descriptions, 33
Job discipline, 56
Job interviews, 213-214
Joblessness, 220
Job loss, 49, 52, 262
Job markets, 146, *see also* Labor markets
Job opportunities, 126
Job preservation, 234
Jobs
    autonomy, challenge, enrichment, and
      promotions in, 59
    dead-end, 123
    full-time, 56, 257
    growth in numbers of, 52, 270
    part-time, 258
Job searches, 210, 212-213, 215
Job sharing, 56
Job skills, technical, 214, 270
Job-specific skills, 209, 215
Job training, 1-3, 33, 129, 133, 136, 169-
    177, 212
    the effects of, 149-164, 170, 173
Job-training programs, 16, 33, 207
Job turnover, 210
Johnson, Lyndon Baines, 19
Joint Economic Committee of Congress,
    23, 27-28
Junior Chamber of Commerce, 76
Juvenile delinquents, 59, 116, 119

K

Kamer, Pearl, 263
Katz, Michael, 131-132
Kay, James, 39
Kennedy, John Fitzgerald, 19, 117
Keynes, John Maynard, 10, 23-28, 31
Kingsley, Charles, 54
Kirby, John, 42
Korea, South, 10, 267
Ku Klux Klan, 75

L

Labor, 49, 54, 60, 65, 118, 267
Labor force, 15, 17, 21, 51, 56, 150, 208,
    210, 228, 239-241, 253-254, 256-258, *see*
    also Work force
Labor market related curricula, 212
Labor markets, 101, 109, 115, 117, 122,
    124, 126-127, 177, 209-212, 215, 217, 265-
    266, *see also* Job markets
    demands of, 230
    deregulation of, 17
    early experiences in, 209

    primary, 169, 174
Labor-saving technologies, 54
Labor unions, *see* Unions
Lazerson, Marvin, 113, 115-128, 292
Leach, James A., 167, 179-193, 292
Leadership, 189
Lecht, Leonard A., 225, 253-273, 293
Legal services, 265, 270
Leisure, 49, 52, 55
Lenin, Nikolai, 51
Levitan, Sar, 208
Lewis, Morgan V., 113, 149-165, 293
Liberals, 51-52
Life adjustment education, 117
Life expectancy, 257
Lifestyles, changes in, 3, 5-13
Local agencies, 253, 260, 264-265, 277-278,
    280-281
Local economies, 261, 264-265
Local governments, 256
Local participation in decision making, 88,
    90
Local school boards, 68
Longevity, 253
Lovejoy, Leroy, 59
Lower income workers, 17, 162
Low-tech work, 16-17

M

Machine Shop Calculations, 136
Machinists, 272
Machinists' Union, 143
Macroeconomics, 16-17, 23, 27-29, 115
Malabre, Alfred, 28
Malaysia, 267
Management, 52, 260
Management by objectives, 33
Manpower and training programs, 18-20
Manpower Development and Training
    Act of 1962 (MDTA), 19, 85, 144, 150-
    163, 172-173, 240, 245
Manual labor, 118
Manual training, 38, 43-45, 115, 129-130
Manufacturers, 38, 41, 43-47, 65, 260-261
March on Washington for Jobs and
    Freedom (1963), 79
Markets, 50-51, 53, 66
Marxists and Karl Marx, 30, 54-55
Mass educational system, 122
Mass production, 38
Materialism, 5, 6, 53
Maurice, Clyde, 225, 275-289, 293
Mechanical arts, 44-45
Mechanical ingenuity, 55
Media, 90
Mencken, H.L., 6

Index

Mertens, Donna M., 113, 149-165, 293
Mexico, 10, 240, 267
Microcomputers, 10-11, 223, 247, 264, 268, 270, *see also* Computers
Microeconomics, 27
Mid State Technical Institute (Wisconsin), 235
Migration, 262-264
Milbergs, Egils, 3, 5-13, 293
Miles, Herbert, 39, 46
Military-industrial complex, 5, 57
Miller, Kelly, 79
Miller, Melvin D., 35, 63-69, 293
Minimum wages, 17-18
Mining, 55
Minorities, 2, 40, 51, 117, 124, 143-144, 147, 182, 185-186, 233, 246
Minority businesses, 181
Minority youth, 124, 145, 240, 245
Mirengoff, William, 83, 85-95, 293
Miseducation, 16
Missionaries, 74, 77
M.I.T. Development Foundation, 30
Mobility, 133-135, 137, 219
Monroe, James, 40
Monthly Labor Review, 261-262, 267
Moonlighting, 56
Moral Re-Armament, 75
Morrill Act (1862), 44
Morrow, Lance, 58
Muhammed, Elijah, 73
Multi-agency system linkages, 275-288
Multinational corporations, 5, 52, 267
Municipal Finance: How Deep the Crisis (Kamer), 263
Murphy, Brian P., 83, 105, 294
Murray, William ("Alfalfa Bill") H. (Governor of Oklahoma), 25
Mutual benefit, 280
Mutual commitment, 286
Mysticism, 57

N

Narcissism, 55
National Advisory Council on Vocational Education, Issue Paper on Self Employment (1979), 183
National Alliance of Businessmen, 144
National Archives, 44
National Association for the Promotion of Technical and Secondary Education, 40
National Association of Colored Women, 73-74
National Association of Manufacturers (NAM), 37, 39-41, 44-45

National Association of State Directors of Vocational Education, 238
National Association of Trade and Technical Schools, 272
National Business League (NBL), 75
National Center for Research in Vocational Education, 248
National Commission for Employment Policy, 87, 144, 152, 157, 162, 173, 177, 209
National Council of Negro Women, 73, 75
National Council on Employment Policy of 1977, 161-163
National Education Association (NEA), 44, 190
National Longitudinal Survey (NLS), 155, 158, 172
National Manpower Advisory Committee, 144
National Manpower Council, 143
National Metal Trades Association, 43, 66
National Negro Business League, 75
National Recovery Act (NRA), 26
National Society for the Promotion of Industrial Education (NSPIE), 37, 39-47, 63-64, 66
National Youth Administration (NYA), Division of Negro Affairs, 73, 75, 116
Negro Business League, 75
Negro institutions for vocational education, 72
Nelson, Robert E., 167, 179-193, 294
Networks, 1-2, 8, 13
New Century Club, Working Women's Guild, 74
New Deal, 26, 116
New Federalism, 86
New left, 50
New York Conference Board, 105-106
New Zealand, 218
Nixon administration, 86
Nkrumah, Kwame, 75
Nuclear power, 6

O

Oberlin College, 72, 74
Obsolete equipment, 267
Obsolete skills, 257, 259
Occupational Health and Safety Administration, 127
Occupational mobility, 219
Occupations, 50, 66-68, 109, 192, 197, 211, 238
Office of Education (U.S.), 245
Office of Management and Budget, 89
Office of Occupational and Adult Educa-

tion, 235
Oglesby, Carl, 49
Ohio State University, 102
Oil, obtaining of with advanced
 technologies, 264-265
Old Age and Survivors insurance benefits,
 255
Older manufacturing centers, 260-261
Older persons, 52, 124, 253-260
 working, 15, 255, 257, 259
Old manufacturing industries, 266
On-the-job training (OJT), 100, 174-176,
 218-219, 242, 247
Opportunities Industrialization Centers of
 America (OIC), 73, 76, 79-80
Opportunity, equalization of, 126
Optimism, 71-73, 80
Opulent societies, 50-51, 56
Organizational relations, 233, 281-283, 286
Out-of-school training programs, 120, 125
Over-educated persons, 16, 31-32, 115, 118

P

Parents, working, 58
Parry, David, 41
Part-time jobs, 33, 211, 258
Passive resistance, 57
Paul, Krishan K., 225, 227-236, 294
Penalties, short term, 52
Pensions, 255-257
Personal development, dignity, or en-
 richment, 52, 59, 259
Personnel, 265, 286
Phase-downs in CETA, 94
Phillips curve, 24
Placement assistance, 259
Planning, 239
 contingency, 13
 in vocational education, 253, 266, 272
Plant closures, 52
A Policy for Scientific and Skilled Man-
 power, (National Manpower Council),
 143
Political influence, loss of by older
 regions, 264
Political jurisdictions, 265
Population, 58, 129, 256-258, 262, 264
Portland Community College (PCC), 232-
 233
Postindustrial societies, 28, 270
Postsecondary education, 158, 160-161,
 266, see also Higher education
Poverty, 17, 19, 51, 76, 143
Powell, Adam Clayton, Jr., 73
Practical experience as part of vocational
 education, 67

Pragmatism, 57
Predestination, 53
Present shock, 58
Primary labor markets, 169, 174
Private enterprise, 5, 51, 109
Private Industry Councils (PICs), 147, 249
Private proprietary schools, 272
The Problem of Vocational Education
 (Snedden), 44
Proceedings of the Organizational Meeting
 (NSPIE), 40
Production, 38, 55, 272
Production workers in manufacturing, 269
Productivity, 11, 28, 51, 60
Productivity growth, 6, 8-9, 49, 60, 266-268
Professional job skills, 270
Profit, 52-54
Program abuses, 90, 93
Program blocking, 199
Programmable manufacturing systems, 268
Progressive Era, 116, 118, 123
Project Baseline, 172
Proletariat, industrial, 31, 133, 135
Promotions, 59
Proprietary training schools, 126
Prosser, Charles, 43, 45-46, 63-68
Protest, 57
Protestant-controlled reformatories, 38
Protestant ethic, 49
Public education, 68, 134
Public Education in the United States
 (Cubberly), 40
Public employees, 255
Public policy, 16, 253, 255
Public relations services, 270
Public schools, 64, 116, 120, 122-133
Public sector, 51
Public service employment (PSE), 86
Public vocational institutions, 272
Pump-priming, 26
Purchasing power, 255-256
Purdue University, 102

Q

Quality control, 60, 267-268
Quality of life, 227

R

Racism, 49, 57, 124
Radical revisionists, 131-132, 134-135
Railroads, 266
Randolph, A. Phillip, 73
Reagan administration, 19, 85, 94
Reauthorization Act of 1978 (CETA),
 91-93

Index

Recapitalization, 28
Recessions, 9, 23, 244
Recreation, 259, 265
Redfield, W.C., 65
Regional growth, 260-261, 264-265
Regional patterns of employment, 260, 262
Rehabilitation, vocational, 20
Reindustrialization, 28, 225, 237, 239, 242-243, 246-247
Reinvestment, 52
Religion, 53, 57, 259
Remedial education, 58, 212
Repair skills, 259, 270-272
Report of the Commission on National Aid to Vocational Education (Commission on National Aid to Vocational Education), 46, 63, 65-66, 68
Republicans, 18-19, 23-24, 86
Research and development (R&D), 68-69, 247-248, 250
Resources, 5, 10-11
Responsibility accounting, 33
Retirement, 253-258
Retraining, 33, 242-243
Reubens, Beatrice, 98, 145, 195, 217-223, 294
Revitalization, 28, 243
Revolution, working class, 55
Rewards of culture, 52
Rice, H.H., 66
Richards, C.R., 41
Ringel, Paul Joseph, 113, 129-141, 294
Risk-free societies, 52
Ritter, Thomas (Reverend), 79
Robinson, Dolores M., 195, 207-217, 294
Robots, 55, 59, 240, 266, 268, 271-272
Roosevelt, Franklin Delano, 25-26, 28
Roosevelt, Theodore, 39
Roots of Crisis: American Education in the Twentieth Century (Karier, Violas, and Spring, eds.), 133-134
Ruggles, Richard, 208
Russel Report, 116-117

S

Safety, environmental, 269
Samuelson, Paul, 24
Scandinavia, 218, 221
Schneider, Herman, 137
Scholastic Aptitude Tests (SATs), 59
School-based programs, 125-126
School boards, local, 68
Schools
  industrial, 38, 67
  private proprietary, 126, 272
  public, 64, 116, 120, 122-123

stratification in, 126
systematic cooperation of, 67
trade, 41, 44
urban, 58
vocational-technical, 101
School-to-work transition, 207-209
Schumpeter, Joseph, 26
Science, persons with graduate degrees in, 50, 271
Second Plenary Council of American Bishops (1886), 38
Secondary education, 151, 217-223, 272, *see also* High schools
Secretary of Commerce (U.S.), 65
Selective Patronage Campaign, 76
Self-employment, 32, 155, 179, 183-187, *see also* Entrepreneurs
Self-enrichment practices of American management, 52
Self interest, 50, 52-53, 56
Semi-skilled workers, 266, 269-270, *see also* Blue-collar workers
Senate (U.S.), 24, 28, 45, 181, *see also* Congress
  Select Committee on Small Business, 181
  Subcommittee on Education and Employment, 247
Senegal, 77
Seniority, 257
Sensuality, 57
Sex stereotyping, 118
Sheehy, Gail, 58
Silicon valley, 11, 15
Single-company towns, 52
Skill adjustment, 16
Skilled labor, 55, 130, 248, 265
Skills, 55
  basic, 157, 169, 209-210
  deficient, 222
  industry-specific, 175-176
  interpersonal, 211, 214, 259
  obsolete, 257, 259
  professional, 270
  required by new firms, 264
  up-to-date, 255
Skills training, 172, 175, 219, 232
Skinkle, John D., 195, 197-205, 295
Slow track, 16-18, 20-21
Small Business Administration (SBA), 125, 179, 185
Small Business Development Act of 1980, 182
Small Business Development Centers (SBDCs), 182
Small Business Encouragement and Rescue Program (New York), 235

Small businesses, 8, 30, 179-182
Smith, Adam, 53-54
Smith, Hoke, 45
Smith-Hughes Act, 44, 46, 63, 66-69, 229
Smith-Hughes funds, 39
Snedden, David, 44, 63-64, 66-68
Social Control, 39
Social Darwinists, 53
Social reformers, 116
Social Security, 124, 254-256
Societal growth, 50
Society for the Promotion of Manual
    Labor in Literary Institutions, 40
South Africa, 74
South Korea, 10, 267
"Spaceship-earth economy," 7
Spanish-speaking person, 58, 124
Specialization, 7-8
Spivey, Donald, 39
Stagflation, 9, 24, 266
Stagnation, economic, 24, 26
Standards of living, 8, 65
State advisory councils, 278
State apprenticeship agencies, 99
State divisions of vocational education
    (SDVE), 278
State economic development efforts, 264
State employment service agencies, 278
State governments, 256
State grant programs in adult education,
    258
State legislatures, 278
State vocational education agencies, 253
Statistical Abstract (1979), 261
Status systems, 52-53
Stockmarket, collapse of the, 24
Stone, Sonja H., 35, 71-81, 295
Stratification in the schools, 126
Structural defects in the economy, 26
Student assaults on teachers, 58
Student enrollments, 59
Student protests, 57
Students
    disadvantaged or handicapped, 118
    high school, 59, 211, see also High
    schools; Secondary education
    nontraditional groups of, 260
    part-time working, 33
    in vocational programs, 253, 266
Students for Democratic Society (SDS), 49
Substitution of PSE for local resources,
    90
Suburbs, 262-264, 266
Sullivan, Leon Howard (Reverend), 72-
    73, 76-81
Suicide, 58

Sultan, Paul, 35, 49-61, 295
Supply-side economics, 3, 23-33, 50
Support payments, 51
Surplus value, 54-55
Survival, 54, 57
Swanson, Richard A., 83, 105, 295
Switzerland, 217, 220-221

T

Taiwan, 10, 267
Task Force on Youth Employment (1980),
    170-171, 209
Taxes, reduction of, 51
Taxpayer revolts, 115
Tax write-offs, 264
Taylor, Frederick, 41-42
Teachers, 66-67, 211, 255, 258
Technical education, 253
Technical institutions, 156, 271
Technical job skills, 214, 270
Technical workers, 265
Technological changes, 10, 255, 260
Technology, 5-6, 9, 13, 29, 54-55, 59-60,
    265, 270-271
    automated processing, 9
    high, 15, 50, 262, 266, 268
    industrial, 130
    labor saving, 54
    new, 264, 270-271
    for obtaining oil, 264-265
Teenage unemployment, 207, 214, see also
    Youth: unemployment of
Theory of Moral Sentiment (Smith), 53
"The Third Wave," 29
Third World nations, 7, 52, see also
    Underdeveloped nations
The Three Fishers (Kingsley), 54
Toffler, Alvin, 29
Tourism, 265
Trade protectionism, 7
Trades as work, 66-68
Trade schools, 41, 44
"Trade Schools or Vocational Education,"
    44
Traditional work values, 221
Training
    assertiveness, 243
    definition of, 105
    for industry and business, 105-111, 235-
    236
    industry-based, 217
    job, see Job training
    manual skills, 38, 43-45, 115, 129-130
    motivational, 108
    occupational, 219, 238
    on-the-job, 100, 174-176, 218-219, 242, 247

Index

out-of-school, 120-125
performance-based, 104
in the private sector, 109-111
school-based, 125
team-building, 108
for women, 40
work-study, 98, 272
Training coordinators, 111
Training programs, 18-20, 125-126, 231
Training-related placement, 153
Training terminology, 38
Travel and recreation specialists, 265
Truants, 116
Turnover on jobs, 210
Tuskegee Institute, 72, 75
Typists, 260, 272

U

The Uncommon Man, (Greenwalt), 129
Under-consumption, 25
Underdeveloped nations, 223, *see also*
Third World nations
Under-educated youths, 118
Underground Railroad, 73
Unemployed persons, 55-56, 58, 93, 233
Unemployed youth, *see* Youth: unemployment of
Unemployment, 23, 26-28, 49-50, 118,
121, 125, 150-151, 159, 208-210, 222-223,
235, 239
cyclical, 90, 93
frictional, 209-210
structural, 18, 85, 93, 95, 161
technological, 117, 119
Unemployment rates, 17, 20-21, 79, 115,
117-118, 125, 127, 172, 210, 262, 264
of blacks, 265
high, 266
low, 220
Unemployment statistics, 207-208, 210
Unions, 41, 74, 116, 143, 255, 264
United Brotherhood of Carpenters and
Joiners, 41
Universities, *see* Higher education
Unskilled workers, 16, 20, 270
Unsubsidized employment, 94
Upper Valley Joint Vocational School
(Ohio), 234-235
Urban centers, 29
Urban schools, 58
Urban working class, 45

V

Values, 6-7, 58
Van Cleave, James, 37-38, 44

Variety of Retirement Ages (President's
Commission on Pension Policy, 254
Vice President's Commission on Youth
Employment (1977), 120
Vietnam war, 57
Violas, Paul C., 40, 133-136
Violence, 57
Vocational education
alternatives to, 103
effectiveness of, 113, 115-165
state boards for, 278
underlying values of, 63-69
Vocational education agencies, 253, 265
Vocational Educational Act of 1963,
117-118, 121, 149, 245
Vocational education networks, 83, 278
Vocational Education Study of 1980,
151-156, 159-160
Vocationalism, 117, 121-122, 126, 132
Vocational rehabilitation programs, 20
Vocational retraining, 118
Vocational training, non-school, 116
Voltaire, 54
Voluntary simplicity, 6
Volunteer work, 258
Voting behavior, 158

W

Wages, 9, 17-18, 50, 92, 255, 257, 267
Wallace, Henry, 45
War on poverty, 19
Washington, Booker Taliafero, 72-78,
80-81
Watson, Tom, 240
Wealth of Nations (Smith), 53
Weiner, Norbert, 50
Welfare, 19-20
"We Shall Overcome," 77
West Africa, 77
Westchester Community College (New
York), 235
Western region of the United States, 229,
260-263
West Germany, 9, 11, 59, 235, 266-267,
see also Germany
What Went Wrong, 32
White-collar occupations, 137-138
White House Conference on Small
Business of 1980, 179, 181-182
Wilde, Oscar, 31
Women, 2, 147, 173, 176, 180-182, 249,
253
apprenticeships for, 100
entrepreneurial training for, 180, 185-
186
families headed by, 17

lack of geographical mobility of, 190
and role models, 192
training for, 40
in vocational education administration,
189-193
in the work force, 15, 21, 56, 64, 180,
192, 240-242, 257, 270
Women's Exchange and Girls' Home, 74
Women's movement, 6, 15, 81
Women workers, 15, 21, 64, 167, 192, 257
Woodworking skills, 259
Word processors, 17, 260, 265, 272
Work
attraction to, 56
education for, 1, 35, 109
environment for, 60
low-tech, 16-17
preparation for, 63-64
volunteer, 258
world of, 259
Workers, 55
administrative, 265
clerical, 265
discouraged, 208
lower income, 17, 162
part-time, 212
permanently unemployed, 55
production, 269
semi-skilled, 260, 266, 270, 280
technical, 265
Third World, 52
unskilled, 16, 20, 270
women, 15, 21, 56, 64, 167, 192, 257
Workers' Conference, 75
Workers' productivity, 18
Work ethic, 8, 35, 49-61
Work experience, 66-68, 218, 222
Workfare, 19-21
Work force, 57-59, 118, 257, 260, *see also*
Labor force
women in the, 15, 21, 56, 64, 180, 192,
240-242, 257, 270
Work guarantees, 255
Work habits, 210, 214
Work histories, 259
Work Incentive Program (WIN), 20
Working class, 45, 55, 115, 137-138, *see
also* Blue-collar workers
Working conditions, 64
Working Women's Guild, New Century
Club, 74
Work module method, 33
Work opportunities, 52
Work Progress Administration (WPA), 18,
116, 119
Work-study training, 98, 272

Work training programs, 18-19
Work values, 221
World of work, 259
World War I, 130, 237
World War II, 5, 23, 117, 122, 143, 238-
239, 242, 247
era after, 115, 123-124, 254, 257, 269

Y

Younger students, 260
Young persons, *see also* Youth
decline in numbers of, 258
of immigrant backgrounds, 116
of the lower classes, 116
of minority groups, 124, 145, 240, 245
Young workers, 15-16, 18, 240-242, 246,
255, 257, 261
Your Job Search (1978), 212
Youth, 57, 64, 76, 171, 253, 257, 259, 264
employment of, 120, 124, 170-171, 173,
209
innocence of, 57
in-school, *see* Students
in the labor force, 218, 257
out-of-school, 64, 147, 212
preparation of for employment, 59, 113
problems of, 57, 115-127
undereducated, 55
unemployment of, 58, 115, 120, 123-
126, 207-218, 220, 240-241, *see also*
Teenage unemployment
Youth Employment and Demonstration
Project Act (YEDPA), 87, 126, 246
Youth Employment Service, 76
Youth Opportunity Center counselors, 211

Z

Zion Baptist Church (Philadelphia), 73, 75